SAGE was founded in 1965 by Sara Miller McCune to support the dissemination of usable knowledge by publishing innovative and high-quality research and teaching content. Today, we publish over 900 journals, including those of more than 400 learned societies, more than 800 new books per year, and a growing range of library products including archives, data, case studies, reports, and video. SAGE remains majority-owned by our founder, and after Sara's lifetime will become owned by a charitable trust that secures our continued independence.

Los Angeles | London | New Delhi | Singapore | Washington DC | Melbourne

Empowering
MARGINALIZED COMMUNITIES IN INDIA

Empowering MARGINALIZED COMMUNITIES IN INDIA

The Impact of Higher Education

EDITED BY
M. J. VINOD
S. Y. SURENDRA KUMAR

Los Angeles | London | New Delhi
Singapore | Washington DC | Melbourne

Copyright © M. J. Vinod and S. Y. Surendra Kumar, 2021

All rights reserved. No part of this book may be reproduced or utilised in any form or by any means, electronic or mechanical, including photocopying, recording, or by any information storage or retrieval system, without permission in writing from the publisher.

First published in 2021 by

SAGE Publications India Pvt Ltd
B1/I-1 Mohan Cooperative Industrial Area
Mathura Road, New Delhi 110 044, India
www.sagepub.in

SAGE Publications Inc
2455 Teller Road
Thousand Oaks, California 91320, USA

SAGE Publications Ltd
1 Oliver's Yard, 55 City Road
London EC1Y 1SP, United Kingdom

SAGE Publications Asia-Pacific Pte Ltd
18 Cross Street #10-10/11/12
China Square Central
Singapore 048423

Published by Vivek Mehra for SAGE Publications India Pvt Ltd. Typeset in 10.5/13 pt Sabon by AG Infographics, Delhi.

Library of Congress Control Number: 2021942203

ISBN: 978-93-91370-23-7 (HB)

SAGE Team: Aarooshi Garg, Shipra Pant, Shivani A. Damle and Rajinder Kaur

*To All those who strive to
make Indian higher education truly inclusive*

Thank you for choosing a SAGE product!
If you have any comment, observation or feedback,
I would like to personally hear from you.

Please write to me at **contactceo@sagepub.in**

Vivek Mehra, Managing Director and CEO, SAGE India.

Bulk Sales

SAGE India offers special discounts
for purchase of books in bulk.
We also make available special imprints
and excerpts from our books on demand.

For orders and enquiries, write to us at

Marketing Department
SAGE Publications India Pvt Ltd
B1/I-1, Mohan Cooperative Industrial Area
Mathura Road, Post Bag 7
New Delhi 110044, India

E-mail us at **marketing@sagepub.in**

Subscribe to our mailing list
Write to **marketing@sagepub.in**

This book is also available as an e-book.

CONTENTS

List of Figures ix
List of Tables xi
List of Abbreviations xiii
Acknowledgements xvii

Introduction 1
M. J. Vinod and S. Y. Surendra Kumar

Part I: Contextualizing Indian Higher Education

1 State of Higher Education in India 21
   Prakash Desai

2 Equity and Higher Education Policies in India: Perspectives on National Education Policy 2020 38
   Chetan Singai

Part II: Dalits and Higher Education

3 Social Advantage and Hermeneutical Injustice in the Realm of Education 59
   Krishnaswamy Dara

4 Higher Education Status among Scheduled Castes in India 68
   T. Brahmanandam

5 Caste Discrimination and Exclusion in Higher Education 88
   Areesh Kumar Karamala

Part III: Minorities and Higher Education

6 Muslim's Inclusion in Indian Higher Education: An Analysis 105
   K. M. Ziyauddin

7   Reaching the Unreachable: Jesuit Worldwide Learning—Higher
    Education at the Margins   125
    Maxim Dias and Alphonse Pius Fernandes

Part IV: Persons with Disabilities and Higher Education

8   Indian Higher Education and PwD: Issue of Access
    and Opportunities   139
    S. Y. Surendra Kumar

9   Right to Higher Education of PwD: Critical Reflections   155
    Sanjay Jain

10 Assistive Technology in Higher Education   209
    Udaya Kiran K. T.

Part V: Women and Higher Education

11 Locating Women in India's Higher Education   225
    Vagishwari S. P.

12 Addressing Gender Parity in Higher Education:
    Challenges and Concerns   239
    Priyanca Mathur and Roshni Sharma

Part VI: Prospects of Indian Higher Education

13 Marginalized Communities and Higher Education:
    The Way Forward   255
    D. Jeevan Kumar

    About the Editors and Contributors   268
    Index   273

LIST OF FIGURES

5.1 Social Category-wise Distribution of Teaching Staff in India's Higher Educational Institutions   96
5.2 Social Category-wise Distribution of Non-teaching Staff in India's Higher Educational Institutions   97
5.3 Gross Enrolment Ratio in India's Higher-educational Institutions   98

LIST OF TABLES

2.1	Illustration of Key Policies and Committees on Higher Education	41
4.1	SC Enrolment with Comparison to Total Enrolment	73
4.2	SC/ST Proportion with Non-SC/STs students in Higher Education in Different Academic Disciplines from 1966–67 to 2014–15	75
4.3	Implementation of Reservation in Admissions for SC/ST	76
4.4	Implementation of Reservation in Employment for SC/ST	78
4.5	Number of Teaching Community among Various Social Categories and Gender in Higher Education (in %)	84
5.1	List of Dalit Students Committing Suicide in India's Higher-educational Institutions	93
9.1	No. of Scholarship Provided to PwD (Caste Wise)	160
9.2	Governmental Schemes and Programmes in Higher Education	178

LIST OF ABBREVIATIONS

AIIMS	All India Institute of Medical Sciences
AISHE	All India Survey on Higher Education
BA-SD	BA sustainable development
BJP	Bharatiya Janata Party
CABE	Central Advisory Board of Education
CPD	Compensatory/protective discrimination
CRC	Convention on the Rights of the Child
DBT	Duxbury Braille Translation
DEPWD	Department of Empowerment of PWD
DPSP	Directive Principles of State Policy
ECDA	Empowerment cell for differently abled
EOC	Equal Opportunity Cell
ESC	European Social Charter
FoF	Forum of Federations
GBP	Great Britain Pound Sterling
GEL	Global English Language
GER	Gross enrolment ratio
GOI	Government of India
GST	Goods and services tax
HCU	Hyderabad Central University
HECI	Higher Education Commission of India
HEI	Higher education in India
HEIs	Higher education institutions
HEPSN	Higher Education for Persons with Special Needs
ICESCR	International Covenant on Economic, Social and Cultural Rights
ICHR	Indian Council of Historical Research
ICSSR	Indian Council of Social Science Research
ICT	Information and communications technology
IEDC	Integrated Education for Disabled Children
IIM	Indian Institute of Management

IIT	Indian Institute of Technology
IOS	iPhone Operating System
IPP	Ignatian Pedagogical Paradigm
JAWS	Job Access with Speech
JC	Jesuit Commons
HEM	Higher Education at the Margins
JEE	Joint Entrance Examination
JMI	Jamia Millia Islamia
JNU	Jawaharlal Nehru University
JR	Junior research
JRS	Jesuit Refugee Service
JWL	Jesuit Worldwide Learning
LMS	Learning management system
MHRD	Ministry of Human Resource Development
MNCs	Multinational corporations
NCM	National Commission for Minorities
NCPEDP	National Centre for Promoting of Employment of Disabled People
NDA	National Democratic Alliance
NEP 2020	National Education Policy 2020
NEP	National Education Policy
NHEP	National higher education policy
NKC	National Knowledge Commission
NMDFC	National Minorities Development and Finance Corporation
NPE 1986	National Policy on Education, 1986
NSSO	National Sample Survey Office
OBC	Other Backward Class
OCR	Optical character recognition
pa	Per annum
PMS	Post-matric Scholarship
PoA	Programme of Action
PwD	Persons with disabilities
RA	Reasonable Accommodation
RPwD	Rights of Persons with Disabilities
RUSA	Rashtriya Uchchatar Shiksha Abhiyan
SC	Scheduled Caste

SDGs	Sustainable Development Goals
SEDGs	Socio-economically Disadvantaged Groups
SJC	St Joseph's College
SR	Senior research
ST	Scheduled Tribe
STEM	Science, technology, engineering and mathematics
TISS	Tata Institute of Social Sciences
UGC	University Grants Commission
UN	United Nations
UNCRPD	United Nations Convention on the Rights of Persons with Disabilities
UNDP	United Nations Development Programme
UNESCO	United Nations Educational, Scientific and Cultural Organization
UPA	United Progressive Alliance
UPSC	Union Public Service Commission
VC	Vice chancellor
VMMC	Vardhman Mahavir Medical College
VTU	Visvesvaraya Technological University
WCAG	Web Content Accessibility Guidelines
XUB	Xavier University Bhubaneswar

ACKNOWLEDGEMENTS

We place on record our sincere thanks to each one of the contributors to this volume, for their unstinted support and cooperation. Our special thanks to Professor K. R. Venugopal, Vice-Chancellor, Bangalore University, and Professor B. K. Ravi, former Registrar, Bangalore University, Bengaluru, for encouraging and supporting us to work on 'higher education and marginalized communities in India'.

We also thank Mr Rajesh Dey, Managing Editor—Commissioning, SAGE, for the support that he provided us in the publication of this volume.

Introduction

M. J. Vinod and S. Y. Surendra Kumar

Higher education in India is in a state of ferment and undergoing unprecedented transformation. The impact of the transition from a welfare state philosophy to a market-oriented one is particularly being felt in the educational sector. This has raised the issue of accessibility and systemic inequalities. Higher education ought to be a medium for overcoming social barriers and marginality. The challenge lies in the politics of polarization. The linkage between margins as space, marginality as social dimensions and marginalization as a process needs to be addressed.

How Inclusive Is Higher Education in India?

Inequality of growth and access constitutes a major challenge facing higher education in India. The representation of the weaker sections especially Scheduled Caste (SC), Scheduled Tribe (ST), Other Backward Class (OBC), women, persons with disabilities (PwD) and minorities in colleges and universities still remains low. Rural students are particularly at a disadvantage. There is wide disparity in enrolments across social categories, rural and urban areas and gender variations. In India, spending on higher education is largely by the central and state governments as well as households.

A large part of the growth of higher education in the last three decades has been the mushrooming of private unaided colleges/ universities. Nearly 85 per cent of the engineering colleges are private self-financed institutions. Though this has brought some relief for the government, yet it can be at a huge social and human cost. The challenge has been to ensure equity, transparency and propriety, especially in the days of globalization, liberalization, privatization and corporatization and its impact on higher education. The revolution in information and communications technology (ICT) along with the changing nature of the market and conflicting interests have added to this state of flux in higher education. Change in the realm of education is not a choice and has to happen by design. The Indian higher education system which is at the crossroads, faces many challenges and opportunities. Higher education has not necessarily kept pace with qualitative standards the world over. Unlike India, many Chinese universities are today in the list of major global universities. This has been a matter of concern, and India has no choice but to quantitatively and qualitatively strengthen its higher education system simultaneously.

Marginalization and Higher Education

Education is a catalyst for economic growth, poverty reduction and social change, along with fulfilling the physical, intellectual, social, economic, emotional or other needs and conditions. In this context, marginalization can be perceived as an acute and persistent disadvantage rooted in underlying social inequalities. Marginalization can be both an abstract and complex concept. It has been used in a variety of ways and in different contexts and disciplines. The present volume attempts to conceptualize and analyse the problem of access and marginality in higher education in the Indian context. The focus is on the socially and economically disadvantaged and the people with disabilities. The experiences of marginalization are also addressed, given its sociological and psychological implications. Lack of access to higher education can be considered as an ultimate form of marginalization.

The United Nations Development Programme (UNDP) has argued that marginality is the state of being considered unwanted, undesirable and insignificant, which results in inequity, unfairness, deprivation and enforced lack of access to power and resources. Marginalization is basically a global problem which varies in terms of degree. It contributes to widening socioeconomic inequalities. All countries face a variety of challenges to guarantee all its citizens equal access to higher education. Children with disabilities are among the most marginalized. The marginalized are obviously left behind, and this is a major cause for concern. By including them, we are able to create an inclusive, meaningful environment. The needs of those who are vulnerable to marginalization cannot be discounted.

The rapidity with which the world is changing, perhaps, poses the biggest challenge to higher education. The software revolution has transformed the traditional perceptions and requirement of jobs in the world. Many of our educational institutions are yet to come to terms with these changes. Traditional jobs are fast disappearing, and hence, inequalities in terms of opportunities are increasing. The larger issue relates to the extent to which educational institutions contribute to compounding systemic inequalities.

The larger debate about marginalization in the realm of education centres on the question of marginalization from what. There are many reasons for concern. Well-being is affected by a cluster of experiences. The pace of change in the economy clearly impacts educational models all over the world. The reality of change has to be faced. The present scenario poses both challenges and opportunities. The challenge lies in thinking of ways and means by which we can create spaces for the marginalized in higher education. There is need for a socially inclusive pedagogy. In most domestic societies, higher education is not necessarily a representative sample of the larger demographic base. For example, in Australia, the indigenous Australians are very poorly represented in the institutions of higher education. Polarization across the global landscape has largely taken place on the basis of race, caste, class, religion, gender, language and ethnicity. Needless to say, poverty and unemployment are major reasons for marginalization. In recent times, migrant and immigrant children constitute a marginalized category too. An increased understanding of reasons for marginality can positively impact educational policies and strategies. Higher education is a medium through which social barriers and marginality can be overcome.

Democratic citizenship in theory and practice becomes meaningful if individuals are involved and valued. In some communities, though the state may provide for greater access to mainstream education, yet social, cultural practices, beliefs and institutions can create barriers. Change in mindsets and perceptions also matter. In that sense, marginalization can work both ways. The time has come to think beyond the framework of a monolithic community and focus on a pluralistic and inclusive possibility.

Evolution and Growth of Higher Education in India

In this context, it will be useful to take a bird's eye view of the evolution and growth of higher education in India. Development of higher education has been one of the most important priorities in the development agenda of successive governments in post-Independence India. The country has witnessed the explosive growth of higher education, though not without challenges. The British authorities developed the university system in India, though it was largely used as a tool of cultural colonization. Much has happened since the establishment of the Asiatic society of Bengal in 1784, Fort William College in 1800 up to Macaulay's famous Minutes on education in 1835. After the first War of Indian Independence in 1857 three universities were established in Bombay, Calcutta and Madras. The initial steps towards the Indianization of the Indian higher education system commenced with the Government of India Act of 1935. At the time of independence, India had 20 universities and 496 colleges spread across the length and breadth of the country.

The post-Independence phase witnessed a variety of initiatives being taken by various governments. In the earlier days, Nehru government established the University Education Commission in 1948 under the chairmanship of Dr S. Radhakrishnan. The commission assessed the status of university education and made a variety of proposals. The Education Commission (1964–1966) is very significant. Popularly called as the Kothari Commission, it made the most comprehensive assessment as well as a blueprint for the development of education. It suggested restructuring education through the 10 + 2 + 3 pattern. National Education Policy of 1968 was the outcome of the Kothari Commission. Subsequently in 1976, the Parliament passed the 42nd amendment whereby education was removed from the State List and shifted to the Concurrent List. The next significant landmark was the National Policy on Education 1986. It primarily focused on raising standards and increasing access. The revised Programme of Action (1992) proposed education for quality. Over the years, state support for higher education widened and deepened along with co-opting the private sector. Thus, the phenomenon of private-aided and grant-in-aid institutions began to grow and flourish.

The New Education Policy (NEP) 2020 contends that it will 'contribute directly to transforming our nation into an India-centred education system that contributes directly to transforming our nation sustainably into an equitable and vibrant knowledge society by providing high quality education for all'. NEP 2020 replaces the 1986 policy. NEP 2020 represents a bundle of hopes and perceives education as an organic continuum that involves both knowledge as well as development of cognitive skills, thereby it removes unnecessary hierarchy of subjects and provides equal importance to curricular, extra-curricular and co-curricular activities. The emphasis will also be on multidisciplinary study options. It hopes to universalize pre-primary education and provide foundational literacy for all by 2025. The overall focus is on *universal, equitable and inclusive education.* The transformations are a combination of governance reforms, academic interventions and enhancing the learning outcomes for the students. Undoubtedly, there are huge challenges ahead involving a variety of structural issues as well as funding. Even in the realm of research, the thrust is on the need for a strong public-benefit mandate. The major strength of NEP 2020 is the emphasis on liberal education and professional education. Though many questions remain unanswered, yet NEP 2020 seems to provide for a hopeful vision for the future.

Higher education in India, today, has elicited a variety of policy discourses. It is caught between conflicting interests of the State on the one hand and that of the market on the other. It has simultaneously raised issues and concerns relating to expansion, excellence, equity and ethics. Over the last few decades, the higher-education sector in India has grown in terms of enrolment, institutional capacity and better student–teacher ratios. Education is now being increasingly perceived from the perspective of socio-economic mobility in the country.

Up-skilling the youth to make them employable is a major challenge facing the system today. The major challenges include privatization and commercialization of higher education, mushrooming of low-quality, money-making institutes, teacher vacancies, need for qualitative teaching, problem of financial constraints, lack of employable skills and the importance of multitasking, especially among the marginalized youth. Ultimately, the system has to ensure that the country's human resources are used to the maximum possible extent. We need holistic, flexible and multi-disciplinary education. Let us not forget that *education is a public good*. Hence, *access, affordability, equity, quality and accountability* ought to remain the main pillars of higher education.

Challenges Facing the Marginalized in Higher Education

The Indian higher education system, which is the third largest in the world, is at the crossroads. In terms of enrolment, the numbers have gone up, but issues of representation continue to be debated. Two of the most pervasive forms of inequality in the

Indian context have been caste and gender. Though conscious attempts are being made by the state to address these issues yet change in societal perceptions and attitudes are required to make these efforts truly meaningful. The state is increasingly providing subsidies in higher education for the education of the weaker sections in particular. The challenges of access to higher education also have to do with financial constraints, inadequate infrastructure, lack of skilled and trained faculty and systemic overload in terms of syllabus. All these and more add to the crisis of higher education in the country.

Concerns in terms of staffing patterns and recruitment, employability of graduates and knowledge/skills have surfaced. Under-performance of colleges and universities cannot go unnoticed. Needless to say, there have been islands of excellence too. The University Grants Commission (UGC) has tried to address these issues over the years by innovative practices and structural innovations such as autonomous colleges, deemed universities, cluster universities, private universities and so on. The challenge is to raise equity aspirations and, at the same time, maintain academic standards. Higher education is vital to India's economic and social progress.

The educational disadvantage is complex and multidimensional. States and societies need to come up with strategies accordingly. Education can be perceived as a basic human right. Learning opportunities should be available to everybody regardless of individual differences and disabilities. Persistent gaps in education, income and wealth are matters of concern. Increased understanding of marginality can impact educational policies and strategies. Higher education is a medium through which social barriers and marginality can be overcome. The intersection of race, class, gender, ethnicity, disability and lack of access to material well-being need to be examined. Many countries like India have resorted to reservation/affirmative action policies to bridge these divides. This is even done by lowering the eligibility criteria for specific marginalized groups. Gendered inequality has also been a challenge which is being addressed. Higher-educational institutions are expected to address the well-being of the marginalized. Though there are no quick-fix solutions, yet we need to reiterate certain guiding principles, namely, equity, access and quality. Education and economic opportunities are closely intertwined. The need to enhance equity in higher education also raises many ethical issues and concerns.

Marginalization tends to keep people powerless. Education is indispensable for well-being of the marginalized. The question is whether higher education mirrors rather than remedies inequality. This is because well-being can be affected by a cluster of experiences. The practical proposition of pluralism makes sure everyone is involved. The challenge lies in the politics of polarization. It is in the interests of any society to be as pluralistic and inclusive as possible. Inclusion should be celebrated and not merely because it is a rule. A positive educational experience is crucial for the marginalized. For education to be meaningful, it has an important role to play in achieving greater equity and social justice which has to do with fairness. Any major transformation in higher education should not result in imbalances and incongruities in the system.

All India Survey on Higher Education (AISHE), 2019, conducted by the Department of Higher Education, Ministry of Human Resource Development (MHRD), states that there are 993 universities (central, state, deemed and private) and more than 39,931 colleges; however, it also found that the enrolment of Dalits, Muslims, women and PwDs in higher education and their representation in teaching and administrative jobs are way below their population. The SC population is 16.6 per cent, ST is 8.6 per cent and Muslims is 14.2 per cent. Some of these issues deserve a deeper analysis.

Dalits and Higher Education

The centrality of caste to understand Indian social reality cannot go unnoticed. Though caste is very ancient, it seems to be very present. To engage caste, one would have to navigate a variety of questions, situations and experiences. The core arguments of Phule and Ambedkar emphasize the importance of humanization, social justice and self-actualization. Their writings reflected their life experiences too. The social spaces of Dalits have become an enduring theme in the milieu of Indian politics and social life. Hence, caste-based discrimination has often determined the status and mobility of Dalit students. Caste discrimination and marginalization tends to exist both as a visible and hidden form of prejudice.

Dr B. R. Ambedkar had stressed that 'Dalithood' emphasized *life conditions*. Hence, he provided a radical slogan, namely, 'educate, agitate and organize' for the upliftment of the Dalits. Caste-based discrimination in higher education is now being seriously addressed. Higher education is one of the leading instruments to either prevent or promote social mobility. Exclusionary practices of Dalits, especially in professional educational institutions at multiple levels such as admission, pedagogy and learning approach, have been an area of concern. Some studies have shown that while overt acts of discrimination based on a student's caste are negligible, lower-caste students often experience limited access to the networks that create social capital. Needless to say, institutional efforts to enhance social capital would help students from the disadvantaged sections of society to overcome less obvious forms of discrimination. This helps to enhance their self-esteem and, consequently, performance levels in colleges and universities.

Different states have varied experiences. In Karnataka, more SC/ST students tend to enrol in government degree colleges and state universities than in aided colleges and private universities. Some sample surveys have shown that the dropout rate in the SC/ST community tends to increase with levels of education. The gap in the performance of the SC/ST students is again a matter of concern. In Tamil Nadu, the social justice movement has resulted in OBCs' monopolizing 54.4 per cent of the higher-education teaching jobs in the state. SC and ST enrolment across the country falls short of the mandated quota of 15 per cent and 7.5 per cent, respectively. In states like Tamil Nadu, Uttar Pradesh,

Kerala and Bihar, less than 20 per cent of the students enrolled in higher education are SCs and STs. Among the top-10 universities, only three have 22.5 per cent of SC/ST students. Among the IITs, under 19 per cent of enrolled students were SC or ST and an even lesser percentage were female. The Dalits have a higher dropout rate in the IITs, and this largely tends to happen because of caste-based discrimination and poor academic performance. The scenario is more or less the same in the IIMs and All India Institutes of Medical Sciences.

Muslims and Higher Education

Muslim representation in higher-educational institutions is way below their demographic base. The Sachar Committee on social, economic and educational condition of Muslims shows that they are way behind other religious minorities. Muslims seem to be broadly located in the informal sector labour force, small peasantry, petty production and small trades and artisanal industries. Indian Muslims are one of the most educationally backward and economically deprived groups. These low levels of socio-economic deprivation often do not get articulated in political discourses. The AISHE point out that Muslim enrolment is only around 5 per cent, which is less than that of the SC and ST.

They constitute only 2.5 per cent of the bureaucracy and 4.6 per cent of university teachers. Enrolment of Muslims in minority institutions is high—Jamia Milia Islamia, 50 per cent and in Aligarh Muslim University, 75 per cent. However, in non-minority institutions the figure comes down to as low as 1–3 per cent. In states where there is OBC domination politically and economically, we see the lower castes and Muslims being sidelined. AISHE data shows that Muslims are most underrepresented at both the national and state levels. The proliferation of madrasa form of education further hinders Muslims from getting the benefit of higher education. Mainstreaming does not necessarily mean loss of identity. Traditional madrasas could add to their woes. Many progressive Muslims contend that the time has come to train the imams of mosques to recognize the importance of modern education. Even the literacy rate among Muslims which stands at 60 per cent is way behind other religious minorities. Muslims have lagged in terms of development due to poor educational levels.

Overall, most studies tend to show the following reasons for backwardness among Muslims, namely, the large family size, lack of a link between modern education and madrasa education, economic poverty and negative attitude towards girls' education and the overall lack of a progressive leadership among the Muslim community. Such a progressive leadership is also required to mobilize support for greater equity in modern education, health, income and employment, rather than merely focusing on fatwas, personal laws and issues of identity, which may be necessary but not sufficient for their growth and well-being.

Women and Higher Education

The status of women in higher education cannot be perceived different from the overall status of women in society. The enrolment of women in higher education has gone up from 1.2 million women in 2010–2011 to 17.4 million in 2017–2018. However, the overall growth of women's education in rural India is very slow. Gender enrolment is not uniform across the country. States like Kerala, Goa, Himachal Pradesh and Union Territories like Lakshadweep are ahead of states like West Bengal, Tripura, Maharashtra, Madhya Pradesh and Bihar.

Enrolment of women in IITs and IIMs is lower than men. Due to certain relaxations provided by the government, women's enrolment for the PhD programmes has rapidly gone up. The rising enrolment of women in higher education has led to an improvement in the Gender Parity Index. Yet much remains to be done in terms of recruitment and placement for women in both the teaching and non-teaching staff in higher-education institutes.

It is time to get more women into leadership positions in higher education. The pipeline myth that there are few qualified women does not hold water any longer. In recent times, women have broken through various glass ceilings. The greatest challenge is to break through the rigidity of structures, systems, mindsets, biases and stereotypes. These systemic and cultural challenges often result in a loss of talent to institutions of higher education right across the global landscape. In the USA, for example, less than a third of the college or university presidents are women, and a majority of them White women. Denial of leadership opportunities means loss of opportunities too. The need of the hour is to create workplaces that are more inclusive, respectful and productive. Ultimately, what is required is not just an increase in terms of numbers but also the development of a culture of equality. Women's empowerment and sustainable development go together.

PwDs and Higher Education

PwDs have, over the years, remained a silent, invisible and marginalized populace. The time has come to provide them wings to achieve their dreams. The rights of the disabled have to do with the debate over 'equality of fair opportunities', the use of a *right-based framework* and the creation of an *inclusive culture* personally and institutionally. Article 21 of the Indian Constitution provides for the right to live with human dignity free from exploitation. All avenues of life ought to be made accessible and inclusive for the disabled. This will empower them with economic security and human dignity.

The Rights of Persons with Disabilities Act, 2016, provides for reservation of not less than 5 per cent seats for the PwDs. The Supreme Court in a landmark judgment in 2017 observed that people with disability have the right to access higher education and that action needs to be taken against defaulting institutions. This is required for the disabled to lead an independent, dignified, economically self-sufficient and fully participatory life. To do this, all possible barriers and obstacles to accessibility have to be removed.

Affirmative action is essential to empower the disabled realize their full potential and also experience their well-being. The main barriers to education faced by the PwDs include social exclusion, physical inaccessibility and even lack of individualized support. Hence, all infrastructural and social barriers to their inclusion and accessibility need to be removed. Not providing for this ipso facto amounts to discrimination and insensitivity. The importance of inclusive values demands an individualized, need-based approach along with sensitization of the stakeholders.

Against this background, the volume attempts to critically analyse the impact of higher education on the marginalized communities in India and suggests suitable policy measures to ensure Indian higher education becomes more inclusive and empowers marginalized communities.

Structure and Contents

The book contains a total of 13 chapters which are divided into six parts: (a) background, (b) Dalits and higher education, (c) minorities and higher education, (d) persons with disabilities and higher education, (e) women and higher education and (f) the way forward.

In the first section, Prakash Desai attempts to critically examine the evolution of state higher education in India. He has made an effort to understand the process of commercialization and communalization of higher education in India. Against this background, the chapter focuses on critical issues like market and higher education; private universities and freedom of social research; higher education and communal agenda and the political consensus on commercialization of higher education. Thus, the author's arguments form a basis for examining the status of marginalized communities in higher education. Chetan Singai emphasizes that after 34 years a new policy has been envisaged for reforming higher education in India. Access to higher education has improved over the past decades; however, equity continues to be a challenge. There exist myriad barriers for equity, especially for successful completion of higher education mainly due to gender, caste, physical abilities, religion, rural and urban and regional, amplifying the issue of equity. Arguably, such barriers tend to persist beyond enrolment. Policies need to be cognizant of such evidence(s). In this context, the chapter provides a descriptive analysis of key policies and committee on higher education from 1947 to 2020 to provide a systematic and systemic analysis of complex interpretation of equity in India's higher education.

In the second section, Krishnaswamy Dara explores the various ways and complex mechanisms that work to create an unjust environment for members of Dalit communities. In the process, the issue of testimonial injustice, which plays a central role in sustaining and perpetuating all forms of social injustice, is critically examined. Finally, the author argues that the efforts in the form of celebrating Ambedkar Jayanti, Sir Syed day, beef festival, etc., are in the right direction where students from the subaltern classes are made invisible and are a constant ridicule. Overall, the chapter provides a theatrical understanding of the concept of 'injustice'. T Brahmanandam argues that apart from social discrimination, personal struggle has been part of Dalits in higher education. Dalits, being weaker in their socio-economic profile, cannot afford to subscribe the mainstream culture which is otherwise very expensive. In this context, the author examines the higher education status among the SCs in India, since its independence, by analysing the available data on SCs ennoblement in primary, secondary and higher education. He also compares the proportion of non-SCs/STs in higher education, particularly different academic discipline and their presence in premier institutions like IITs, through affirmative action like reservations and its implementations. The prevailing deep-rooted rigid forms in institutional practices that have hampered the progress of Dalits in higher education are critically analysed. Areesh Kumar Karamala emphasize that the social stratification and hierarchical differences have consistently placed a large section of marginalized communities at the periphery, particularly the Dalits. The chapter attempts to analyse the concept of social inclusion within the framework of higher-educational institutions. It also concentrates on various forms of caste-based discrimination in higher education spaces like universities and inspects the challenges marginalized students experience in the academic spaces. Finally, the chapter analyses the legal frameworks to forbid exclusionary practices in the universities and also critically analyses the attempt to dilute the functioning of inclusive policies in an effective manner in the universities.

In the third section, K. M. Ziyauddin's chapter attempts to take the reference of Muslim community as a minority population but not an equal representation to other five minorities in order to understand and examine the questions of minorities in higher education. He argues that the discourse of equal opportunity is not to be seen only for a few but for all the communities that lag behind. Therefore, the chapter does intend to bring the challenges of minorities and especially Muslims in higher education with the underlying fact that they are the largest marginalized community in various parameters. Finally, the paper contextualizes in the perspectives of inclusion and exclusion and how the social distance is created over a period of time between the similar groups of citizenship on the line of religion and language. Maxim Dias and Alphonse Pius Fernandes discuss the critical role played by the Jesuit Worldwide Learning (JWL) in ensuring accessible education for the marginalized communities. The authors tend to argue that the Jesuit education, having a tradition of close to 500 years, has survived in quality and competence due to its capacity to adapt itself to the changing needs of the society. They justify the unique role that JWL has taken 'teaching-learning' process beyond the walls of classrooms to open spaces of domination of discrimination (refugees and marginalized), has ensured its survival. Even in the context of the commercialization of education, the authors explain how JWL's philosophy of teaching–learning acts as a counter-cultural movement, consciously using institutions for the benefits of the marginalized and less privileged. Finally, they conclude that, to a certain extent, JWL is a revolution in education but is not free from limitations.

In the fourth section, S. Y. Surendra Kumar explains that from time to time, various international conventions, declarations and resolutions have emphasized on inclusive education, so that the disadvantaged groups like the PwD would benefit. India's commitment to ensure PwD's access to education is well reflected by being part of the international provisions. Despite this, the percentage of PwD in higher education in India continues to be less than 5 per cent. In this context, the chapter attempts to examine the international community and India's efforts to make education accessible to PwD. The issues confronting the Indian education system in general and particularly the PwD in higher education are also analysed. Finally, the chapter identifies the necessary measures that need to be adopted to ensure PwD have access to higher education without any hurdles. Sanjay Jain makes an attempt to examine the role of higher education as an enabler in the lives of PwD. The author argues that although there are a lot of articles and books emphasizing and highlighting the role of accessibility in higher education, there are very few studies dealing with the fundamental question, what difference higher education can make in the lives of PWD? Thus, the main objective of this chapter is to analyse whether higher education is a value addition in the quality of lives of PWD. Subsequently, it also demonstrates that higher education apart from empowering the PWD is also an enabler in opening numerous vistas of career for them. Udaya Kiran K., being a visually impaired, has discussed the available assistive technology in higher education. The different types of devices based on disability, application, manufacturing and low and high technology are explained in detail. Thus, the author attempts to argue that even the visually impaired students can pursue higher education without any major hurdles through the use of available assistive technologies. At the same time, the limitations of assistive technologies are discussed in detail.

In the fifth section, Vagishwari S. P. writes that transparency, clear demarcation of rules of selection and policy statements of an inclusive culture alone do not provide satisfactory results for women empowerment. There needs to be a paradigm shift, in organizational structures and approaches, towards making higher education truly inclusive in nature. The chapter attempts to understand the entire discourse of women in higher education from a framework of postcolonialism and modernism perspective. Finally, it suggests that the academic audits in higher education spaces need to be redesigned, wherein individual strengths and institutional experiences will emerge as major qualifying determinants. At the same time, strict adherence to gender ratio, in terms of leadership, within an organization will also be a positive step towards women benefiting from higher education. Priyanca Mathur and Roshni Sharma's chapter seeks to interrogate the reasons behind the low representation of women in leadership roles as vice chancellors and administrators within higher education, despite studies showing a worldwide boom in higher education of women. The critical questions addressed in the chapter include why this 'gap' exists even after a rise in the enrolment of women in higher education. Finally, the authors also identify the root causes and look at measures that address the same.

The last section focuses on the way forward for marginalized communities in India and the impact of higher education. D. Jeevan Kumar intends to look at the current education scenario in India from the perspective of the marginalized communities and wonders whether the latest policy initiative in the form of the NEP 2020 has the right prescription to address the ever-elusive goals of access, inclusion and equity. Also, the chapter attempts an analysis of what ails our educational ecosystem and identifies a way forward that can only come from a deeper introspection of the roots of structural inequality and violence that is inherent in our social and cultural ethos.

We hope the readers will appreciate the modest attempt to critically analyse the impact of Indian higher education to empower the marginalized communities, especially Dalits, minorities, PwDs and women.

PART I

Contextualizing Indian Higher Education

Chapter 1
State of Higher Education in India
Prakash Desai

Chapter 2
Equity and Higher Education Policies in India:
Perspectives on National Education Policy 2020
Chetan Singai

1

State of Higher Education in India

Prakash Desai

Higher education is an important means of bringing about comprehensive development in any society. Any country which has a strong foundation of higher education can realize progress in different spheres of life. A strong foundation and growth of higher education have been the main factors which identify many Western countries as developed countries. This is not the story in the case of developing countries like India. Though higher education received some attention in the early decades after Independence, it has not yet received genuine attention on the part of both the Central government and the state governments. Consequently, it has not reached every section of the society, especially the marginalized. Moreover, whatever little bit progress was made has been eroded due to several factors such as corruption, nepotism in recruitment, political interference and many others. The quality of teaching and research has come down,[1] and there is no botheration about these developments on the part of respective governments and larger society.

From 1948 to 1990, a number of higher education learning centres such as Indian Institutes of Technology, Indian Institutes of Management, central universities and regional universities were established. However, they did not become educational agencies to accommodate and include students from every section of the society. The strategy of state-centric development was not able to make education as a public good in genuine sense. It did not realize the connection between primary and higher education. The people and areas which did not have access to primary education were deprived of access to higher education. The vast mass of children belonging to the deprived communities need to go to good schools and only then they can enter universities and institutes of higher education (Borooah, 2010).

The New Economic Policy (NEP) that was introduced in 1991 has its implications for higher education also (Kesar et al., 2019). The introduction of new economic reform policies that included stabilization and structural adjustment had tremendous impact on higher education (Jandhyala, 2004). Educational marginality of socially marginalized people, a kind of alliance between crony capitalism and communal forces,[2] and communalization of education are some of the developments that have been taking place for even longer than the two and a half decades. The capitalist forces and communal forces have been emerging as dominant forces in India. The capitalists are expanding their scope of capital investment and receiving direct and indirect support from the communal forces. Their activities are in tandem destroying the very idea of higher education. In this paper, an effort has been made to understand the process of commercialization and communalization of higher education in India. In this direction, the sub-themes covered in this paper are as follows: (a) market and higher education, (b) private universities and freedom of social research, (c) higher education and communal agenda and (d) the political consensus on commercialization of higher education.

Market and Higher Education

For longer than the two decades, higher education in India has been following the path of commercialization and trying its best to cater to the market needs. Both private and public institutions of higher education are trying hard to attract students for their market-oriented programmes like management, technical and medical education. These programmes are very expensive and students from socially and economically marginalized sections are not in a position to opt for such programmes. This leads one to believe that the higher education system is not a space that stands for equality, social justice, social inclusiveness and, above all, social democracy. There may be some positive developments, for instance, in the case of increased presence in higher education institutions of students from backward classes, but there are still many problems as far as the presence of students from Muslim minority is concerned (Apoorvanand, 2018). Muslims still do not have much presence in higher education (Apoorvanand, 2018).

There are certain observations to be made about public and private universities in the context of certain developments that are taking place in the country. The experiences of the last 20 odd years show that there have been few vice chancellors who have not spoken much on interconnectedness between market and universities. Many of them have reflected a lot on this and tried to make the university educational system facilitative towards the market and its needs. With this in mind, many new programmes are being offered at the university level. Most of these programmes do not have the philosophical foundations of core disciplines. The example of programmes related to governance and development can be given in this regard. If there are no philosophical basics of economics and political science in the above-mentioned programme, the pertinent questions that arise are: (a) how is development defined? (b) whether the idea of development is to be understood as an idea which facilitates social and economic inclusiveness or whether development is to be treated as a mainstream economic concept which favours only the elite sections of the society. These are difficult questions which need to be answered by the concerned people who have been in the forefront of the attempts to make educational programmes of universities pro market. These questions need to be answered because there is a need for democratizing the teaching in higher education learning centres. Our higher-educational institutions and the people who are heading them have to be socially accountable to the society. It is not just the question of creation of interconnectedness between higher education and industry that has to become the concern; the utmost concern should be creation of interconnectedness between society and higher-educational institutions. Higher-educational institutions should be made socially accountable to the marginalized in the society. There should be interconnectedness between marginalized class, marginalized gender, marginalized caste, marginalized religious groups and higher-educational institutions.[3]

Credit goes to the United Progressive Alliance (UPA) that was in power from 2004 to 2014 for establishing new central universities for many states of the Union. This could be considered a great development for the country. Most of these universities are established in backward regions of the respective states for the benefit of the people. However, if recent developments are taken into consideration, they cannot be considered as agencies of educational development. One can see a number of problems in the functioning of these universities. These universities have given major support to only some programmes such as management and natural sciences. Social science disciplines are getting step-motherly treatment. Thus, the plurality[4] in education in these universities was continuously being neglected during the UPA regime at the Centre. The National Democratic Alliance (NDA) which formed the government at Centre in 2014 has also followed the same approach as far as central universities are concerned. It tried to control and destroy the foundation of social sciences in all old central universities such as Jawaharlal Nehru University.[5] Progressive teachers and student organizations of these universities faced trouble from their administrations,[6] which are guided by the indirect intervention of the government. Where there is a demand for making education inclusive and affordable, the efforts are being made to dismantle the eminent institutions of higher learning (Chirmuley, 2017).

Universities like Jawaharlal Nehru University became targets of the NDA government because of the ideological plurality of their students and teachers.[7] These are public educational institutes where there is no scope for any brand of communalism and sectarianism. The reason for parties like Bharatiya Janata Party (BJP) to target such public educational institutes is explained well by Romila Thapar (Thapar, 2016). The BJP and Rashtriya Swayamsevak Sangh had to face a number of prestigious learning centres where there has been a demand for the right to debate ideas and issues that may be understood to be very critical. When they failed in curbing the demand for debate, the alternative left with them was to dismantle such learning centres by creating disturbances.

There are other worrying developments taking place in higher-educational institutions under the spell of market forces and neoliberal philosophy. Public universities are administered by people who give importance to surveillance, efficiency and techno-managerial solutions (Pathak, 2018). Avijit Pathak has analysed these developments well. He observes that as these 'academic bureaucrats become overwhelmingly powerful, critical pedagogues become marginalised. Idealism dies as fear or forced labour is normalised' (Pathak, 2018). Recognizing the importance of critical pedagogy, he writes, the

> University recovers its soul only through the spirited work of critical pedagogues; and the therapeutic function of critical pedagogy is to learn to redefine the meaning of work and freedom—work as creative play, freedom as engaged responsibility and concern for others and time as enabling, not constraining. (Pathak, 2018)

With regards to such an understanding of research and teaching, it is a general tendency on the part of academic administrators to come up with an argument that universities cannot run with the presence of only some disciplines, however important they may be, and there cannot be proper order in the universities without control, standardization and monitoring (Pathak, 2018). Thus, academic bureaucrats would not like to give importance to critical pedagogy. The effect of such tendency can be seen in the way certain disciplines are treated. The disciplines like philosophy, anthropology, political science, sociology and history are not given much importance because they are the sources of critical thinking and they pave the way for logic, reason, debate and discussion.

Private Universities and Freedom of Social Research

There has been discussion that higher education should be further privatized. One of the observations that is given for privatization of higher education is that publicly provided professional education has not expanded and it has not met the growth in demand (Balakrishnan, 2015). This observation of proponents of private education has its own validity, but there are many problems in privatizing higher education. Higher education is not just about technical education. It comprises natural sciences and social sciences. Our policymakers and political class, those who are involved in educational policy formulation, should understand the nature, scope and importance of higher education. In the private universities which have already come into existence, research related to social sciences is not receiving required encouragement. Though these private universities may claim that they too have social sciences divisions, fundamental and dynamic research related to social sciences is not being undertaken.

There are many private universities in developed Western countries. Though these universities are managed by the private sector, they have retained educational autonomy and freedom. The management is always a great supporter of their autonomy. Many scholars from reputed universities work as faculty members in Indian private universities. These scholars cannot undertake research on the basis of progressive philosophy or approaches. Their research is not supposed to go against the philosophy of the management. Since these universities are managed or owned by industrialists or business firms, any research which questions the philosophy of neoliberalism cannot be conducted without unnecessary interference. For these reasons, it is suggested that the state take the responsibility of the management of institutes of higher education.

The very idea of autonomy being demanded and offered has different objectives in the case of India. The issue of autonomy raised has intention of commercializing education and pushing away disciplines of social sciences from the institutions of higher education. Education loses its purpose if it does not prepare youth for leading a meaningful life. Society not only educates its youth to acquire skills but also to allow the fullest development of the personality in them (Prasad, 2005). Autonomy is actually required for higher-educational institutions in this regard. Autonomy is required for the social sciences to teach and encourage free thinking. 'Education must encourage both competence and critical thinking' (Prasad, 2005). Unfortunately, this is not generally made as a reason for demanding autonomy. It is pertinent to keep in mind here

> That the best institutions of higher education in the world in terms of quality and standards are public institutions or private institutions that are guided by the principles of philanthropy. They are certainly not for-profit institutions. Besides, for-profit institutions are hardly inclusive in providing access to higher education. As a matter of fact, they are clearly exclusionary in nature. (Jandhyala, 2012)

In the name of autonomy, crucial role of higher education is getting forgotten. The role that higher-educational institutions are there for teaching and following the idea of inclusive societal development that results in inclusive society and inclusive democracy is not being given much importance.

Constructing the notion of what should constitute higher education is working in tandem with institutional agendas and societal aspirations. Educational institutions are setting and following the agendas of what is considered important education for human life, and, at the individual level, parents are responding to such notions by imposing these agendas by forcing their children to be the experiments. Regarding the nature of success associated with education, it is observed that in the age of trade and economic utility the success is based on the hierarchy of disciplines (Pathak, 2018). Disciplines like science and commerce are considered as superior and moneymaking whereas a negative orientation is attached to arts and humanities (Pathak, 2018). The thinking is such that arts and humanities have no future; so bright students are not supposed to study and opt for such branches of knowledge (Pathak, 2018). This is a very regressive and totalizing thinking in the sense that it would not allow aspirants of knowledge to get exposed to the branches of knowledge which plays an important role in building a humane and democratic society that further makes the world cosmopolitan and harmonious without facilitating any scope for ethnocentric tendencies and regressive thinking.

It is common knowledge that many of teachers and parents pressurize children to opt for disciplines which they think would help children's lives. Children are not given the chance to think about their choice of education and career. This could be considered as the beginning of some kind of isolation or detachment in the life of children (Pathak, 2018). When friends, neighbours and relatives, as a part of society, put restrictions on children's imagination, children's anxiety and fear are further intensified, and this condition makes them to believe that life is necessarily dark and bleak without medical, technological and management studies (Pathak, 2018). As a solution to this problem, Avijit Pathak suggests that teachers, educationists and adults in general need to tell children the importance of inner fulfilment (Pathak, 2018). To become successful, one needs to find happiness and meaning in any profession that is voluntarily opted. The profession may be farming, nursing or teaching. Second, he suggests that for a mature society all kinds of professions are required. It is the task of teachers to make child understand his or her potential (Pathak, 2018). Society cannot run merely relying on one particular profession. For its vibrancy, it needs the presence of many professions. As engineers and doctors are required for society, in the same way, historians, filmmakers, economists and many more are required. Pathak's third prescription is very meaningful and philosophical. There should be encouragement for youngsters to think differently, to take a risky path and experiment with life. Continuous pressure to remain normal and opt safe path does not empower youngsters to make life meaningful (Pathak, 2018).

Higher Education and Communal Agenda

Direct and indirect interference of communal forces in policy formulation and implementation with respect to higher education is another problem to be concerned about. The University Grants Commission (UGC) is one of the major sources of finance for universities. Apart from the UGC, universities apply for financial support from the Indian Council of Social Science Research (ICSSR), the Indian Council of Historical Research (ICHR) and other institutions associated with the Central government, in order to undertake research activities. If these institutions are headed by people who come from the background of communal philosophy and organizations, one cannot expect liberal and autonomous decisions from them with respect to any academic activity. Academic activities like seminars and projects which explore liberal and progressive ideas may not get support from funding councils if they are under the control of people with certain ideological or communal approach. The issue of concern in universities is with respect to faculty recruitment.[8] If universities are headed by people with an ideological bias, faculty recruitment for universities may not be purely on the basis of merit. Rather, it can happen on the basis of communal considerations.

Introducing Indian philosophy, culture, civilization, religions and history to the world and Indian students has always been one of the objectives of higher education in India. In this direction, several disciplines and subjects were introduced in the country's various universities and research centres. The general idea which guided these disciplines and subjects did not have any hidden agenda to fulfil. Overall, these disciplines and subjects were studied and researched with the support of all philosophical approaches without any bias. This has not been the case when the BJP came to the power. It tried to bring in its own ideological biases in the process of understanding the areas of Indic studies mentioned above. It made an effort to distort the facts and tried to give a distorted understanding of Indic thought and life. BJP, which came to power at the Centre in 2014, gave enough scope to such activities of distorted understanding of Indic thought. The process of popularizing the Indic thought by the scholars who are influenced by the rightist ideology received enough support in the period of the BJP's government at the Centre from 2014 to 2019.

There is nothing wrong in giving importance to Indic thought in higher-educational institutions, but the problem lies in the way these ideas are understood and researched. The trend in Indic ideas in recent times is that they are studied, researched and debated with two main philosophical bases, either Vedic or Shramanic. There are ideas and existence beyond Vedic and Shramanic bases. Our Adivasi life and philosophy, our non-Vedic life and philosophy have their own significance and relevance. Ideas beyond Vedic and Shramanic are very much Indian and need to be discussed and researched. Unfortunately, even progressive scholars are not giving the required attention to this lacuna. Our higher-educational institutions are supposed to give importance to research on such life and philosophy so that they become known at national and international level. Many among us do not know the life and philosophy of the people living in different regions of the country. Cultures, religions, social visions of our own several communities are missing in the knowledge and awareness of our many people including educated and highly educated. There is total ignorance and illiteracy about our own regions in the country. This ignorance is causing the prejudices and divisions in the country. The process of constructing other within our own is mainly due to our ignorance and illiteracy about our own people, their culture, language and their philosophy of life.

It needs to be emphasized that the idea of India is not sectarian and exclusive. The idea of India is open and gives space for several voices (Ganeri, 2009). These voices might be orthodox and dissenting of different regions, ages and affiliations (Ganeri, 2009). Any direct or indirect threat to this civilizational foundation cannot be sustained but remains as an unwarranted phase in our history for the future. India as a civilization has received many ideas from the world and has contributed many ideas to the world. This is the reason that India is not just known as Bharat, it is Vishwabharati—Vishwabharati of Rabindranath, Discovered Bharat of Nehru and Prabuddha Bharat of Ambedkar. Bharat of Rabindranath, Nehru and Ambedkar is a confluence of several streams of ideas.

The Political Consensus on Commercialization of Higher Education

The discussion on privatizing higher education began during the period of the NDA government (1999–2004). The special subject group established under the leadership of Mukesh Ambani by this government had advised private finance in higher education (Sharma, 2001). In actuality, in the name of the knowledge economy, this special group was hinting at commercialization of higher education (Sharma, 2001). The report submitted to the Prime Minister's Council on Trade and Industry by Mukesh Ambani and Kumar Mangalam Birla in April 2000 'sought to convert the entire system of higher education in the country into a market where profit making would be the only consideration' (Sharma, 2010).

After the NDA experiment, the UPA, which came to power at the Centre in 2004, set up the National Knowledge Commission. This commission came up with a number of good suggestions, but it did not remain free from the idea of private finance in education. The commission recommended 'the expansion of the number of universities to 1,500 in the country' (Jandhyala, 2007). There was a belief that it 'would enable India to attain a gross enrolment ratio of at least 15 percent by 2015' (Jandhyala, 2007). Consequently, both the Central government and many state governments have established universities. However, if one looks at the state of these newly established universities, there are many problems to be tackled. Universities are facing the problem of basic infrastructure facilities. It is a widely known fact that many teaching and non-teaching positions are vacant. Whatever recruitment has taken place has also been widely criticized because of certain unfair practices. The other recommendation of the commission was 'autonomy for the universities to set student fee levels, tap other sources, and also for the commercial use of university facilities' (Jandhyala, 2007, p. 632). Thus, the overall approach adopted by the commission was 'largely pro-private, and even anti-public' (Jandhyala, 2007).

The NDA that came to power in 2014 was in the news for its many controversial policy formulations and implementations regarding higher education.

> The most controversial decision in the realm of higher education was the selection of 'Institutions of Eminence'. In the 2016 budget, the government announced it would select 20 institutions, 10 each in the public and private sector, which would get funds and greater administrative autonomy to achieve top-500 positions in international university rankings. (Chowdhury, 2019)

In the direction of this decision, the government 'announced the names of six institutions of higher education—three each in public and private sectors—that have been granted the status' (Choudhury, 2018), the status of Institutions of Eminence. Interestingly, one of them was 'Jio Institute, an institution proposed to be set up by Reliance Foundation, led by Nita Ambani' (Choudhury, 2018). The selection of this non-existent institute sparked controversy (*Indian Express*, 2018). Discussions and criticisms were raised regarding the rationale behind the selection of this institute.

The other issue that received attention was the government's effort to withdraw finance to higher education.

> The withdrawal of university grants came with the idea of pushing institutions to raise funds from the market. For this, the Higher Education Finance Agency was created in November 2017. It is a non-banking finance corporation that gives infrastructure loans to universities and colleges. The institutions are expected to repay the principal amount within 10 years, while the government pays the interest. (Chowdhury, 2019)

The universities which opt for such loans 'will have to raise their own funds through fees and research earnings to pay the loans back' (Jha & Jamil, 2018). In this way, universities would become 'corporate entities, entangled in a web of real-estate and finance dealings' (Jha & Jamil, 2018). It would adversely affect students and parents who come from socio-economically disadvantaged backgrounds.

These developments show a clear political consensus on the part of political parties towards commercializing and privatizing the higher education. When a political establishment plays with the issues of the common people, the public has to play a greater role. Every citizen has to engage with the establishment to teach it the grammar of democracy. Every Indian citizen has to ensure that the government gives priority to public interests and protects public services like health and education. There has been a problem with the funding of education and health. They have continued to remain not properly supported (Chattopadhyay, 2020). Citizens should make the government to protect services like these from onslaught by the forces which propagate 'the ideology of the marketplace as the solution to every issue' (Sharma, 2005).

The BJP, which again came to power in 2019, is emphasizing on reforms in higher education. The new National Education Policy is being discussed and reviewed by the government (*Indian Express*, 2020). Some of the stated objectives of this new process are to bring higher education at par with the highest global standards, providing education, which is effective, inclusive and contemporary, rooted in the Indian culture and ethos (*Indian Express*, 2020). These objectives can be appreciated but the problem is with respect to bringing them into practice. India's record of implementing the principle of good-quality education is not satisfactory (Jha & Parvati, 2019). It needs to be seen how the government and future governments are going to implement the stated principles of the process. They should not become like pre-election manifesto promises which can be brushed aside (Deshpande, 2019).

Certain concerns have already been expressed regarding the draft National Education Policy 2019, which is being discussed by the government and all the concerned (Roy, 2019). It was observed that 'the policy envisages a centralised and tightly structured system that will be under the direct control of political leaders of the government of the day' (Robinson, 2019). The other observation regarding the policy is 'autonomy and academic freedom popularly understood would become casualties to the changes in the regulatory regime and governance structure it lays down' (Bohidar, 2019). It is to be noted that the report of India's first Education Commission emphasized teachers and students as a learning society to retain 'their independence from interference by political and market forces, from pressures of governmental, administrative and financial intervention, and the prejudices of socio-religious ideologies' (Prasad, 2019).

Whether the government at the centre is the UPA or the NDA, their educational approach to a large extent has remained the same and is causing great destruction of higher education. It has become difficult to identify the political forces which stand for inclusive and democratic higher education. If market principles are applied to education, the very objective of education is lost (Chattopadhyay, 2009). There is danger in treating education as any other consumption good (Chattopadhyay, 2009). The process of making education as any other good causes education to lose its vital role—its role 'in building up of a democratic, humane, and inclusive society' (Chattopadhyay, 2009). The narratives on the part of political forces in India clearly convey that they are not serious about the future course of action on higher education. Some might be in favour of mere privatization of higher education, but some are very clear about their agenda of privatizing and communalizing higher education.

Notes

1. See Bhoite (2009).
2. To know how political elites, including in the Bharatiya Janata Party, have given importance to market and globalization, read Priya Chacko (2019). Also read Hansen (1996, 2015).
3. Read the project discussed in the article by Divya Trivedi (2018).
4. To know more about the importance of pluralism in universities, read Ramchandra Guha (2007).

5. To know how some universities faced certain problems in last few years, read Arunima (2017).
6. See Sanjaya Baru (2018).
7. To know more about diversity, democracy and dissent in JNU, read Jean-Thomas Martelli and Khaliq Parkar (2018).
8. See, Kumar Buradikatti (2020). One such example of the violation of norms and procedures is given here. There are many more such developments that happened in last many years.

References

Apoorvanand. (2018, 8 December). A higher exclusion. *The Indian Express.* https://indianexpress.com/article/opinion/columns/a-higher-exclusion-obc-dalit-muslim-quota-student-reservation-indian-university-campus-5483776/

Arunima, G. (2017, November). Thought, policies and politics: How may we imagine the public university in India? *Kronos,* 43 165–184. https://www.jstor.org/stable/44646202

Balakrishnan, P. (2015, 10 May). The case against privatisation of education. *The Hindu.* https://www.thehindu.com/opinion/op-ed/The-case-against-privatisation-of-education/article11640719.ece

Baru, S. (2018, 7 August). Don't destroy my university. *The Indian Express.* https://indianexpress.com/article/opinion/columns/higher-studies-jawaharlal-nehru-university-indian-students-stduying-abroad-5294734/

Bhoite, U. B. (2009). Higher education in India: A system on the verge of chaos. *Sociological Bulletin,* 58(2), 151. https://www.jstor.org/stable/23620683

Bohidar, S. K. (2019). Corporate route in higher education. *Frontline.* https://frontline.thehindu.com/cover-story/article28259190.ece

Borooah, V. K. (2010). Social exclusion and jobs reservation in India. *Economic & Political Weekly,* 45(52), 35. https://www.jstor.org/stable/27917960

Buradikatti, K. (2020, 2 March). Violation of UGC norms alleged in CUK recruitment process. *The Hindu.* https://www.thehindu.com/news/national/karnataka/violation-of-ugc-norms-alleged-in-cuk-recruitment-process/article30964818.ece

Chacko, P. (2019, March). Marketizing *Hindutva*: The state, society, and markets in Hindu nationalism. *Modern Asian Studies,* 53(2), 377–410.

Chattopadhyay, S. (2009). The market in higher education: Concern for equity and quality. *Economic & Political Weekly,* 44(29), 60. https://www.jstor.org/stable/40279288

Chattopadhyay, S. (2020, 11 January). Public funding of universities: In pursuit of efficiency, equity and excellence. *Economic & Political Weekly, IV*(2), 32.

Chirmuley, P. (2017, 21 September). The business of learning. *The Indian Express*. https://indianexpress.com/article/opinion/columns/the-business-of-learning-higher-education-iit-iim-education-sector-4853416/

Choudhury, S. R. (2018, 9 July). Reliance's Jio Institute gets government's Institution of Eminence status but it's yet to be set up. *Scroll.in*. https://scroll.in/article/885897/reliances-jio-university-gets-governments-institute-of-eminence-status-but-its-yet-to-be-set-up

Chowdhury, S. R. (2019, 5 February). The Modi years: What has the government done to improve higher education in India? *Scroll.in*. https://scroll.in/article/909668/the-modi-years-what-has-the-government-done-to-improve-higher-education-in-india

Deshpande, S. (2019, 14 June). Like election manifestos, draft NEP is merely a statement of intent. *The Indian Express*. https://indianexpress.com/article/opinion/columns/too-good-to-be-true-national-education-policy-5779613/

Editorial. (2018, 3 September). Open the black box. *The Indian Express*. https://indianexpress.com/article/opinion/editorials/institutions-of-eminence-jio-university-hrd-prakash-javadekar-5336477/

Ganeri, J. (2009, Spring). Intellectual India: Reason, identity, dissent. *New Literary History, 40*(2), 262. https://www.jstor.org/stable/27760257

Guha, R. (2007, 17 February). Pluralism in the Indian University. *Economic & Political Weekly, 42*(7), 564–570.

Hansen, T. B. (1996). The ethics of Hindutva and the spirit of capitalism. In T. B. Hansen & C. Jaffrelot (Eds.), *BJP and the compulsions of politics*. Oxford University Press.

Hansen, T. B. (2015, October). *Communalism, democracy and Indian capitalism*. Seminar. http://www.india-seminar.com/2015/674/674_thomas_blom_hansen.htm

Jandhyala B. G. T. (2004). Absence of policy and perspective in higher education. *Economic & Political Weekly, 39*(21), 2160. https://www.jstor.org/stable/4415064

Jandhyala, B. G. T. (2007). Knowledge commission and higher education. *Economic & Political Weekly, 42*(8), 630. http://www.jstor.org/stable/4419273

Jandhyala, B. G. T. (2012). Higher education policy in India in transition. *Economic & Political Weekly, xlvii*(13), 39. https://www.jstor.org/stable/23214708

Jha, M. K., & Jamil, G. (2018, 26 October). Dismantling the public university. *Indian Express*, https://indianexpress.com/article/opinion/columns/higher-education-india-hrd-prakash-javadekar-ugc-autonomy-of-universities-5363404/

Jha, P., & Parvati, P. (2019, 29 June). A country in search of an education policy. *Economic & Political Weekly, IIV*(26 & 27), 16.

Kesar, S., Dutt, D., & Dasgupta, Z. (2019, 20 December). Higher education: Privatizing a public good. *Frontline*. https://frontline.thehindu.com/the-nation/article30147154.ece

Martelli, J. T., & Parkar, K. (2018, 17 March). Diversity, democracy, and dissent: A study on student politics in JNU. *Economic & Political Weekly (engage)*, *53*(11). https://www.epw.in/engage/article/diversity-democracy-dissent-study-student-politics-JNU

Pathak, A. (2018, 30 May). A sick society that manufactures failures—The true face of education in India. *The Wire*. https://thewire.in/education/the-true-face-of-indias-education-system

Pathak, A. (2018, 23 July). The danger that lies in academic bureaucrats taking over our universities. *The Wire*. https://thewire.in/education/academic-bureaucrats-critical-pedagogues-and-our-universities

Prasad, M. (2005, November–December). Autonomy and the commercialization of higher education. *Social Scientist*, *33*(11/12), 43. https://www.jstor.org/stable/3518065

Prasad, M. (2019, 19 July). NEP 2019: The devil in the detail. *Frontline*. https://frontline.thehindu.com/cover-story/article28259123.ece

Robinson, R. (2017, July). An academic's response: Draft National Education Policy, 2019. *Economic & Political Weekly*, *IIV*(30), 32.

Roy, K. (2019, June). Examining the Draft National Education Policy, 2019. *Economic & Political Weekly (engage)*, *54*(25). https://www.epw.in/engage/article/examining-draft-national-education-policy-2019

Sharma, V. (2001, 25 March). Reject Ambani-Birla report education. *People's Democracy*, *XXV*(12). https://archives.peoplesdemocracy.in/2001/march25/march25_vijender.htm

Sharma, V. (2005, September–October). Commercialisation of higher education in India. *Social Scientist*, *33*(9/10), 73. https://www.jstor.org/stable/3518092

Sharma, V. (2010, September–December). UPA's agenda of academic 'reforms' facilitating trade in higher education. *Social Scientist*, *38*(9/12), 92. https://www.jstor.org/stable/27896291

Thapar, R. (2016). Targeting institutions of higher education: Fear of the intellectual. *Economic & Political Weekly*, *LI*(10), 20.

The Indian Express. (2020, 2 May). PM Modi holds education sector review meeting, focus to make India 'global knowledge power'. https://indianexpress.com/article/education/pm-modi-holds-education-sector-review-meeting-focus-to-make-india-global-knowledge-power-6389917/

Trivedi, D. (2018, 30 March). Inclusive universities. *Frontline*. https://frontline.thehindu.com/the-nation/inclusive-universities/article10092263.ece?homepage=true

2

Equity and Higher Education Policies in India
Perspectives on National Education Policy 2020

Chetan Singai

Introduction

In the last seven decades, higher education in India (HEI) has witnessed unprecedented growth and transformation. Currently, 37.4 million students enrolled in 993 universities and 39,931 colleges (Ministry of Human Resource Development [MHRD], 2019, p. i) as compared to 3.69 million students studying in 27 universities and 695 colleges at the time of Independence (Agarwal & Kamalakar, 2009, p. 152). Arguably, decisive policy interventions and reforms towards expansion, equity and excellence have been instrumental in transforming the system of higher education and its institutions, particularly in the last three decades. Since Independence, the principles of 'expansion, equity and excellence' are the foundation for the overall evolution of higher education system and its policy reforms in India (Tilak, 2013, p. 22).

To this end, the main aim of the chapter is to examine the key policy reports on higher education from 1947 to 2016, while examining the perspectives of National Education Policy 2020 (NEP 2020). In other words, analysing the content and context of the recommendations of national higher education policy (NHEP) reports (n = 29), the chapter exemplifies certain policy constants, changes and contradictions. The NHEP reports are listed into two temporalities—the pre-liberalization and post-liberalization era, 1947–1989 (15 policy reports) and 1990–2016 (14 policy reports) (see Table 2.1). A review of the recent 'themes and questions for policy consultation on higher education' (MHRD, 2015) does not surface a coherent underlying framework (Kumkum, 2015). No underlying logic is evident, the list appears to be ad hoc. There is an urgent need for a comprehensive framework; for without one, neither the retrospective analysis nor the projection can be systemic or systematic. In this backdrop, the chapter provides a brief discussion on linking the key interpretations to the issue of equity in higher education as envisaged in the NEP 2020.

Higher Education Policies in India: The Setting

As a result of constant planning and policy interventions, the higher education sector in India has witnessed unprecedented expansion. According to J. B. G. Tilak, given the total number of students enrolled in higher education, India is the third largest in the world, followed by China and the USA (Tilak, 2013). Further, expansion in the number of institutions since Independence makes India one of the largest in the world (University Grants Commission, 2011). However, scholars in the domain of education policy in India were critical on such a quantitative shift in higher education. Periodic assessment of higher education by policies and committees on higher education suggested lapses in systemic reforms (Agarwal, 2009) followed by concerns of deteriorating standards and inclusiveness in higher education due to uncontrolled and unplanned expansion (Rizvi, 2012). According to J. N. Kaul (1988), HEI has witnessed a phenomenon of 'planned drift' in implementing the reforms suggested over several decades. Further, according to Philip Altbach (2009), in addition to deteriorating standards within the higher education system, the government has failed to 'act' upon the recommendations of education commission(s) since Independence.

In retrospect, the higher education system and its institutions have deep-rooted impressions from the colonial past. Immediately after Independence, examining the need for and status of higher education, various reports of the committees and policies, over a decade, emphasized on three core principles of expansion, equity and excellence. However, the prioritization of these principles witnessed variations by respective policies and committee recommendations. To this end, the chapter illustrates the trajectory of the core principles in higher education.

While the country is witnessing series of reforms in higher education, there exists a crisis in the institutions (Tilak, 2013). For instance, previously, policies lacked an implementation framework in addressing issues related to access and equity. Arguably, most of the higher education institutions in the country, over a period, have adopted self-styled modes of practising equity and accessibility. There exists a gap between policies, guidelines and programme between the government and the institutions. Such a gap is compounded by myriad types of higher education institutions—public-state, private-state, public-central, private deemed-to-be, public deemed-to-be, institutions of national importance, public-state open universities and public-central open universities and private-aided and un-aided affiliating and autonomous colleges. Majority of the NHEP reports have ignored such complex realities or evidence at the institutional level.

Misguided policies have manifested the higher education sector and its institutions in the last few decades; hence, a new national education policy is much needed (Roy, 2015). The much celebrated and awaited NEP 2020 addresses the issue of equity at the level of the policy, seeking inputs from the state of the practice and the state of the need, for instance, nation-wide consultations with stakeholders to examine the role and relevance of equity in higher education and its institutions.

Higher Education and Nation-building from 1947 to 2016

A shift from the British legacy to Independence observed specific changes as well as continuity (Chitnis, 1993). In other words, the higher education sector was deep-rooted into the vestiges of colonial interventions, while envisioning the project of modernity and nation-building.

In this part, the chapter aims to examine 29 NHEP reports and not the consequent operational policies of the Government of India ministries, regulatory agencies and accreditation bodies. The NHEP reports are divided into two temporal components: (a) the period between 1947 to 1989 (n = 15) and (b) the period from 1990–2016 (n = 14). Table 2.1 illustrates NHEP recommendation listed across the two phases.

Table 2.1 *Illustration of Key Policies and Committees on Higher Education*

1947–1989 ($n = 15$)	1990–Present ($n = 14$)
• The University Education Commission of 1948/ Dr Radhakrishnan Commission (1948)	• Gnanam Committee on 'Alternate Models of Management'/'New education management' in higher education (1990)
• Committee on higher education for rural areas, rural institutions/Shri K. L. Shrimali Committee (1954)	• National Policy on Education (Programme of Action) (1992)
• The National Committee on Women's Education (1958)	• *Justice Punnayya Committee Report on UGC Funding of Institutions of Higher Education (1992–1993)*
• Review Committee on Education/Saiyidain Committee (1960)	
• Kothari Committee on Model Act for Universities (1961)	• Ramlal Parikh Committee for reforms in appointment of vice chancellors in Indian universities (1993)

1947–1989 (n = 15)	1990–Present (n = 14)
• Education Commission or Kothari Commission (1964–1966) • Committee of Members of Parliament on Education (1967) • National Policy on Education (1968) • Committee on Governance of Universities and Colleges (1969) • Gajendragadkar Committee on Governance of Universities and Colleges (1971) • *Towards a Socially Relevant Legal Education (UGC) (1975–1977)* • *Report of The Committee to Enquire into the Working of Central Universities (1984)* • National Policy on Education (1986) • *Report of the Expert Committee on the Minimum Qualifications and Workload etc. for Librarians and Directors of Physical Education in Universities and Colleges (1987)* • *Report of the Taskforce on the Code of Professional Ethics for University and College Teachers (1989)*	• UGC Commonwealth Secretariat Workshop on Women and Management in Higher Education (1997) • *Report of the Committee to Curb the Menace of Ragging in Universities/Educational Institutions (1999)* • CABE report on autonomy in higher education, MHRD, GOI (2005) • National Knowledge Commission recommendations on higher education (2006) • The Yashpal Committee Report/Committee to Advise on Renovation and Rejuvenation of Higher Education (2008) • Indian Institutes of Management (IIMs) Review Committee, MHRD, GoI (2008) • Action Plan for Academic and Administrative Reforms (2009) • Recommendations on the guidelines for implementation of programmes and schemes under Scheduled Castes Sub Plan and Tribal Sub Plan in the Ministry of Human Resource Development (2010) • Rashtriya Uchchattar Shiksha Abhiyan (2013) • *T. S. R. Subramanian Committee Report of the Committee for the Evolution of the New Education Policy (2015)*

Source: Ramaprasad et al. (2016, p. 12).

Policy Dispositions in the Post-Independence Era (1947–1989): Expansion with Equity

Expansion followed by the equity in higher education was considered to be the policy priority by members of the core committees and policies between 1947–1989. The policy dispositions envisaged during this period emphasized on the spirit of reforms in higher education aligned to the vestiges of the colonial system and aspiration of a 'new' India (Singai, 2018). During this period, the Radhakrishnan Commission—1948, the Kothari Commission—1964, the National Policy on Education—1968, Committee on Governance of the Universities and Colleges—1969, the Gajendragadkar Committee—1971 and the National Policy on Education—1986 (NPE 1986) have been critical for the overall development and conceptualization of policy landscape and interventions for higher education in the post-independent India.

The Radhakrishnan Committee, also known as the University Education Commission of 1948–1949, was committed to providing policy direction to the university education system in line with the priorities of the nation and its project of development (Ayyar, 2017). The commission identified the importance of expansion of higher education institutions as a policy priority to address the issue of accessibility and equity. In particular, the commission recommended provision for various provisions to students through scholarship, hostels, the role of vernacular languages in teaching and learning, establishment of HEIs in rural areas and so on. As an emerging independent nation, such prioritization was inevitable and, hence, apropos to the aspirations of the new and young India.

In order to engage with the recommendations of the Radhakrishnan Commission, following committees—the Shrimali Committee, 1954; National Committee on Women's Education, 1958; and Kothari Committee on Model Act for Universities, 1961—provided inputs in shaping the higher education sector in the country. The members associated with these committees recognized the importance of expansion as one of the key reform areas in higher education aligned with the socio-economic–cultural diversity of the country.

Amidst major political and economic transformations witnessed by the Second Five-year Plan (1956–1961) leading to the Third Five-year Plan (1961–1966), the then Ministry of Education constituted a national-level commission—the Kothari Commission in 1964, a milestone document for visualizing a modern education system for an independent and emerging India (Naik, 1982, p. 18). The core policy objective of the commission was to evolve a 'national strategy for the development of education at all stages and in all aspects' (Ayyar, 2017, p. 48). Further, the commission, while examining the causes for existing inequalities of educational opportunities, identified poverty as one of the core issues affecting access to higher education. The commission suggests that there exists gender disparity between boys and girls at all levels and disciplines of higher education. Further, there are caste-based disparities between the Scheduled Castes (SCs) and Scheduled Tribes (STs). By addressing these issues, the core mission of the commission was to democratize higher education by addressing the main causes of disparities.

While the commission indicates a need for inclusive education, it provides equal stress on the need for quality in and of education. On the one hand, the commission intended overcoming barriers for accessibility in higher education, whereas it recommended 'selective admission' at the degree level, on the other (NCERT, 1970, p. 151). Further, the commission, emphasized role and relevance of research to harness the quantity and quality in the production of knowledge in HEIs. In other words, the commission recommended prioritizing programmes related to qualitative improvement over programmes of expansion, an agenda set by the Radhakrishnan Commission and subsequent committees. A renowned scholar in the field of education policy, J. P. Naik suggests that such an emphasis resulted in the significant lapse in the policy direction. According to him, 'large scale expansion vis-à-vis quality was the need of the hour.' (Naik, 1982, p. 28)

Addressing the aspirations and contradictions discussed in the Kothari Commission's report to the nation, the Committee of Members of Parliament on Education, 1967, whilst evaluating the commission's report, expressed its discontent with the core recommendations. The committee, while acknowledging the commission's vision for creating a national system of education, it expressed dissent regarding prioritizing quality improvement at the cost of inclusion and expansion. Thus, the committee recommended, rather unanimously, to revisit recommendations of Radhakrishnan Commission and subsequent committee reports, endorsing expansion and inclusion as a policy priority (Powar, 2000, p. 34).

Between the period from 1967 to 1985, the country witnessed a series of social, political and economic changes. Specific interventions were suggested in higher education and its institutions during this period. For instance, to review and reform the governance of universities and colleges, the ministry constituted the Gajendragadkar Committee, 1969, and Committee to Enquire into the Working of Central Universities in 1984. The two committees, arguably, for the first time, were attempts to organize and streamline higher education institutions and their governance.

After two decades from the preceding national policy on education, the ministry constituted NPE 1986. The NPE 1986, in the preamble, mentions that 'Education in India stands at the crossroads today. Neither normal linear expansion nor the existing pace and nature of improvement can meet the needs of the situation' (MHRD, 1986, p. 2). Further, NPE 1986 in its preamble provides a cautionary note that the education sector in the country continues to be in crisis. As such, indicating the fact that recommendations of previous NHEP reports, especially the Kothari Commission, 1964, has little or no impact in implementing a robust system of education in the country (MHRD, 1986, p. 3).

Before the NPE 1986 was constituted, the country witnessed a significant social movement persuading the government to constitute the Mandal Commission in 1979, to 'study and identify socially and economically backward classes.' One of the core recommendations of the Mandal Commission was to ensure access to higher education for the socially and economically backward classes by introducing 'quota' for admission. Such an intervention transformed the landscape of HEI. At the systemic level and the level of the institutions, higher education witnessed an unprecedented expansion in terms of increase in student enrolment and higher education institutions. Aligned to the spirit of inclusive education and the concerns expressed by the advocates, activist and analysts associated with education, NPE 1986 recommends that 'the doors of academic institutions should be open to all and must provide for special provisions for the weaker sections of the society' (MHRD, 1986, p. 6). NPE 1986 recommended special provisions to enhance access to institutions of higher education through protective discrimination like reservation, quotas in higher education, scholarship and special incentives. Further, NPE 1986 appreciated the relevance of the open university system and setting up of rural universities in each district in order to expand the scope of higher education to all.

To this end, the discourse emerging from the NHEP reports in the pre-liberalization phase witnessed certain constants, changes and contradiction. The meta-analysis of policies and committee reports between 1947 and 1989 illustrated an emphasis on expanto ensuring equity in higher education as a policy constant while witnessing a gradual shift towards equity with excellence, in the later part of the 1980's. However, such a policy change, especially the Kothari Commission—1964 recommendations, was in contradiction to the need of the hour for the nation, during the period of social, political and economic transitions witnessed by the country since Independence to 1989–1990s. However, after 1964, the NHEP reports revert to the policy constant, that is, emphasis on expansion to ensure accessibility and equity.

Policy Dispositions and the Post-liberalization Era (1990–2016): A Curious Case for Excellence and Equity

The 1990s witnessed the rise of new India, with the coming of the New Economic Policy in 1991. The New Economic Policy aligned to the spirit of liberalization, privatization and globalization suggested specific reforms in higher education. Reforms in higher education were associated with decentralization and deregulation. Aligned to this, the government constituted several committees and a Programme of Action (PoA) 1992 to address the need for a 'new' and 'vibrant' higher education system for the country. With decentralization and deregulation as a significant reform direction, the higher education sector witnessed a series of reform initiatives. For instance, post-1990s, higher-education sector witnessed the rise of a large number of private-owned (not-for-profit) private colleges and universities. PoA 1992 envisaged a policy for higher education that integrated the aspirations of the past, present and the future by harmonizing various types and forms of colleges and universities aligned to the distinctive character of the nation (Powar, 2002).

Given the significant shifts in the overall policy orientation as a result of structural changes, the policy dispositions on higher education during the period witnessed a transition from a socialist framework to a more liberalized framework. NHEP reports ponder upon the importance of managerialism in higher education and its institutions, linkages of universities and colleges for economic growth and development.

PoA 1992 provided an implementation framework to the recommendations of NPE 1986 in reforming the university system. The Gnanam Committee, 1990, and the PoA 1992 prioritized on recommending a robust framework for the governance of universities and colleges, making them efficient, outcome oriented and insulated from politicization. The Gnanam Committee aspired to convert universities as 'centres of excellence' for teaching, research and extension. To this end, the committee made a series of recommendations, on the lines of autonomy, accountability and transparency, to review and redefine the vision/mission and objectives of higher education institutions and their governance.

The next significant policy intervention promulgated by the government was to rejuvenate the Central Advisory Board of Education (CABE), Government of India. CABE, in 2005, provided a detailed report on reforming the MHRD, the UGC and Centre–State relation regarding higher education. One of the key recommendations of CABE, 2005, was to evolve central legislation into streamline establishment and governance of private, higher-education institutions. With an unprecedented demand for higher education and a gradual decline in public expenditure in higher education, the contribution of the private sector to accommodate growing demand was inevitable. Such was the scenario across the globe, and India was no exception to it. To substantiate this, according to Rajani Naidoo (2007, p. 11), 'the wave of privatisation and liberalisation across the globe has enabled nation-states to adopt a mixed model of governing higher education, i.e., the state funding public universities amidst mushrooming private institutions per appropriate regulations.'

CABE, 2005, advised public state universities to introduce 'self-financing' courses to seek financial resources, internally, arguably leading to a significant shift in the policy orientation towards financial viability and sustainability by the institutions. Post 1990s, the demand for higher education increased while public expenditure on higher education was gradually declining. As an alternative to CABE, 2005, considered it appropriate to consider the role of private institutions to accommodate the increasing demand in higher education. As a result of this, a shift in the emphasis on privatization, self-financing courses in public universities and promoting non-government agencies whilst streamlining on regulation continues to exist. In other words, the higher education sector, at this juncture, oscillated between regulation and deregulation. Such a scenario is well characterized by Kapur and Mehta (2004, p. 13) as 'half-baked socialism to half-baked capitalism'.

With CABE and other committees, private-sector participation in higher education unpacked series of barriers and drivers for accessibility and equity, respectively, in higher education. Given the weakening public expenditure for higher education, the rise of private sector to cater to the increasing demand for higher education in the country, on the one hand, and the access to private institutions, on the other, was limited mostly to the urban, neo-middle class, second- or third-generation learners.

Against this backdrop, the National Knowledge Commission (NKC), 2006 was constituted. NKC recommended a series of reforms in expanding the higher education system by threefold to overcome the challenge of accessibility for all. The NKC believed in establishing 1,500 universities to increase in the gross enrolment ratio (GER) by 2015. To regulate the anticipated expansion, NKC recommended the Constitution of an Independent Regulatory Authority for Higher Education. Further, NKC laid equal emphasis on excellence through research in higher education and its institutions. To this end, NKC suggested streamlining governance in HEIs by promoting autonomy and accountability. On a similar note, the Committee to Advise on Renovation and Rejuvenation of Higher Education was constituted in 2008. According to the committee, higher education since Independence was the primary responsibility of the state, and it continues to be so. The committee recommended an increased focus on research vis-à-vis teaching and extension across HEIs by creating a comprehensive body—the National Commission for Higher Education and Research—governing higher education in the country. The committee has made detailed recommendations in ensuring quality in higher education while addressing the aspect of equity.

Subsequent to this, MHRD launched the Rashtriya Uchchatar Shiksha Abhiyan (RUSA) in 2013. RUSA envisaged the need to increase financial allocation for public institutions, rejuvenate the system of affiliation, address the issues related to equity for the disadvantaged communities and to take stock of regional imbalances in ensuring access to higher education for all. Realizing the need for a national policy on education after a long gap of 30 years, MHRD constituted the T. S. R Subramanian committee to draft the New Education Policy in 2016. Whilst the committee continued to emphasize issues related to accessibility, equity and expansion with excellence, the committee made special reference internationalization in higher education, professional education system and the need for a national fund.

The policy recommendations of the 29 reports mapped in this paper are spread over a long period. They were formulated independently by different individuals and committees. They were not designed to be incremental and to build upon one another systematically; they were more ad hoc, designed to address an issue or a set of issues at a point in time. Issues were identified by experience and expertise, not much on the evidence. As a result of this, the NHEP reports lacked temporality and evidence along with specific projections to shape the higher education system in the country.

NEP 2020: Tryst with Equity

NEP 2020 provides empirical insights into the preceding national policies on education, whilst evaluating the new opportunities and challenges emerging in the intervening years. NEP 2020 believes in the fact that erstwhile policies have been 'preoccupied largely with issues of access and equity and have unfortunately dropped the baton concerning the quality of education' (MHRD, 2020). To this end, NEP 2020 envisages the following policy objective for higher education: 'Revamp the higher education system, create world-class multidisciplinary higher education institutions across the country—increase GER to at least 50% by 2035' (MHRD, 2020), for a new and forward-looking India's higher education system.

Tryst with Equity

NEP 2020 is grounded in the guiding goals of access, equity, quality, affordability and accountability. At the outset, NEP 2020 engages with the question of equity in higher education to issues associated with limited accessibility at the primary- and secondary-education level. According to NEP 2020, 'education is the single greatest tool for achieving social justice and equality for inclusive and equitable education' (MHRD, 2020).

NEP 2020 appropriately identifies the need to address barriers for enrolment and completion at the secondary-education level, to address the issue of accessibility and equity. NEP 2020 acknowledges the fact that there exist myriad barriers in higher education for aspiring minds belonging to the marginalized communities (MHRD, 2020). NEP 2020, examining the current GER in higher education, aims for GER to reach 50 per cent by 2035, a twofold increase, in order to fulfil the aspirations of our youth and to form the basis for a vibrant society and economy (MHRD, 2020). NEP 2020 states that 'there must be continuity across the stages to ensure sustainable reform. Thus, the policy initiatives required to meet the goals of equity and inclusion in higher education should be appreciated in conjunction with those for school education' (MHRD, 2020).

In order to facilitate interventions beyond access, NEP 2020 recommends administrative, financial and academic autonomy to HEIs, to develop and sustain an inclusive ecosystem for under-represented groups entering the portals of HEIs. Given the rise of private sector participation in higher education and the perceived anxiety regarding affordability, equity, accessibility and accountability, NEP 2020 makes a series of interventions. NEP 2020 reaffirms the need for, and improvement of, public HEIs and the commitment to the national importance of public education in the public education investment has a direct impact on equity outcomes.

NEP 2020 engages with issues of access, affordability and equity by recommending a robust intervention for open and distance learning (ODL) to improve access and equity in higher education. In other words, the NEP 2020 suggests that the ODL programmes will be reimagined to ensure that their quality is equivalent to the best in-class programmes. ODL will help expand the reach of higher education and, thus, improve access and equity (NEP 2020).

Subsequently, because private sector participation in higher education is critical to address the increasing demand for higher education with a share of public funding being limited, NEP 2020 recommends encouragement of 'public-spirited' private philanthropic contributions. NEP 2020 proposes to establish the Higher Education Commission of India (HECI) 'for a synergistic functioning of India's education system, to deliver equity and excellence at all levels, from vision to implementation' (MHRD,

2020, p. 391). Arguably, the current governance of education in this country falls far short of being able to achieve this goal. Consecutively, this will create additional complexities and challenges in the implementation of this policy. In this backdrop, there is a need to revisit the existing system of governance, its structures and leadership mechanisms.

NEP 2020 recommends transformation in the existing institutional architecture from myriad types of institutions based on ownership (private, public–state and central and so on) to research, teaching and degree-granting autonomous colleges aligned to the core functions of the HEIs. In order to ensure accessibility, NEP 2020 recommends for 'disadvantaged geographies to be a priority—there will be at least one Type 1–3 institution for every district' (MHRD, 2020. p. 219). NEP 2020 aims to streamline institutional priorities to harness quality while appreciating equity in higher education.

Finally, NEP 2020 makes an insightful policy intervention in acknowledging 'the need for engaging and supporting learning environment for all students to succeed, irrespective of any discrimination' (MHRD, 2020). This is one of the most critical and novel policy interventions amongst others, vis-à-vis erstwhile policies and policy reports, hitherto. Lack of encouraging institutional environment is one of the significant barriers for ensuing equity in higher education and its institutions (Singai, 2019).

In order to bridge the gap between policy and practice, NEP 2020 envisages mechanisms at the level of government and institution to address issues related to equity in higher education. NEP 2020 recommends earmarking suitable government funds for the education of socio-economically disadvantaged groups (SEDGs) while establishing high-quality HEIs in aspirational districts and special education zones. At the institutional level, NEP 2020 envisages a more inclusive admission process, makes the curriculum more inclusive, ensures sensitization of faculty and develops Institutional Development Plans that contain specific plans for action on increasing participation from SEDGs.

The Way Forward: Policy versus Practice Conundrum

Post-Independence, NHEP reports indicate a series of interventions regarding expansion, equity and excellence at the systemic and institutional level. However, such interventions have had limited impact on addressing the problem of equity and inclusion in higher education in the country. The gap between accessibility (expansion) and equity in higher education and its institutions persists, hitherto, as a perennial crisis.

At the level of practice, equity and accessibility are often perceived to be two different entities. Equity entails an impartial, or fair, decision. Accessibility is the right, or privilege, to make use of something (Reid & Wankhede, 2017, p. 21). In other words, equity is not about expansion; it is about the experience of being included with all fairness in an institution after enrolment. However, at the level of policy, such a distinction, especially in the Indian context, gets limited attention. Arguably, policymakers believed in enhancing accessibility, that is, expansion will ensure inclusive education, that is, equity. For instance, in the early period of NPE 1986 and NKC, 2006, it was envisaged to establish a more significant number of universities and colleges across the country, with emphasis on rural India. An agenda for expanding the number of institutions to enhance accessibility to all eligible students aligned to the core mandate of our Constitution. Whilst there was some impact on enhancing enrolment, institutions had a limited role in providing an inclusive educational experience. Hierarchies and divisions based on caste, gender and so on continue to thrive hindering an inclusive ecosystem in majority of the higher-education institutions (Singai, 2019). Evidence of a major gap between the aspiration of policies and realities at the level of institution still exists.

NEP 2020 provides 'glimmers of hope and reform' in the country's higher education system (Vasavi, 2019). However, the test of the policy is its implementation framework and the evaluation of the implementation. NEP 2020 provides a vision for the nation. The nation needs to wait and assess the success of the policy and its implementation. However, the overarching intent, ethos and vision of NEP 2020 will help reinforce 'expansion, equity and excellence' in higher education and its institutions. NEP 2020 values education across all levels and all institutions in a continuum, affecting equity along with expansion and excellence.

References

Agarwal, P. (2009). Indian higher education: Envisioning the future. SAGE Publications.
Agarwal, P., & Kamalakar, G. (2013). Indian higher education: Envisioning the future. The Indian Economic Journal, 61(1), 151–155.
Altbach, P. G. (2009). The giants awake: Higher education systems in China and India. Economic & Political Weekly, 44(23), 39–51.
Ayyar, R. V. (2017). History of *education policymaking* in India, 1947–2016. Oxford University Press.
Chitnis, S. (1993). Gearing a colonial system of education to take independent India towards development. Higher Education, 26(1), 21–41.
Kapur, D., & Mehta, P. B. (2004). *Indian higher education reform: From half-baked socialism to half-baked capitalism* (Working Paper). Center for International Development, *103*, 1–65. http://citeseerx.ist.psu.edu/viewdoc/download?doi=10.1.1.472.6367&rep=rep1&type=pdf
Kaul, J. N. (1988). Governance of *universities*: Autonomy of the *university community*. Abhinav Publications.
Ministry of Human Resource Development (MHRD). (1986). National Policy on Education, 1986. Ministry of Education. https://mhrd.gov.in/sites/upload_files/mhrd/files/upload_document/npe.pdf
Ministry of Human Resource Development, Department of Higher Education (MHRD). (2015, Pg. 2). Themes and questions for Policy Consultation on Higher Education (Annexure-II). http://mhrd.gov.in/sites/upload_files/mhrd/files/upload_document/Themes_questions_HE.pdf
Ministry of Human Resource Development (MHRD) (2019). All India Survey of Higher Education (AISHE), 2018–*2019*. Department of Higher Education. https://mhrd.gov.in/sites/upload_files/mhrd/files/statistics-new/AISHE%20Final%20Report%202018-19.pdf
Ministry of Human Resource Development (MHRD). (2020). National Education Policy-2020. *MHRD, GOI*. https://www.mhrd.gov.in/sites/upload_files/mhrd/files/NEP_Final_English_0.pdf
Naidoo, R. (2007, p. 26). Higher education as a global commodity: The perils and promises for developing countries. The Observatory on Borderless Higher Education. London.

Naik, J. P. (1982). *The Education Commission and after*. Allied Publishers.
National Council of Educational Research and Training (NCERT). (1970). *Education and national development*—Report of the Education Commission 1964–1968. Ministry of Education, Government of India. http://dise.in/Downloads/KothariCommissionVol.1pp.1-287.pdf
Powar, K. B. (2000). *Reforms and innovations in higher education in India: The relevance and role of research*. Association of Indian Universities.
Powar, K. B. (2002, p. 76). *Indian higher education: A conglomerate of concepts, facts and practices*. Concept Publishing Company.
Ramaprasad, A., Singai, C. B., Hasan, T., Syn, T., & Thirumalai, M. (2016). India's National Higher Education Policy recommendations since Independence. *Journal of Educational Planning and Administration*, 30(1), 5.
Rizvi, F. (2012, p. 6). Challenges of modernization in higher education in Altbach, P. G. (2012). *A half-century of Indian higher education: Essays by Philip G Altbach*. SAGE Publications India.
Roy, K. (2015). Decoding 'New Education Policy'. *Economic & Political Weekly*, 50(19). https://www.epw.in/journal/2015/19/web-exclusives/decoding-new-education-policy.html
Singai, C. (2018). *Higher education and university governance in India: A case study of two universities in Karnataka* (Unpublished doctoral dissertation). National Institute of Advanced Studies & Manipal Academy of Higher Education.
Singai, C. (2019). Public and private dichotomy: An empirical insight into the university governance in India. In S. Babu. (Ed.), *Education and the public sphere: Exploring the structures of mediation in post-colonial India* (pp. 74–92). Routledge.
Tilak, J. B. (Ed.). (2013). *Higher education in India: In search of equality, quality and quantity*. Orient BlackSwan.
University Grants Commission. (2011). *Inclusive and qualitative expansion of higher education*. Compilation based on the deliberations of the Working Group for Higher Education in the 12th Five-Year Plan (2012–2017). University Grants Commission.
Vasavi, A. (2019, 6 June). Glimmers of hope and reform in the National Education Policy draft. *The Wire*. https://thewire.in/education/national-education-policy-draft-2019
Wankhede, G., & Reid, I. (Eds.). (2017). *Accessing higher education: Footprints of marginalised groups*. Aakar Books.

PART II
Dalits and Higher Education

Chapter 3
Social Advantage and Hermeneutical Injustice
in the Realm of Education
Krishnaswamy Dara

Chapter 4
Higher Education Status among Scheduled Castes in India
T. Brahmanandam

Chapter 5
Caste Discrimination and Exclusion in Higher Education
Areesh Kumar Karamala

3

Social Advantage and Hermeneutical Injustice in the Realm of Education

Krishnaswamy Dara

Introduction

Discrimination and disadvantage are an enduring presence in the Dalit predicament. These are and have been a harsh reality for Dalits and other marginalized sections of the society that come to institutions of higher education. There are, in my view (not fully worked out) broadly three arenas of discrimination in India's educational institutions. One is in the formal arenas or settings (classroom, seminars and academic discourses). Then there is the administrative arena, the rules and regulations along with the conventions.

The last but most important one is the informal spaces like hostels, university campus and its politics, the student life in campus, etc. When one talks of discrimination, one needs to look at all the spheres plus how they intersect and reinforce prejudice and discrimination in the pedagogic apparatus. Its pedagogic exercise is seen as where society recreates or reproduces itself. This is an arena that is much neglected by most subaltern intellectuals and activists to bring about serious administrative and cultural change academically. There is no novelty when we say there are overt and covert forms of disadvantage that affects the marginalized. What is all the more shocking or indigestible is the gap between the rhetoric and practice by the privileged within these institutions. One can call this structural violence. When those who have no place demand a place to speak, there are various mechanisms discursively put to silence and humiliate them. Even many innocuous (apparently) procedures and practices have been set against the disadvantaged. These practices and conventions are so seductive that even conscious progressive intellectuals and activists have been seduced by them and end up defending them. Meritocracy is one such practice. The way merit is understood and projected has been a raging debate between the upper castes and lower castes in India. Here again, the discourse introduces what has now become popular in the discrimination literature as hermeneutical injustice.

Hermeneutical Injustice: Testimonial Injustice— Credibility Deficit/Prejudice and Stereotyping

This chapter uses the concepts developed by Miranda Fricker. Her concept of social power and its subspecies of identity power in the argument are as follows (Fricker, 2007). Hermeneutical injustice can occur when there is not a 'collective hermeneutical resource'. It happens when the marginalized do not have a community which can provide the above resource. For example, in the Indian context, we can take the distinction between positive discrimination and negative discrimination. Here, I want to use the concept of positive discrimination not to the existing affirmative policies or reservation but to discrimination and harm that is deliberately inflicted on people coming from the marginalized sections. And by contrasting it with negative discrimination that affects the disadvantaged negatively, here, the perpetrator is not interested in harming the Dalit or female victim but favours people from his/her own caste, class, race or sex. This framework is missing and neglected (probably deliberately), particularly in educational institutions where many favours are done to the so-called blue-eyed boys mostly from upper castes and privileged backgrounds.

This is generally called or named as favouritism but not discrimination against other people. However, a sense of injustice is felt by the person and sometimes implicit in it. Generally, discrimination is considered an act/acts done deliberately towards Dalits rather than an action which is not done. It is a form of discrimination at a massive scale in our day-to-day life in all public and private institutions, particularly so in educational institutions. By and large, students coming from harsh backgrounds have lot of psychological issues which need to be addressed both by psychological experts and intellectual efforts which need a lot of empathy towards these students. But the mainstream culture's language of competency and efficacy, which includes masculine standards, makes a mockery of such appeals and arguments as excuses for various weaknesses. This can constitute what Miranda Fricker calls hermeneutical injustice where the predicament of students coming from non-privileged backgrounds and their concerns are not understood (much more, ignored).

Systematic Testimonial Injustice

Miranda Fricker also deals with the issue of testimonial injustice. She writes, 'The idea that (what I am calling) testimonial injustice constitutes an ethical wrong that can be non-trivial, indeed profoundly damaging, and even systematically connected with other forms of injustice in society, is not much appreciated' (Fricker, 2007, p. 40). She further writes,

> Systematic testimonial injustices then, are produced not by prejudice simpliciter, but specifically by those prejudices that 'track' the subject through different dimensions of social activity—economic, educational, professional, sexual, legal, political, religious, and so on. Being subject to a tracker prejudice renders one susceptible not only to testimonial injustice but to a gamut of different injustices, and so when such a prejudice generates a testimonial injustice, that injustice is systematically connected with other kinds of actual or potential injustice. (Fricker, 2007, p. 27)

This systematic testimonial injustice can be seen when the prejudice that is held by the majority in an institution plays a role in producing administrative injustice. As Fricker says, testimonial injustice flows into every dimension of social injustice. As she is inspired by Judith Shklar, we need to focus on social injustice much more than social justice. And we cannot reduce injustice as the opposite of justice. Fricker writes, 'The exploration is orientated not to justice, but rather to injustice. As Judith Shklar points out, philosophy talks a lot about justice, and very little about injustice' (Fricker, 2007). She further writes, 'Philosophers are very keen to understand what it is to get things right. That's fine, but we should not stop there if we also want to understand the human practices that may only very patchily approximate the rational ideal.' We will now move on to the topic of administrative injustice.

Administrative Injustice

It is a subspecies of legal injustice or what is commonly referred to as the failure of the legal system to protect the marginalized. Here, we can focus on the law of public administration. Dalit scholars have focused on constitutional law but ignored administrative law. Dalit and other activists have focused on the question of how one can get the marginalized into institutions that were exclusively in the hands of the dominant groups but what happens to those who manage to get into these institutions is mostly ignored. Administrative law in India has grown from its colonial origins to its postcolonial avatars. This law has been used effectively for various concerns. What we are concerned about here is its use for curtailing the growth of Dalit and other minorities in the system. Numerous techniques have been used, which we cannot go into every aspect right now. For example, if we take the case of when 'employees' file' in the government system, it is a powerful tool in the hands of administrative officers higher up to check the voices of Dalit employees who are showing red flag against administrative misconduct. (Even the SC/ST commission seems to be not able to intervene unless they can find some severe inflexion or moral outrage.) Although Blacks and women have questioned the way administrative law is deployed, the focus mostly has been on criminal law and incarceration injustices. There is an urgent need to interrogate public administration, and administrative law is taught to our students. False charges of corruption and misdemeanour against Dalit employees and staff is the go-to strategy by upper-caste groups within the system. The famous case Devyani Khobragade, an Indian Foreign Service officer deployed in the USA experienced humiliation when an upper caste American citizen of Indian origin used American law against abuse of domestic servants to target her selectively. This was done to humiliate and harass a Dalit woman whose success could not be digested by the upper caste Indian. Law enforcement, which is primarily controlled by upper castes, is a weapon to sustain and reinforce social domination using the state's arms. There is also a need to thoughtfully critique the concepts and categories that form the backbone of administrative law in India.

Upendra Baxi, in his famous piece on administrative law, takes a very high critical tone in describing administrative law as it is practised in India. He argues that courts have gone beyond tackling the issue of arbitrariness and applied the principles of natural justice to administrative law cases. He cites various court decisions where the courts have applied the principles of natural justice to provide remedies to individuals and groups affected by administrative actions and decisions. He writes,

> Simple negation of arbitrariness is, however, not enough to preserve the rule of law values. Indian courts have gone further to insist on specific positive content of the rule of law obligations. These include the rules of natural justice which have to be followed not just in quasi-jurisdiction but often also merely administrative action. (Upendra, 1982)

He further writes, 'This is not to say that Indian courts have never invalidated what appeared to them to be genuinely arbitrary conferrals of discretionary power. But they have done so only where the arbitrariness of the conferral is writ large on the face of the provision.' In fact, the courts have given in 'a very large number of instances where discretionary powers conferred in wide terms have been sustained. Very often, the general objective and policy of the statute are considered as sufficient.' The courts have, thus, also played a negative role when discretionary power is exercised with malicious intentions. One of the critical drawbacks of Upendra Baxi's criticism is that he keeps the critique at a general level without going into the sociological underpinnings that produce skewed understandings and interpretations of the administrative law by the courts and the whole law-enforcing establishment. It does not get into questions of race, caste and gender as a serious analytical tool to understand the pitfalls in the Indian legal system. particularly in the administrative law.

Coming back to the issue of epistemic injustice and its embeddedness in the legal philosophy among its practitioners of administrative law and law in general, we come across the big idea of reasonableness: the un-thought. The textbooks both critical and status quoist are always concerned with the misuse of law. What is considered as proper use and misuse is that which the majority in that society believe. Legal discourse reflects this inherent majoritarian social bias. What is considered criminal and unethical is socially determined rather than formal rationality. Even academic discourse both when it focuses itself on analysing and study of society and also when analysing self-reflectively tends to be influenced by the mainstream dominant perceptions in and of society. One classic example of this is the policy of reservation in India (also loosely called affirmative action or positive discrimination). Predominant academic discussions in the past decades sustained mainstream upper-caste society's prejudice against the policy. This produced hermeneutical injustice for candidates who benefited with the help of the above policy. These candidates or students were seen as unjust usurpers of seats meant for meritorious candidates generally from upper-caste backgrounds. This caused severe moral harm to these candidates, thereby producing stigmatization and undervaluing their performance. Their voices were also suppressed because they lack merit and the appropriate moral stamina to study in these institutions. This produces interpretive harm towards the marginalized sections of the population.

Apart from this particular harm being the harm in itself, it also contributes to other harms. It produces harms like stigma and contempt for groups that benefit from the policy of reservation. This in turn leads to general indifference and complicity in other forms of discriminations and humiliations inflicted on the marginalized by the dominant groups in public institutions, in particular, academic and other higher-educational institutions. Putting it in a more technical register, epistemic injustice produces hermeneutical injustice, which is a major contributor to social injustice. The issue of 'law's misuse or abuse' has frequently raised as a counter charge whenever demands for better and stringent law to protect against institutional and societal discrimination in the favour of the marginalized are made. We will now deal with this issue in the next section.

'Misuse of law', Administrative Complacency and Hermeneutical injustice—the Supreme Court of India, in its most recent infamous case *Dr Subash Kashinath Mahajan v. State of Maharashtra and others* under the judgeship of Justice Mishra rejected a special provision of pre-emptive bail to protect Dalits in public institutions. Before we grapple with the issue, let us first look at what the court said,

> It is thus pretend that in cases under the atrocities act, exclusion of right of anticipatory bail is applicable only if the case is shown to be bona fide and that prima facie it [alts under the atrocities act and not otherwise. Section 18 does not apply where there is no prima facie case or to cases of patent false implication or when the allegation is motivated for extraneous reasons. We approve the view of Gujarat High Court in Pankaj d Suthar and Dr NT Desai. We clarify the judgments in Balothia and Manju Devi to this effect. (Simzkaur4, n.d.)

It is clear from the *ratio decidendi* of the judgment that the judges see that the complaint is motivated by extraneous reasons and cases of 'patent false implication'. Since we cannot go deeper into details and the issues as to why the court has come to the above conclusion, we can simply say that the court has committed hermeneutical harm to the Dalit who complained against his bosses for discriminating against him. Moreover, it also did it to all Dalits by accusing that Dalits tend to misuse the law. Misuse of law is the most abused trope in Indian society today. It is set against women, Dalits and other socially disadvantaged strategically whenever they demand the assertion of their rights through legal means. Madhu Kishwar has argued why the misuse of law is always evoked only when women's issues are in question. It does not get used when dominant groups use law as a means to maintain their power over the lower classes and appropriation of public resources for private gains. Legal discourse in India is filled with debilitating and humiliating rhetoric of defending the rights of the marginalized coupled with a polemic of abuse of the law by the marginalized.

Courts in India like the United States' courts have played a very damaging role in misinterpreting the Dalit predicament and history when it comes to the question of affirmative action. The issue of stigmatization has often been invoked by the Supreme Court to show the harmful impact of affirmative policies. To this, the beneficiaries themselves have taken in the criticism seriously. At the same time, the dynamics of the process of stigmatization is a complex process. The courts, instead of going into this dynamic, produced and participated in stigmatization by taking a polemic against stigmatization itself. This further is picked up by upper-caste teachers, colleagues and administrators in the higher education system in India to perpetuate a hostile climate and let various forms of contempt and discriminatory practices in the system. This also reflects in the important way society and its dynamics are taught to young, impressable students in schools and particularly in institutions of higher learning.

Conclusion

In this chapter, we explored the various ways and complex mechanisms that work to create an unjust environment for members of disadvantaged communities in a new way. We looked at the issues of testimonial injustice which comes under the broader category of epistemic injustice. Testimonial injustice plays a very central role in sustaining and perpetuating all forms of social injustice. The prejudice, which is a testimonial injustice, also plays a key role in administrative injustice where the mechanisms that are provided by the state through various legal means fail because of this phenomenon. In particular, in educational institutions, these insidious forms of misinterpretations and prejudices perpetuate layered and complex forms of injustices for the socially marginalized. Scholars paid little attention to this phenomenon and did not engage in a systematic and scholarly manner. Coming to the informal side, this is where a lot of work is needed. The basic assumptions and what Heidegger would call '*dasein* or being there' or the cultural and pre-understandings in our daily life have a significant effect on all kinds of discourses of social justice and simultaneously injustices. Efforts in the form of celebrating Ambedkar Jayanti, Sir Syed's Day, beef festival, etc., are in the right direction where students from the subaltern classes are made invisible and are constant ridicule.

References

Fricker, M. (2007). *Epistemic injustice: Power and the ethics of knowing.* Clarendon Press.

Simzkaur4. (n.d.). The SC and ST Prevention of Atrocities Act, 1989—Latest Judgments. *Legal Service India.* http://www.legalserviceindia.com/legal/article-223-the-sc-and-st-prevention-of-atrocities-act-1989-latest-judgments.html

Upendra, B. (1982). Developments in Indian administration. In A. G. Noorani (Ed.), *Public law in India* (p. 125). Vikas Publishing House.

4

Higher Education Status among Scheduled Castes in India

T. Brahmanandam

The Hindu religious texts such as the Vedas and the Shastras have divided the society into hierarchical order. The 10th chapter of Rigveda in its 91st hymn (Kumar, 2014, p. 36) reveals that there are four *varnas* in a hierarchical order and they are: the Brahmins, the Kshatriyas, the Vaishyas and Sudras. All these four *varnas* are called twice born or *savarna*. The concept of twice born is applicable to the above-mentioned castes, that is, four castes only. The theory of twice born is linked to the people whose occupations are clean and unclean. It means coming back again to purity and pollution notions only (Chanana, 1993, p. 70). The castes that are outside the savarna are considered as avarana (without any varna) and they are Untouchables or Harijans (Gandhian concept) and are Dalits in modern India. The Untouchables are not homogeneous castes[1] and they are divided into a number of endogamous sub-castes which were again arranged in a hierarchy like the rest of the castes[2] in the society. The greatest error of these texts was leaving the untouchables from this social order (Desai & Kulkarni, 2008, p. 246).

As per Vivek Kumar's observation, it was anthropologists and sociologists who included the untouchables as fifth group—the *ashprishyas or asprustha*,[3] (literary translation is 'untouchables') better known as Dalits in the Hindu social order. Thus, the Hindu social order has five major social groups arranged in a hierarchical manner with Brahmins at the top and Dalits at the bottom. He further says that Hindu social order has also prescribed certain socio-economic, political, educational and religious functions for each *varna* to attain renunciation and to escape from the death-and-birth cycle. However, the untouchables (Dalits) have been completely excluded from this cycle of renunciation in every sphere of Hindu social order (Kumar, 2014, p. 36). Further, the same social order assigned certain rights and privileges to these twice born, and the same privileges were denied to those groups who are out of the pale of *varna* scheme. This unequal distribution of rights and privileges had the religious sanctity that produced the extreme form of inequality in Indian society. This indicates that the Scheduled Castes (SCs) for generations together were/are made to live in these polluted occupations without freedom, dignity and property.

Untouchables are traditionally outside the Hindu social order and face social, economic, political and religious segregation. (Corrie, 1995, p. 395). Many theoretical explanations also attributed to their low status in Hindu society. One among these attributions is that these groups or sects, from time immemorial, are engaged in certain unclean occupations (Chanana, 1993, p. 70) that are considered to be the most polluting or profane occupations such as skinning animal carcasses, butchery of animals, removal of human waste, attendance at cremation grounds, washing clothes and fishing (Desai & Kulkarni, 2008, p. 247). These SCs have been facing the inhuman treatment just because they are untouchables, which is the most extreme form of denial of human dignity and social oppression (Sankaran, 1998, p. 209), and their residential segregation is strictly enforced in rural areas even today (Benjamin, 2008, p. 628).

In such situations, it is worth mentioning 'Dharwad Case', where education was denied to an untouchable boy. In 1854, a low-caste boy sought permission for admission in a government school at Dharwad. The school administration failed to give admission on a pretext that if the lower-caste boy is admitted into school, children of upper-caste Hindus would withdraw from the school and would virtually lead to the closure of the institution. However, the matter was brought to the notice of government, and then it was referred to the board of directors of the company. The directors opined that permission could not be denied on the grounds of caste, and the educational institutions of government were kept open to all castes, and it could not depart from a principle which was of utmost importance. If the wealthier class were not willing to accept the essential principle like open to all, they were at liberty, and they could drop and set up their own schools exclusively for them. In view of the opinion expressed by the Court of Directors, the first Indian Education Commission in 1882 recommended that 'all primary schools wholly maintained at the cost of school boards and all primary schools that are aided from the same fund and are not registered as special schools, should open to all castes and class of the community'.

Despite this, the colonial administration failed to promote education among the lower castes. The reason for such non-committal attitude of the administration was due to the severity of untouchability prevalent in the country, and any attempt to promote education among them would be inviting wrath from the high-caste Hindus. More than that, the British were not interested in disturbing the existing land relations based on the caste system. Therefore, a small section of the Untouchables could only receive education extended by colonial administration. This vindictive attitude of Brahmins on marginal sections from ancient days onwards has been spelt out by Shills in one of his writings that 'no other country can quite match this picture of a continuing intellectual tradition carried so long by a single section of the population' (Shills, 1961, p. 21).

Under these cumulative disadvantages, committees like Miller Committee in Mysore and O. H. B. Starte Committee in Bombay had recommended special facilities to the 'Depressed, Aboriginal', Hill Tribes and Other Backward Classes' in education. However, such facilities were already extending to these groups at Kolhapur (1902), Travancore (1926) and Baroda (1931). Despite these facilities, the literacy rate among this section was just 1.9 per cent in 1931 (Pandey, 1986, p. 59; Sahoo, 2009, p. 64). There were a number of factors which played against these groups and, due to that, they are in an unimaginable level. The factors are as follows: majority of them were poor, their illiteracy level compelled them not to access productive resources because they did not possess requisite skills to compete in the modern world or in open market.

All these factors forced these groups to remain deeply tied to land and transitional occupations which offer very limited possibilities of upward mobility (Benjamin, 2008, p. 630). In these depressing conditions, many national leaders and social reformers of India such as B. R. Ambedkar, Nehru, Azad, Ram Mohan Roy, Swami Vivekananda and Rabindranath Tagore (NCSC report, 2004–2005, p. 115) thought that only education can bring occupational, economic mobility and positive change in marginalized groups (Choudhary, 2007, p. 3), particularly with SCs, and this may even be the foundation vehicle for emancipation of the deprived sections of society in general and the SCs in particular (Chitnis, 1972, p. 1675).

Prior to Independence, the British government had introduced post-matric scholarship to the SCs in 1944, with an idea to bring a change in their numbers in higher education. The post-matric scholarship induced the Indian political leaders to introduce certain constitutional provisions or preferential treatment policies for the betterment of SCs[4]. These preferential treatment policies might ensure them to participate in a newly emerging social order, and the state would certainly secure economic, educational and political justice to them. Soon after Independence, the government explicitly and clearly adopted the principle of promoting social equality through preferential-treatment policies. This led to the incorporation of a number of constitutionally guaranteed rights to the Dalits, which include education also. On the educational front, 'the state shall take special care of the educational and economic interest of the weaker sections of the people and in particular of the Scheduled Castes and Scheduled Tribes and shall protect them from social injustice and all forms of exploitation' (Pandey, 1986, p. 61). Article 29(2) prohibits discrimination in government-aided educational institutions.

Although the reservation of seats at higher-educational institutions for SC and ST students was established as a national policy in the early 1950s, its actual implementation was delayed in educational institutions (Weisskopf, 2004, p. 4340) because it did not specify any such measure to be adopted by the government. Therefore, it led to the amendment of the Constitution in 1951 through the inclusion of Clause 4 to the Article 15(4). This clause empowered the states to make a special provision to reserve 20 *per cent seats for SCs and STs in educational* institutions including technical and professional institutions for the development of SC's and ST's educational. Again, the same provision was modified to have 15 per cent for the SCs and 5 per cent for the STs in 1962 (Shaoo, 2012, p. 63).

Addition to these provisions, a massive scheme like post-matric scholarship scheme was continued by the then government with an intention to promote education among SCs and ST. The purpose of this scheme was to enhance their enrolment and improve their performance in education. The post-matric scholarship budgetary allocations had led to a conspicuous increase on SC's enrolment in higher education. The actual expenditure incurred on SC scholarship during 1944 to 1950–1951 has come to an extent of ₹2,963,843. This includes the expenditure of 22 scholars who were sent abroad for higher studies in 1945–1946 (NCSC, 2005–2006, p. 26). Even if you take the scholarship holders alone into consideration, one may find a massive increase from 1,316 scholarships holders in colleges in 1950–1951 to 42,071 by 1960–1961, and it further went up to 157,000 in 1970–1971 (Chitnis, 1972, p. 1676). Despite this massive scholarship programme, the number of graduates from all streams (BA, BSc and BCom) of Indian higher-educational institutions rose from 0.9 per cent in 1961 to 3.3 per cent in

Table 4.1	SC Enrolment with Comparison to Total Enrolment		
Year	Total Enrolment	SC Enrolment	%
1978–1979	2,543,449	180,058	7.08
1995–1996	7,955,811	1,058,514	13.30
2002–2003	9,516,773	1,076,996	11.32
2014–2015	34,211,637 (51.6)	4,618,535	13.5*

Source: NCSC report, 2004–2005.
Note: *All India Survey on Higher Education (AISHE) (2014–2015).

1981. This increase was far below than their share of the total population, and details can be obtained from below-mentioned Table 4.1 (Weisskopf, 2004, p. 4340). Nonetheless, Chitnis' study concludes that it was the scholarship scheme which made their presence in a significant way in colleges which were almost unrepresented by this community to be noted as a measure of success by the post-matric scholarship.

The post-matric scholarships have, no doubt, brought a substantial increase in their enrolment in higher education, particularly in public institutions. Admission to reserved seats enhanced the ability of SC/ST students to gain access to financial and other forms of government aid without which staying and continuing their studies in institution may prove to be very difficult. The government provision of scholarships, special hostels and supply of books has enabled many SC and ST students to enter and pursue their higher education. However, Weisskopf expressed the view that enough data is not available on this matter, particularly the number of people got benefited with this scheme. The difficulty of such identification was due to the scarcity of detailed data on the composition of higher-educational enrolments. It is also due to the complexity of the way in which India's reservation policies in the educational sphere are structured and administered. He further held that all these policies only apply to public institutions and not to private institutions, where the number of private institutions is rapidly increasing after economic reforms.

Moreover, the SC and ST students were never admitted under general category even if they scored with high qualifying marks in their entrance examination. To this point, a conjecture can be drawn from Patwardhan and Palshikar's (1992) study at regional medical college in Pune, Maharashtra. Thus, reservation policies gave big boost to SC and ST students to get enrolled and pursue their higher education.

Table 4.2 provides a comparative assessment between non-SC/ST and SC/ST students in their enrolment in higher education over a period of four decades. Among these academic disciplines, engineering and medicine are the most lucrative and respectable professional disciplines. In these disciplines, the SC and ST participation was around 3.8 and 0.7 per cent in 1966, respectively. By 1998, their participation had gone up to 8.5 and 2.4 per cent, which was a modest progress but fell short of reaching the halfway mark of their population share. In contrast, the non-SC/ST groups continue to overwhelmingly dominate even after four decades (2004–2005), and particularly with professional courses, the picture is more glaring even in 2014–2015 also. At PhD/DPhil level, the SC and ST group's ration has not changed much, and they are at 8.77 and 3.2 in 2014–2015. The SC/ST performance had steadily increased in the case of liberal arts courses rather than science, engineering and commerce.

The SCs are found to be crowding more in liberal arts degrees than professional courses, which generally facilitate them in better job opportunity. At the doctoral (PhD) level, in 2014–2015, they (SC) were standing at 8.7 per cent and STs were at 3.2 per cent (students who registered at various educational institutions). These numbers are below the share of their population. Importantly, in none of the faculties, except in the Master of Arts, SCs are nowhere near to their share of population. The implementation of reservations in premier institution like Indian Institutes of Technology (IITs) is also not full-fledged owing to a number of factors such as merit of students, attitude of institutes and sociocultural background of marginalized groups, which ultimately affect their participation in specialized courses in IITs.

Table 4.2 SC/ST Proportion with Non-SC/STs students in Higher Education in Different Academic Disciplines from 1966–67 to 2014–15

Stages	Non-SC/ST				SC				ST			
	1966–1967	1998–1999	2004–2005	2014–2015	1966–1967	1998–1999	2004–2005	2014–2015	1966–1967	1998–1999	2004–2005	2014–2015
BA (Honours)	93.4	85.2	80.3	78.50	5.2	10.5	15	12.14	1.4	4.3	5	8.9
BSc	–	97.6	87.2	82.74	–	11.3	10	13.12	–	1.7	3	4.07
BCom	94.5	92.5	89.4	86.22	4.1	6	8	10.61	0.6	1.5	3	3.16
BE/Eng/BArch	94.5	88	88.4	88	3.8	8.5	7	9.94	0.7	2.4	3	2.05
BEd/BT	–	84.4	81.2	77.23	–	11.4	13	17.12	–	2.2	6	5.64
MBBS/Ayurved	93	88	85	–	6.1	9	11.5	–	1.1	3.1	4	–
MA	–	82	79.6	79.73	–	14.4	16.2	14.3	–	4	5	5.94
MSc	–	90	87	85.38	–	8	10.4	11.23	–	2.3	3	3.37
MCom	–	90.2	88	87.53	–	7.8	9	9.55	–	2	3	2.9
PhD/DPhil	–	94.3	92	88.01	–	4.1	6	8.77	–	1.6	2.4	3.2
Teacher's training	91.6	79.5	82.4	–	6.9	13.6	11.5	–	1.5	7	6.1	–
Polytechnic	–	87.2	88.5	–	–	10	9.7	–	–	3	3.3	–
Technical, Industrial, arts, crafts	98	82.6	78	–	1.7	11.94	14.7	–	0.5	5.4	7.2	–

Source: GOI, MHRD (1966–1967; 1998–1999; 2004–2005 and 2014–2015).

Trends and Participation of SC/ST in IITs

The IITs have been offering reservation to SCs and STs since 1973 as per constitutional provisions that allocate 15 per cent to SC and 7.2 per cent to ST. Although the IITs are bound to fill these seats, many of these seats remain vacant because of the criteria of the selection process.[5]

The Constitution mandates 22.2 per cent reservation to SC and ST in all the centrally funded institutes including IITs and Indian Institutes of Management. However, these institutes failed to comply with the mandatory reservation for these communities because of their own admission policy which is an injurious policy to these communities. It together, that is, all the IITs combined, provided only 12 per cent for SCs and 4 per cent ST students in 2005–2006 (See table 4.3). In economic terms, the SC and ST are also contributing to national budget in the form of direct and indirect taxes under uniformed tax laws to all the citizens of the nation. In the same way, governments also make allocations under the same purview to these institutes; however,

Table 4.3 Implementation of Reservation in Admissions for SC/ST

IITs	Year	% of Seats Filled for SCs	% of Seats Filled for STs
IIT Kharagpur	2004–2005	12.0	3.2
IIT Mumbai	2004–2005	9.1	2.5
IIT Chennai	2004–2005	14.0	3.7
IIT Delhi	2004–2005	10.6	2.4
IIT Kanpur	2004–2005	9.2	2.0
IIT Guwahati	2004–2005	9.4	4.3
IIT Roorkee	2004–2005	10.6	3.7
All IITs	2005–2006	12.00	4.00

Source: Indiastasts.com

the SC and ST students failed to get benefited from these allocations because IITs follow their own or unique admission policy, where its adversely affecting the SC and ST's enrolment into these institutions, and therefore, the said communities failed to get benefited from their own share in these institutions. Due to this, most people from marginalized caste/groups are unable to reach these institutions of higher education. Thus, the sizable numbers of SC/ST students lose their opportunity under the above circumstances.

The faculty-recruitment policy at premier institutes like IITs also adversely affect the opportunities of SC and ST communities. This may be noticed from Shri Udit Raj (former Lok Sabha Member of Parliament), who sought information from Ministry of Human Resources Development. The information provided to Shri Udit Raj in the Lok Sabha suggests that only 2,813 faculty positions are vacant against the total sanctioned positions of 8,856 in all the 23 IITs combined. Out of 6,043 faculty members, only 149 are SC and 21 from the ST category are working at these institutions. This indicates that only 2.81 per cent of teachers belonging to SC and ST are currently working at IITs (*Wire*, 2015). Details are given in Table 4.4.

The minister said in the Parliament,

> IITs follow flexible cadre system for appointment of faculty. Therefore, the sanctioned strength of faculty at different grades i.e Professor, Associate Professor and Assistant Professor is not fixed. Under the flexible cadre system, IITs are free to recruit any grade of faculty, depending upon requirement, availability of eligible candidates subject to the condition that the overall strength will not exceed the standard ratio of 1:10.

Despite all, the literacy rate of SCs remains below national average, and the seats reserved for SCs are not filled in centrally funded institutes. All these pit falls were/are due to deep-rooted rigid norms of institutional practices that have adversely impacted their educational backwardness in the society. In the case of indifferent attitude of teachers towards SC students, an inference

Table 4.4 Implementation of Reservation in Employment for SC/ST

S. No.	Name of the Institute	Sanctioned Posts	Post Earmarked For		Posts Filled	
			SC	ST	SC	ST
1	IIT Kharagpur	1,203	*	*	8	0
2	IIT Mumbai	1,034			5	0
3	IIT Chennai	800			13	2
4	IIT Delhi	776			10	2
5	IIT Kanpur	694			3	0
6	IIT Roorkee	745			10	2
7	IIT Guwahati	596			16	3
8	IIT BHU	556			19	3
9	IIT Jodhpur	90			2	0
10	IIT Ropar	150			4	0
11	IIT Indore	150			2	0
12	IIT Patna	155			6	0
13	IIT Gandhinagar	160			1	0
14	IIT Hyderabad	254			6	1
15	IIT Bhubaneswar	170			4	0
16	IIT Mandi	125			0	0
17	IIT Dhanbad	711			29	6
18	IIT Jammu	93			1	0
19	IIT Tirupati	93			2	1
20	IIT Palakkad	93			4	0
21	IIT Dharwad	93			1	1
22	IIT Goa	45			1	0
23	IIT Bhilai	70			2	0
	Total	8,856			149	21

Source: Government of India, MHRD.
Note: *IITs follow flexible cadre system for appointment of faculty.

can be drawn from S. K. Thorat Committee Report on All India Institute of Medical Sciences:

> That nearly 69 percent of SC/ST students reported that they do not receive adequate supports from their upper caste teachers. They also categorically said that it was because of their social status, the teachers are indifferent and inaccessible. Therefore, given the dependence of students on teachers for learning and the inaccessibility of teachers to the SC/ST students got reflected in their performance and also psychological problems. As they lacked close contact with their teachers and it directly impacts in their examination and valuation of papers and they invariable get less marks both in theory and practical. (Maurya, 2018, p. 21)

Some of the Deep-rooted Rigid Forms of Institutional Practices That Have Negatively Impacted on SCs in Higher Education

The letter of the first Prime Minister of India, Jawaharlal Nehru, to the chief ministers on 27 June 1961 can be cited as an example for the deep-rooted detrimental attitude towards Dalits and tribal in India. In the words of Nehru (1989),

> I have referred above efficiency and to our getting out our traditional ruts... It is true that we are tied up with certain rules and conventions about helping the Scheduled Castes and Tribes. They deserve help but, even so, I dislike any kind of reservation, more particularly in service... if we go in for reservations on communal and caste basis we swamp the bright and able people and remain second-rate of third-rate. I am grieved to learn of how far this business of reservation will go on based on communal consideration. It has amazed me to learn that even promotions are based on communal or caste consideration.
>
> This way lies not only folly, but disaster. (Kumar, 2001, p. 19)

From this observation, people can understand the level of commitment rendered to reservation policy by the political elite of this country, and this may be the first injurious step (immediately after Independence) towards the welfare of SC and ST of this country. Even after 75 years the political elite are not able to see the truth that 3,000 years' old discriminatory system (*Manu samskruti*) has not ended. In fact, it allowed other communities to agitate for their due share in the society by way of demanding reservations to them and examples are: Kapu reservation movement in Andhra Pradesh, Gujjar in Rajasthan, Patels in Gujarat and Marathas in Maharashtra.

In spite of reservation since independence, a large section of SCs is still lingering behind Other Backward Classes (OBCs). In this context, the bureaucracy had to address itself and ponder over the following issues: (a) while the framers of the Constitution were sensible enough to make adequate provisions in the Constitution for the advancement of the SCs, the bureaucracy has not been equally sensible to implement these provisions with true spirit. (b) If it is so, how to sensitize them to uphold the visions of the framers of the Constitution? (c) If the bureaucracy is already sensitized, or can be sensitized, there can be other social factors or forces beyond its control which prevented them from doing so and what prevents the SCs from taking advantage of the constitutional provisions. These are most pertinent issues that need to be addressed for the proper implementation of reservations to the SCs and ST (Rajgopal, 2002, p. 654). It is not just bureaucracy, even the upper-caste academia is also not interested to uplift SC and ST from their traditional occupations, and this may be observed from M. N. Srinivas' writings in 1950s, particularly on caste at village level, and he suggests that 'caste is an institution of prodigious strength and it will take a lot of beating before it will die.' He further says that to enforce anti-untouchability laws in the country, there must be caste clashes, and these clashes may even increase at times in the society.

Therefore, by way of bloodshed only the constitutional guarantees can be translated into reality (Srinivas, 1955, p. 1231). Along with that, he also highlighted that the castes relations in the village are interdependent across the castes like those between master and servant, landlord and tenant, creditor and debtor, and patron and client cut across the division of castes. From these observations, he wants that the institution of *caste* should continue to exist to the extent of gross violation of basic human rights of the marginalized groups in the society. If one accepts his argument, it would be difficult to achieve development in the society and nation.

Another notable example for upper-caste academia's antipathy in higher-learning institutions towards Dalits can be drawn from University of Hyderabad, that is, Madari Venkatesh's *suicide on 24 November 2014*. Madari Venkatesh was a postgraduate researcher scholar in school of chemistry at the University of Hyderabad. He consumed poison on the campus. As per Justice K. Ramaswamy committee, Venkatesh was not allotted a supervisor since he joined the school of chemistry despite several efforts, including a letter to the then Vice Chancellor Professor Ramakrishna Ramaswamy. The committee noted,

> No Doctoral Committee was constituted to supervise his research which is mandatory. Though six faculty members from School of Chemistry were available, none was willing to supervise his research. Whatever research he had done, it was only by his self effort .... (Times of India, 2014)

He was discriminated on the ground of caste consideration.

Its report stated, 'It is the consequence of institutional discrimination and systematic exercise of exclusive and oppressive behavior of the Institution and the faculty of the School of Chemistry.' It further observed, 'The antagonism, antipathy and insensitive mindset of the faculty, especially with School of Chemistry ... towards the student belonging to marginalized social groups is clearly apparent.' Justice Ramaswamy also noted that the suggestions made by the V. Pavarala and V. Sri Krishna committees were not implemented in full (Times of India (Hyderabad Edition), 2013).

The curriculum taught at different stages is always alien to the SC and ST students. The proceedings of the several committees appointed by the government to reform the content and quality of textbooks simply ignored the life and worldview of SC and ST. Since independence, the curriculum taught in our schools and colleges is always versatile to those groups who enjoy power over others and get larger share, and the groups that lack power may get a token of representation or none at all (Kumar, 1983, pp. 1567–1568). It was due to this the Fifth Schedule Areas where the more number of tribal habitations continue to perform very low. They are Jharkhand (57.1%), Madhya Pradesh (50.6%), Orissa (52.2%), Rajasthan (52.2%) and Andhra Pradesh (49.2%) (Brahmanandam & Bosu Babu, 2016, p. 77).

The exclusive feature of higher education is another glaring example where 13.5 per cent and 4 per cent of the students belonging to SC and ST respectively are admitted to our higher-educational institutes. This point proves that our higher education system lacks diversity (Kumar, 2016, p. 12). In India, higher-educational institutions are not inclusive and democratic in respect to the appointment of head of the institutes as well as faculties. In this context Vivek (2016) made an observation that out of 46 central universities and one open central university, only one vice chancellor belongs to ST. In 25 state universities of Uttar Pradesh, there is no one from SC category. In the same way, according to information obtained through the Right to Information Act, the University Grants Commission revealed that till 2009–2010, out of 1,688 sanctioned posts of professors and 3,298 associate professors, there were only 24 professors and 90 associate professors from the SC category employed at central universities. In terms of percentage, it is 2.73 per cent and 4.4 per cent respectively against the constitutionally mandated 15 per cent reservation for SCs (Kumar, 2016, p. 12).

From the very beginning, the process of modernization in Indian society has directly impacted Dalits in losing their traditional and hereditary occupations. However, the reservations have given a respite. With the process of globalization, job opportunities have started shrinking and the policy of reservation becomes defunct. Moreover, Dalits were not prepared to face these new challenges. With globalization, many multinational corporations (MNCs) have entered into Indian markets, and they are looking for technically trained personnel such as management experts, system analysts, software experts, etc. It is very difficult for Dalits to seek job opportunities in these MNCs as they are technically inept for such high-skilled jobs. This is not because they lack capability but because the opportunities are scarce. Second, they were late starters in the realm of education (Kumar, 2001, p. 20).

The allegations of not having merit and skill are attributed to the Dalit community as the arguments against reservations. However, many social scientists have rejected this argument in the name of merit (Kumar, 2005). They have argued that rewards in the educational and economic system are not based on merit. The educational and occupational attainments depend more likely on family background than talent and ability. The educational system has created an illusion of meritocracy in support of the abolition of reservation. Furthermore, he says that India has got 124th position among 174 countries in the Human Development Index. Similarly, in the case of external debt, India is whopping up to ₹511,861 crores. Why is India's economic position in such bad condition, when all the meritorious economists and administrators manage the affairs of the country (Kumar, 2005, p. 804)?

By looking at Table 4.5, progressive states like West Bengal and Kerala also failed to perform better with regard to the SC, ST and OBCs and also Muslims. These groups representation in teaching community is very unimaginable level. This indicates that the progressive states have not been able to create enough opportunities for SC/STs, OBCs and Muslims in higher education. Gujarat, touted as the development model for India, is a complete failure on this count, with only 1.18 per cent of the state's teaching positions in higher education filled by Muslims. Table 4.5 also equally conveys that wherever (states) the OBCs are politically and economically powerful in such states, that is, Bihar and Uttar Pradesh, the SC/STs and Muslims are forcefully kept away from education, particularly in higher education.

Table 4.5 Number of Teaching Community among Various Social Categories and Gender in Higher Education (in %)

State	SCs	STs	OBCs	Muslim	Women
TN	8.35	0.33	54.57	1.97	46.27
UP	5.7	0.31	16.84	4.79	32.80
Rajasthan	5.73	2.86	17.37	1.41	36.83
Punjab	3.96	0.16	1.93	0.24	49
West Bengal	5.49	0.77	2.27	3.01	32.62
Maharashtra	10.57	1.55	16.16	2.26	37.39
Kerala	2.7	0.21	25.04	6.72	56.46
Gujarat	4.79	3.62	13.67	1.18	34.85
Bihar	1.67	0.32	27.06	5.83	19.39
All India	6.95	1.99	21.92	3.09	39.07

Source: AISHE 2012–2013 (Provisional), 2014.

Conclusion

Apart from social discrimination, the story of higher education of Dalits is marked with personal struggle. It has never been an easy journey like others belonging to higher strata. The access to education, especially the higher education, is not independent of political economy and caste society that ultimately determine both opportunities to access and success. Dalits being weaker in their socio-economic profile cannot afford to subscribe the mainstream culture which is otherwise very expensive. Despite the political patronage, the Dalits do not enjoy full support and face difficulties in sending their children to higher education. It is not simply higher education; at the end of education, there has to be corresponding job profile, which is again very unlikely.

Notes

1. The Constitution (SCs) Order, 1950 lists 1,108 sub-castes across 28 states in its First Schedule. As per the latest information (26 October 2017) from the Ministry of Social Justice and Empowerment, GOI notification, nearly 1,252 sub-castes are there within the SCs.

2. While describing the twice-born castes, Shah referred the case of Brahmins. Although the Brahmins were considered the purest caste, a Brahmin priest was purer than ordinary Brahmin. The other Brahmin sub-castes were considered the lowest. Similarly, many non- Brahmin caste members of certain highly Sanskrit sects observed the rules of purity/impurity so meticulously, particularly while worshiping their deities, that they considered the ordinary Brahmins as less pure, if not polluting. Many holy men among lower castes and tribes, such as Bhagats and Bhuvas, also observed the rules of purity/impurity strictly. For details, see Shah (2007).
3. S. M. Mate, a Brahmin social reformer from Maharashtra used the word *asprustha* for Untouchables in the 19th Century.
4. In this connection, S. K. Thorat says that mainstream economic theory indicates that economic, particularly in market, discrimination has multiple consequences. For this, he referred to the Birdsall and Sabot's analysis which says that discrimination hampers economic growth, induces income inequality and creates potential for inter-group conflict by denying equal opportunity to discriminated groups (1991). Therefore, remedies against discrimination—legal, affirmative action or compensatory in nature—are required both for equity and economic growth. Hence, he suggests that India needs a reservation policy even in private sector for reasons of equity as well as economic growth. He further brought the idea that wherever discrimination on the basis of race, religion and ethnicity of national or social origin exists in many nations under diverse social, economic and political systems. In such situations, and also to correct the imbalance in terms of access to capital assets, employment, education, political participation and other spheres, countries have turned to practices of reservation, affirmative action, positive action or equal opportunity policies for these discriminated subgroups in addition to general pro-poor policies. A great majority of these policies and programmes of intervention operates in respect to subgroup populations identified by ethnic, racial, religious or gender characteristics. The examples are not only from the West (USA, UK, Northern Ireland and Yugoslavia) but also from Latin American countries like Brazil, Bolivia, Peru; African countries like Nigeria, Sudan, South Africa and countries like Malaysia, Pakistan, China, Japan and India from Asia. It is surprising that while the affirmative action policy in many of these countries was, to begin with, used for both private and public sector, in India, the same method, that is, positive action or equal opportunity policies, is not followed, particularly in private sector—even though it is the fact of discrimination in private domain that led us to accept the reservation policy for the public sector. For details, see Thorat (2005).
5. While a policy of quota system exists throughout the country for their reservation, a different scheme exists in IITs, as they are defined as Institutes of National Importance. The IITs had initially implemented a quota system, but it was scrapped and modified scheme was introduced in 1988. According to this system, all SC and ST candidates have to appear in joint

entrance tests with the rest of the students. Based on the results of IIT-JEE, those SC/ST candidates that qualify by a relaxed selection criterion of scoring more than two-thirds of the marks scored by the last General category student are admitted directly to IITs. Another slab of candidates who do not meet this relaxed admission criteria are offered a preparatory course of physics, chemistry or mathematics at the IIT concerned. After one year of study, only those candidates who are able to clear a cut-off in the end-semester exams are accepted into regular studies at the IITs. The seat reserved for the SC and ST students are not transferable to General category and roll on to next year's students from the preparatory courses. This procedure was evolved based on the experience of implementing a quota system for 10 years (1973–1983). The students admitted through reserved quota have no relaxation in requirements for passing courses or obtaining their degrees. They are, however, allowed to complete the programme at a slower pace (take longer to get the degree).

References

Government of India, MHRD. *All India Survey on Higher Education (AISHE)*. 1966–67; 1998–99; 2004–05; 2012–13 (Provisional), 2014–2015.

Benjamin, J. (2008, July–September). Dalit and higher education in India. *The Indian Journal of Political Science, 69*(3), 627–642.

Brahmanandam, T., & Bosu, T. B. (2016, July–December). Educational status among the Scheduled Tribes: Issues and challenges. *NEHU Journal, XIV*(2), 69–85.

Chanana, K. (1993). Accessing higher education: The dilemma of schooling women, minorities, Scheduled Castes and Scheduled Tribes in contemporary India. *Higher Education, 26*(1), 69–92.

Chitnis, S. (1972). Education for equality: Case of Scheduled Castes in higher education. *Economic & Political Weekly, 7*(31/33), (Special number) 1675–1681.

Choudhary, S. K. (2007). The Scheduled Castes in higher education. *Mainstream, XLV*(24). https://www.mainstreamweekly.net/rubrique18.html?debut_articles=10#pagination_articles

Corrie, P. B. (1995). A Human Development Index for the Dalit child in India. *Social Indicators Research, 34*(3), 395–409.

Desai, S., & Kulkarni, V. (2008, May). Changing educational inequalities in India in the context of affirmative action. *Demography, 45*(2), 245–270.

Government of India. MHRD. Department Of Higher Education, Lok Sabha Debates, DR. UDIT RAJ, Starred Question No. 267 (Annexure-I). http://164.100.24.220/loksabhaquestions/annex/16/AS267.pdf

Kumar, K. (1983, 3–10 September). Educational experience of Scheduled Castes and Tribes. *Economic & Political Weekly, 18*(36/37), 1566–1572.

Kumar, V. (2001, December). Globalisation and empowerment of Dalits in India. *Indian Anthropologist, 31*(2), 15–25

Kumar, V. (2014). Inequality in India: Caste and Hindu social order. *Transience*, 5(1), 36–52.
Maurya. R. D. (2018). Discrimination and social exclusion against Scheduled Caste students in the institutions of higher learning. In Brahmanandam, & B. Babu (Eds.), *Voices unheard: Methodologically articulated*. Kalpaz Publications.
Nancy Birdsall and Richard Sabo (ed) (1991). The International Bank for Reconstruction and Development, Washington, D.C.
Naryanan, S. V. (2015, 8 September). Higher education is still a bar too high for Muslims, Dalits. *The Wire*. https://thewire.in/education/higher-education-is-still-a-bar-too-high-for-muslims-dalits
National Commission for Scheduled Castes (NCSC). (2004–2005). *Annual report*.
National Commission for Scheduled Castes (NCSC). (2005–2006). *Annual report*.
Nehru, J. (1989). *Letters to Chief Ministers. Vol. 5*. Oxford University Press.
Pandey, B. (1986, February–March). Educational development among Scheduled Castes. *Social Scientist*, 14(2/3), 59–68.
Patwardhan, V., & Palshikar, V. (1992). Reserved seats in medical education: A study. *Journal of Education and Social Change*, 5, 1–117.
Radhakrishnan, P. (2002, 16–22 February). Sensitising officials on Dalits and reservations. *Economic & Political Weekly*, 37(7), 653–659.
Sahoo, N. (2009). *Reservation policy and its implementation across domains in India*. Observer Research Foundation.
Sankaran, S. R. (1998, 31 January). Development of Scheduled Castes in Andhra Pradesh: Emerging issues. *Economic & Political Weekly*, 33(5), 208–211.
Shah, A. M. (2007, September–December). Purity, impurity, untouchability: Then and now. *Sociological Bulletin*, 56(3), 356–358.
Shills, E. (1961). The academic profession in India. In A. Singh. & P. Altbach (Eds.), *The higher learning in India*. Vikas Publishing House.
Srinivas, M. N. (1955, 15 October). Castes: Can they exist in India of tomorrow? *The Economic Weekly*, 7(42), 1230–1231 & 1252.
The Wire. (2019, 2 January). Less than 3% of all faculty members at IITs are SC/ST. https://thewire.in/education/less-than-3-of-all-faculty-members-at-iits-are-sc-st
Times of India (Hyderabad edition). (2014, 26 February). Report on UoH student's suicide within a month. https://timesofindia.indiatimes.com/city/hyderabad/Report-on-UoH-students-suicide-within-a-month/articleshow/31009223.cms accessed on 26 August 2020.
Thorat, S. (2005). *Why reservation is necessary*. Seminar Vol: 549. Seminar Publications https://www.india-seminar.com/semframe.html accessed on 26 September 2020.
Weisskopf, T. (2004, 25 September–1 October). Impact of reservation on admissions to higher education in India. *Economic & Political Weekly*, 39(39), 4339–4349.

5

Caste Discrimination and Exclusion in Higher Education

Areesh Kumar Karamala

Introduction

Inclusion and exclusion are contrary or opposing concepts in the educational discourse. The notion of inclusion, particularly that of social inclusion, is viewed as a multi-layered concept. At this juncture, wherein inclusive policies have gained much prominence, the significance of the same in the educational sphere needs to be recognized. Since universities are part of Indian society, discrimination based on caste too exists in higher-educational spaces. Universities are diverse in terms of demographic composition allowing students from different caste and class, subsequently permeating social customs and traditions in higher-educational spaces. Consequently, social and educational institutions have the capacity to reproduce the caste system.

Every student enters into university with merit or its constitutionally accepted equivalent; it is the administration's responsibility to ensure equal opportunities and free working environment. Articles 15 and 16 of the Indian Constitution guarantee social justice and equality of opportunities to all its citizens. According to Article 46, the state shall take the necessary measures to provide education facilities for marginalized communities, and it is the state's responsibility to protect weaker sections of the society from social injustice and exploitation. Despite implementing several legislations like Article 17 (prohibition of untouchability), Prevention of Atrocities Act, 1989 and National Commission for SC/ST, Dalit students are subjected to exclusion harassment and discrimination based on their identity in higher-educational institutions. Several committees and commissions such as Professor S. K. Thorat Committee (2007) and the Mungekar Committee (2012) were formed to enquire the exclusion and discrimination based on caste in premier higher-education institutions such as All India Institute of Medical Sciences (AIIMS), Indian Institute of Management (IIM), Indian Institute of Technology (IIT), Vardhman Mahavir Medical College (VMMC), Hyderabad Central University (HCU), etc.

Notion of Merit in Higher Education

Time and again, the issue of merit has been put forward by certain sections within as well as outside academia. It is a regular working mechanism by which the ruling elite exploit the ruled or common masses. In its challenging character is understood the meaning that the merit is not a thing of masses; so better, they be satisfied with their present fate and fatalistic destinies. The colloquial universality of the embedded mechanism of merit is that it cannot be attained by one and all but the chosen few (Arya, 2013).

The present Indian society exhibits a peculiar phenomenon when we see merit as a trait concentrated into certain sections of Indian society which is easily identifiable on caste lines. In India, Dalits, backward castes, Muslims and women in particular are said to be lacking merit (Girija, 2016). The types of schooling, parentage, education, etc., most of the marginalized sections receive often come as course of fluke rather than capabilities, potential, talent or worth because society is usually imperfect.

According to Anoop Kumar, 1 merit is the argument held against Dalits. Kumar busts the merit myth in his report on caste discrimination at IIT Delhi. Merit has been reduced to marks at the Joint Entrance Examination (JEE) for IITs, which can supposedly be cracked only by the brightest minds. But the 'brightest minds' are invariably manufactured by a billion-dollar coaching industry, points out Kumar. 'students from the upper castes can afford coaching, while many Dalit students crack the JEE on their own. And yet, because the cut-offs are lower for Dalits, this feeds into the myth that they are not meritorious' (Mukherji, 2014). Girija (2016) argues, if we measure merit in terms of marks obtained, all the Dalit and marginalized students got very good marks up to their intermediate courses and secured admission in higher-educational institutions through entrance and viva voce. All the students who committed suicide, began losing marks (merit) after joining for the higher education.

Merit is simply not merit; it is practically much more sophisticated phenomenon than we understand as a theoretical reality. Merit is not a complete and empirically objective fact. In most of the societies and most of the times, merit developed a false consciousness (Arya, 2013). The elite groups in the society used the concept of merit as political strategy to undermine the marginalized communities. Even in modern times, the notion of merit is used against the affirmative action policies for Dalits in higher education. The construction of this false consciousness in academia as well as in general has constructed pessimistic notions against Dalit students.

Patterns of Caste Discrimination in Higher Education

In the last few decades, higher-educational institutions have evolved into powerful spaces. The combination of knowledge creation and power has turned universities into the most contentious spaces. Increase in diversity has not only created a positive impact but also conflict within universities. The concept of equal opportunities in higher education has been overturned with narratives of 'merit' and 'reverse discrimination' by dominant castes, thus questioning the credibility of Dalit students. This has exposed Dalit students to institutional forms of discrimination and exclusion and discrimination based on caste. The caste power nexus between dominant caste students, faculty and administration in universities has adversely affected Dalit students. Caste is a determinant factor in deciding relationship of students with each other and, vice versa, student and teacher's relationship. The existence of caste practices has exceedingly impacted the interaction, performance and well-being of Dalit students in universities. This discriminatory practice extends to exam evaluation, allotment of hostels, granting fellowships and many others.

According to Professor Thorat (2007), Dalit, Adivasi, OBC and other minority students are experiencing different forms of caste-based discrimination and exclusion in modern higher education system such as segregation in hostel and mess, discrimination in practical and viva voce, denial of fellowship, denial of foreign opportunities, class representatives, evaluation and examination, lack of consultation and interaction with teachers, isolation, anti-quota statements, exclusion from games and cultural activities, denial of research opportunities, denial of SC/ST appointments and promotions, rustication from hostel and library and denial of reservation and admission.

In several universities, hostels are segregated based on caste and religious identities. In Rajasthan University, most of the hostels were divided between Jats, Gujjars, Brahmins and Dalits. J. C. Bose hostel for Brahmins, Swami Vivekananda hostel for Jats, DBN hostel for Gujjars and Aravali hostel for SC students are unofficially allotted by university authorities (Mukherji, 2014). The similar pattern of segregation of hostels based on religion and caste was followed in Patna University.

Dalit Media Network says, Dalit and Adivasi students have to submit coloured application forms for JEE. (For JEE 2000, the colour was pink.) They are then given coloured answer sheets as well, while 'others' get plain white ones (Dalit Media Network, 2001). According to the Thorat Committee report on AIIMS,

72 per cent of students said they faced discrimination, while 88 per cent reported various forms of social isolation, 76 per cent of reserved category students said their papers were not examined properly. The percentage of those who felt discriminated against during practical examination and viva was even higher at 84 per cent. As many as 76 per cent said they were asked about their caste while 85 per cent said they got less time with examiners than higher-caste students (Thorat Committee,2 2007). Discrimination within university spaces and academic exclusion has compelled several Dalit students to discontinue their studies.

Caste-based Discrimination in Higher Education

Caste discrimination against Dalit students on campuses has been prevalent for quite a while. However, in the past two decades, the incidents that have surfaced illustrate the gloomy picture in premier institutions in India. The premier institutions also point towards the kind of caste discrimination prevalent in these campuses where Dalit students are subjected to harassment due to their caste background on a regular basis, not only by their colleagues but also by the faculties and the administration (Insight Foundation, 2011). The academic space in higher education has confined itself to the monotonous discourse of merit and reservation that often targets Dalit students in the campuses. Students availing reservations are often discriminated and targeted by the teachers and fellow students in universities. They are often reminded that they are incompetent and 'non-meritorious.' Anti-reservation and merit narratives in academics have adversely affected the Dalit students in several ways. It is only in the recent past that alternative discourse countering merit has emerged. Several caste-based discrimination cases were reported from premier institutions like AIIMS, IIM, IIT, VMMC, HCU, etc.

Table 5.1 illustrates the caste-based discrimination cases in different universities and premier institutions across India. Dalit students in universities are often subjects to discrimination overtly or covertly. In HCU alone, there have been more

Table 5.1 List of Dalit Students Committing Suicide in India's Higher-educational Institutions

Sl. No.	Name of the Student	Year of Death	Course/Programme	Name of the Institution
1	M. Srikanth	2007	BTech	IIT Bombay
2	Ajay S. Chandra	2007	PhD	IISC Bangalore
3	Jaspreet Singh	2008	MBBS	Govt. Medical College (Chandigarh)
4	Senthil Kumar	2008	PhD	HCU
5	Prasanth Kureel	2008	MTech	IIT Kanpur
6	G. Suman	2009	MTech	IIT Kanpur
7	Ankita Veghda	2009	BSc Nursing	Singhi Institute of Nursing (Ahmedabad)
8	Balmukundh Bharti	2010	MBBS	AIIMS (New Delhi)
9	Madhuri Sale	2010	BTech	IIT Kanpur
10	Manish Kumar	2011	BTech	IIT Roorkee
11	Linesh Mohan Gawle	2011	PhD	National Institute of Immunology (New Delhi)
12	Madari Venkatesh	2013	PhD	HCU
13	Rohith Vemula	2016	PhD	HCU

Source: Death of Merit (2011) and Preeti Biswas (2016).
Note. The list is of reported cases of caste discrimination; however, there are cases unreported as well.

than 10 suicides of Dalit students in the past decade. Most of the students were harassed by not allotting supervisor, delay in providing fellowship, delay in confirmation of synopsis and so on. This pattern of discrimination inevitably affects the performance and mental health of Dalit and other marginalized communities. The exclusionary behaviour and attitude among the faculties as well as students have driven Dalit students to take extreme steps like committing suicides. Suicides of Senthil Kumar and Madari Venkatesh at HCU undoubtedly indicates the discrimination meted against Dalit students in universities. The recent incident of the suicide of Rohit Vemula displays the increasing level of prejudices against Dalit students on campuses (Apurva, 2016; The Death of Merit, 2011). In many of the universities, hostels are invariably allotted on the basis of caste. In institutes like AIIMS, students are often humiliated in class calling them incapable of studying in premier institutions as they avail reservation. Various testimonies of Dalit students reveal the horrifying stories of students that often go unnoticed. Caste is very much a part and parcel of institutes of higher learning. These practices continue to persist in multifarious aspects and levels affecting numerous students from marginalized sections.

In the background of increase in the number of suicides of Dalits students, several official and unofficial committees were formed to study and analyse the caste-based discrimination in India's higher-educational institutions such as Professor S. K. Thorat Committee (2006), the Mungekar Committee (2012) and Professor Faizan Mustafa Committee (2013), besides formulating University Grants Commission Grievance Redressal Regulations (2012); several students and faculty members belonging to SC and ST communities reported caste-based discriminations in AIIMS. Some students committed suicide and many discontinued their studies, and these led to protest demonstrations across the country by various civil society groups and student groups against the AIIMS administration. In 2006, the government set up a committee under the chairmanship of Professor S. K. Thorat to observe and examine the caste-based discrimination practices in AIIMS. With two additional members, Dr K. M. Shyamprasad and Dr R. K. Srivastava, the committee interacted with several faculty members, students and non-teaching staff. Findings of the Thorat Committee report revealed the discrimination meted against the Dalit students in AIIMS. The report mentioned segregation in the hostel and discrimination in teaching, discrimination in the evaluation of theory paper, practical, viva and so on (Thorat, 2007).

A similar incident happened in VMMC, New Delhi. Several Dalit students were repeatedly failed in their subjects. The Mungekar Committee was appointed by the National Commission for Scheduled Castes, to enquire discrimination against Dalit students in VMMC in Delhi. After a year-long investigation, the committee came out with a report, very clearly indicating the VMMC administration discriminated students from the reserved category. The committee exposed the deeply rooted caste-based discrimination and hatred against Dalits in VMMC. The report even named the faculties guilty of such acts and has recommended strong legal action against them. However, to date, no action has been taken against any of the faculty members (Singh & Kumar, 2012). Professor Faizan Mustafa Committee was also constituted to examine the discrimination on campuses. The University Grants Commission (UGC), National Campaign on Dalit Human Rights, National Commission for SC and ST and several other agencies explicitly mentioned the presence of caste-based discrimination against Dalit students on campuses along with numerous recommendations to eradicate it. However, the committee's recommendations have not been considered in the backdrop of implementing an Act.

Lack of representation of Dalit and Adivasi teaching and non-teaching staff is one of the major reasons for the continuing caste discrimination in universities and premier institutes. According to the Ministry of Human Resource Development (MHRD) report on higher education in India, SC, ST, Muslims and OBC teachers are being under-represented in premier institutions. The under-representation of marginalized community faculties has made universities' spaces insecure for Dalit students. The future seems

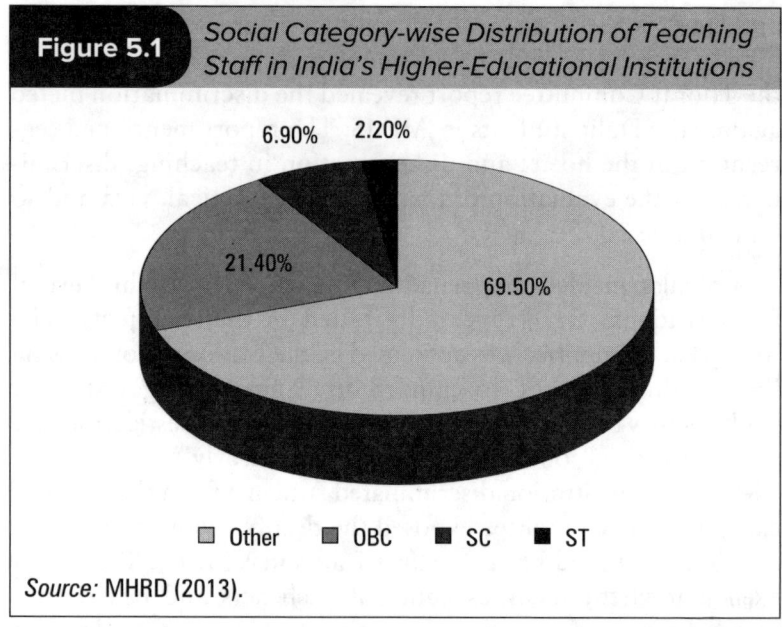

Figure 5.1 Social Category-wise Distribution of Teaching Staff in India's Higher-Educational Institutions

Source: MHRD (2013).

to be uncertain for several Dalit students who are primarily first-generation learners in universities.

Figure 5.1 explains the appointments of teachers in universities, colleges and standalone institutions based on social category. According to MHRD report, SC community constitutes 6.90 per cent, ST (2.20 per cent), OBC (21.40 per cent), whereas 69 per cent of the teaching positions were occupied by other dominant communities (MHRD, 2013). These figures reflect the lack of diversity and representation of marginalized communities. In addition, it also shows the ineffective implementation of reservation in employment which the universities are bound to follow. The report also explored the social category-wise distribution of non-teaching staff in educational institutions.

Figure 5.2 illustrates the over-representation of privileged castes in universities and colleges at different levels of non-teaching positions across the country. The report stated that only 3.70 per cent administration positions were filled by ST community,

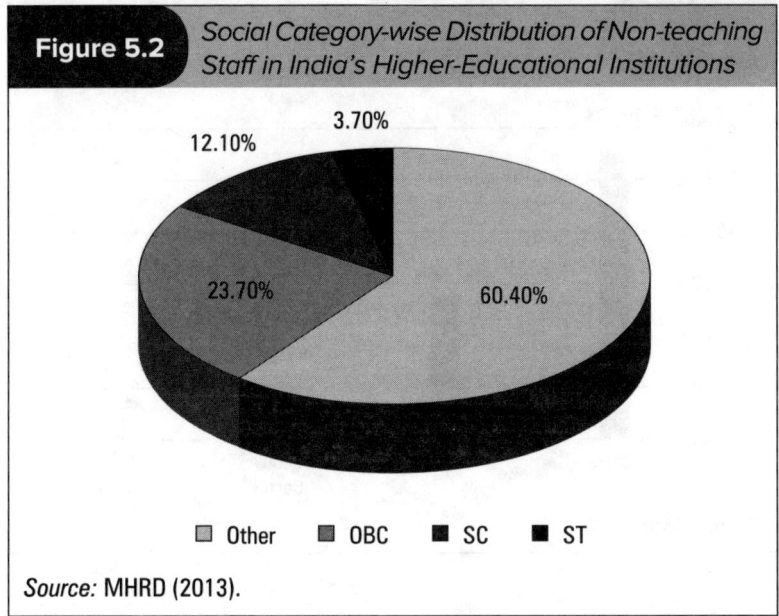

Figure 5.2 Social Category-wise Distribution of Non-teaching Staff in India's Higher-Educational Institutions

Source: MHRD (2013).

12.10 per cent by SC, 23.70 per cent by OBC, whereas more than 60.40 per cent non-teaching and administrative positions are in the hands of privileged groups and others (MHRD, 2013). The unequal distribution of teaching and non-teaching staff inevitably affects the interests of Dalit and other marginalized students in premier institutions. In addition, the impunity and casteist entities in these spaces enjoy the escalated complications that Dalit students experience.

Lack of Dalit, Adivasi and OBC representation in university teaching and non-teaching staff, research committees, review meetings, admission boards and practical and viva-voce examination committees has affected the enrolment of students into higher-education institutions. According to the reports, the representation of marginalized communities in higher education is grim, despite introducing several initiatives such as special programmes, fellowships and legal measures. The enrolment of students from ST into higher-education institutions is 4.4 per cent, while that

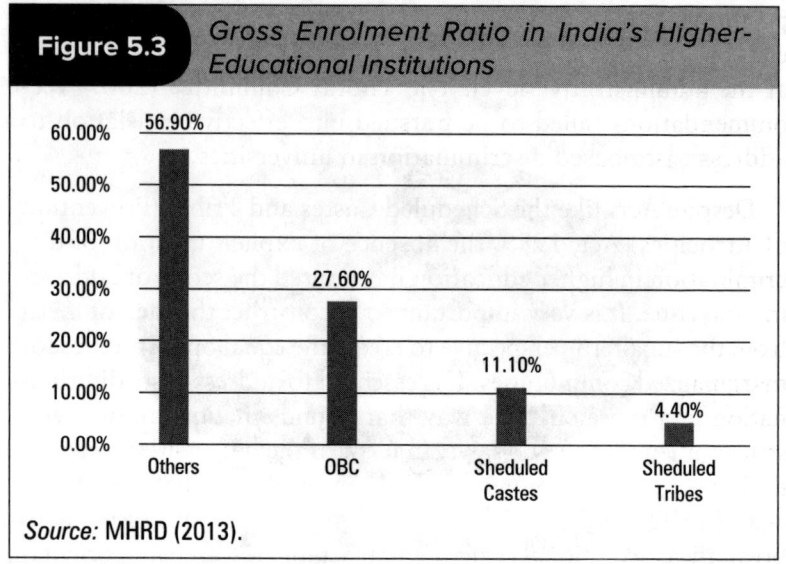

Figure 5.3 Gross Enrolment Ratio in India's Higher-Educational Institutions

Source: MHRD (2013).

of SC constitutes for 11.10 per cent and OBC accounts for 27.60 per cent, whereas other community students' enrolment accounts for 56.90 per cent (MHRD, 2013).

Conclusion

In the recent past, caste has gained a new form of discrimination in modern India. From rural forms of untouchability to caste discrimination has developed into institutionalized form. The subtleness in the way caste and exclusion operates in higher-educational institutions has ignored the existence of the same. The narrative that retreats that caste is a thing of past has further reduced the anti-caste approach addressing discrimination based on caste in premier educational institutions. One of the major challenges in addressing caste-based discrimination effectively in premier institutions is the unwillingness of the administration to handle the issue indisputably. The UGC guidelines are just a mere general rule that doesn't amount to accountability. Similarly, the under-representation of marginalized communities in administrative positions, equal opportunity cells, proctorial enquiry committees, etc., has resulted in the biased decision in case of discrimination at the administrative level. The Thorat Committee (2007) recommendations failed to be pursued into effective legislation to address caste-based discrimination in universities.

Despite Acts like the Scheduled Castes and Tribes (Prevention of Atrocities) Act, 1989, the absence of explicit mention of discrimination in higher education has limited the scope of addressing the issue. It is very important to deconstruct the idea of merit from the subaltern perspective to create the equal opportunities for marginalized communities. It is essential to address caste discrimination in a more effective way that bounds the institutions with stringent legislation and laws. In most of the universities, orientation to students is rudimentary without the mention of the intricacies of marginalization, diversity and many other. It is essential to break the conventional structure of teaching, research and orientation at universities. The incorporation of pedagogy on equality and discrimination in universities will facilitate in evolving the social culture free from caste prejudices. The deepening divide of caste in university spaces has only amplified discrimination and exclusion. It is vital to have an effective intervention from policymakers along with a serious introspection among the privileged communities to address caste hierarchies of which they are torchbearers.

Notes

1. Anoop Kumar, a Dalit advocate based in New Delhi, has documented at least 18 cases of Dalit students committing suicide due to caste-based discrimination in higher-educational institutions since 2007.
2. Thorat committee was formed in 2007 to investigate caste discrimination in higher-educational institutions (AIIMS) in India by the Government of India.

References

Apurva. (2016). Caste came up in 3 suicide probes at Hyderabad University. *The Indian Express*. https://indianexpress.com/article/india/india-news-india/caste-came-up-in-3-suicide-probes-at-hyderabad-university/

Biswas, P. (2016). Nine student suicides in 10 years. *Times of India*. https://timesofindia.indiatimes.com/city/hyderabad/Nine-student-suicides-in-10-years/articleshow/50632151.cms

Dalit Media Network. (2001). Doing Manu Proud academic terrorism, casteism go unnoticed Dalit Media Network, Chennai http://www.ambedkar.org/research/IITs.htm

Deshpande, A.. (2011). *The grammar of caste: Economic discrimination in contemporary India*. Oxford University Press.

Deshpande, S. (2006). Exclusive inequalities: Merit, caste and discrimination in Indian higher education today. *Economic & Political Weekly*, 41(24), 2438–2444.

Editorial. (2007). Caste discrimination in AIIMS [Editorial]. *Economic & Political Weekly*, 42(22), 2032.

Gatade, Subhash. (2016). Condemning caste discrimination in higher education centres that led to Rohith's untimely death. Retrieved 8 February 2016, from http://kafila.org/2016/01/29/condemning-caste-discrimination-in-higher-education-centres-that-led-to-rohiths-untimely-death-students-of-delhi-school-of-economics-delhi-university/

Girija, K. P. (2011). On suicides, caste and higher education insight: Young voices. The Death of Merit. https://thedeathofmeritinindia.wordpress.com/2011/04/26/84/

Girija, K. P. (2016). Dalit suicides in institutes of higher learning. The Death of Merit. https://www.sabrangindia.in/article/death-merit-dalit-suicides-institutes-higher-learning

Human Rights Watch and the Center for Human Rights and Global Justice. (2007). *Hidden apartheid: Caste discrimination against India's 'Untouchables'*. Vol. 19, no. 3. https://www.refworld.org/docid/45eebcdf2.html

IDSN. (2016). Education. http://idsn.org/key-issues/education

Insight Foundation. (2011). On suicides of Dalit students in India's premier educational institutions. *Countercurrents.org*. http://www.countercurrents.org/insight300411.htm

Kumar, A. N. (2013, 15 January). Dissecting the myths of merit and meritocracy. *Countercurrents.org*. http://www.countercurrents.org/arya150113.htm

MHRD. (2013). *All India survey on higher education 2010–2011*. Department of Higher Education, Ministry of Human Resource Development, Government of India. http://mhrd.gov.in/sites/upload_files/mhrd/files/statistics/aishe201011.pdf, 2013.

Mukherji, A. (2014). Degrees of bias. *Times of India*. http://timesofindia.indiatimes.com/home/sunday-times/deep-focus/Degrees-of bias/articleshow/42417903.cms.

Samson, O. V. (2015). *Faces of discrimination in higher education in India: Quota policy, social justice and the Dalits. Routledge Research in Educational Equality and Diversity Series*. Routledge.

Singh, A. K., & Kumar, A. (2012). *Protest against caste discrimination in educational institutions in New Delhi*. Round Table India. http://roundtableindia.co.in/index.php?Itemid=195&catid=129%3Aevents-and activism&id=5853%3Aprotest-against-caste-discrimination-in-educational-institutions-&option=com_content&view=article.

The Death of Merit. (2007). Prof Thorat Committee report on caste discrimination in AIIMS, New Delhi (2007). https://thedeathofmeritinindia.wordpress.com/2011/05/17/prof-thorat-committee-report-on-caste-discrimination-in-aiims-new-delhi.

The Death of Merit. (2011). Manish Kumar (IIT Roorkee) [A Documentary]. https://thedeathofmeritinindia.wordpress.com/.

The Death of Merit. (2011). On suicides, caste and higher education. https://thedeathofmeritinindia.wordpress.com/2011/04/26/84/.

Thorat, S., & Neuman, K. S. (2012). *Blocked by caste: Economic discrimination in modern India*. OUP India.

TNN. (2014, 24 September). Caste divisions of Rajasthan University hostels disturbing. *Times of India*. https://timesofindia.indiatimes.com/city/jaipur/Caste-divisions-of-Rajasthan-University-hostels-disturbing-V-C/articleshow/43270009.cms.

PART III

Minorities and Higher Education

Chapter 6
Muslim's Inclusion in Indian Higher Education: An Analysis
K. M. Ziyauddin

Chapter 7
Reaching the Unreachable: Jesuit Worldwide Learning—Higher Education at the Margins
Maxim Dias and Alphonse Pius Fernandes

6

Muslim's Inclusion in Indian Higher Education
An Analysis

K. M. Ziyauddin

Introduction

India as a nation emerged in a long process of sociopolitical and cultural interaction vis-à-vis assimilation, whereby distinct religious and linguistic communities have lived together for years and decades. The evolution of Indian nation is a sacrosanct outcome to a country that wanted to build a society with a spirit of social democracy and equal opportunity after the attainment of freedom from colonial rule. The struggles between the communities, either religious or various minorities, have not necessarily been in terms of accumulating wealth and capital, rather to strengthen their cultural existence in a new form of democratic social space. However, the post-Independence India shows a very conscious political effort in the forms of making constitutional mandates to reach each and every social group at the margin. Until the government of India accepted the findings of a scientifically studied report popularly known as Sachar Committee (2006) report, the life world of Muslims in India was referred to as the life of an elite and monolith; I see this politically as a metaphor. It may be noted then the Prime Minister of India,

Dr Manmohan Singh constituted a high-level committee to study the socio-economic and educational status of Muslims in India chaired by Justice Rajinder Sachar and so this report is referred as the Sachar Committee Report. This chapter attempts to take the reference of Muslim community as a minority population and not a monolith and does not provide an equal representation to other five minorities in order to understand and examine the questions of minorities in higher education.

The discourse of equal opportunity is not to be seen only for a few but for all the communities that lag behind, for this chapter, in educational attainments too. This is not only true for minorities but also true for Dalits, Adivasis and people with different abilities, etc. Therefore, the chapter does intend to bring the challenges of minorities and especially Muslims in higher education with the underlying fact that they are the largest marginalized community in various parameters. The chapter contextualizes in the perspectives of inclusion and exclusion and how the social distance is created over a period of time between the similar groups of citizenship on the line of religion and language.

Keeping the above discourse in mind, it is important to see the higher education in India as traditional and not only as modern and formal. Before British and Europeans arrived, India also has other schools of providing education through gurukuls (Hindu-run educational institutions), maktabs and madarsas (Muslim-run educational institutions). The British developed, a few argue, imposed and introduced English and formal education, whereby establishment of universities, namely University of Calcutta, University of Bombay and University of Madras were founded in 1857. This period did not find crisis of minority versus majority in terms of development and exclusion, rather the notion of minorities came gradually later, over the period of time when the British ruled India.

Who Are the Minorities in India?

The government of India issued gazette notification on 23 October 1993 that mentions five religious minorities: the Muslims, Christians, Sikhs, Buddhists and Zoroastrians (Parsis).

In another gazette notification, Jains as a 'minority religion' were also given a minority status under the provision of the National Commission for Minorities (NCM) Act, 1992 by Section 2(c), thereby making six religious groups as minority communities in India on 30 January 2014.

However, one needs to locate this group from the fifth session of the Constituent Assembly in India, under the chairman Rajendra Prasad, where he assured that,

> To all the minorities in India we give assurance that they will receive fair and just treatment and there will be no discrimination in any form against them. The religion, their culture and their language are safe and they will enjoy all the right and privileges of citizenship, and will be expected in their turn to render loyalty to the country in which they live and its constitution. To all we give the assurance that it will be our endeavour to end poverty and squalor and companions, hunger and disease, to abolish distinction and exploitation and to ensure decent condition of living.

The constitutional safeguards for the minorities are considered under Article 29 and 304 in Part III of the Constitution of India. While examining the Constitution of India, the expression 'minorities' is used only at four occasions. The head note of Article 295 uses the word minorities and, later, in Article 30 and in sub clause 1 and 2 of Article 306. The concept of minority has got two senses: religious and linguistic expression. But one finds that Britannica defines minorities as 'group held together by ties of common decent, language or religious faith and feeling different in these respects from the inhabitant of a given political entity'.

The sub-commission of the United Nations (UN), on prevention of discrimination of minorities, defines: (a) the minority are those non-documented groups of people which possess and desire to safeguard stable ethnic, religious or linguistic customs and traditions and differ in characteristic from the rest of the inhabitants, (b) these groups of minorities include their adequate number of people having preserved their specific tradition or characteristics and (c) finally, these groups of minority should be loyal to their belonging nations.

However, in sociological context, the concept of minority expresses that 'minority' refers to any group that consists of a population lesser than half of those with whom they differ or differentiate themselves. They may be people of a race, religion, traditions, culture, language and so on. Any such group of people would be in a lesser advantageous social and political location comparing to the dominant group having affluence, influence and prestige.

What Are the Recent Developments for the Minorities?

The purpose is not limited to understanding the minorities and dynamics associated with them but to relate them with the higher education. Seeing the population of minorities gives a picture about the communities and groups and, consequently, helps in understanding their participation and presence in higher education. In the census enumeration data of 2001, five minorities had 18.42 per cent population out of the total population of India. Consequently in 2011, census reports show 18.8 per cent of the six minority population groups: Muslims or the followers of Islam were 38 million (13.4%), Christians were 24 million (2.3%), Sikhs were 19 million (1.9%), Buddhists were 8 million (0.80%) and Jains were 4 million (0.4%). The number of people in this category is significant to understand the dynamics and social concerns embedded in the life of minority population in India. This chapter focuses on one of them, that is, Muslims as a case to examine and contextualize the problem.

The government has set up the National Minorities Development and Finance Corporation (NMDFC) that was linked with 15-point programme by the office of the prime minister. Just after the Sachar Committee recommendations, the Ministry of Minority Affairs allocated an increased fund to NMDFC to fulfil the desired goals of 15-point programme and increase the coverage of population. The data shows that NMDFC assisted to 335,000 beneficiaries from Muslims, Christians, Sikhs, Buddhists and Parsis to the total amount 916 million.

The above elaboration is one example of opening the window of support towards minorities only. Even a few state governments like Telangana has taken some initiatives to study the socio-economic and educational status of Muslim in the state, popularly referred to as the Sudheer Commission Report (2016). But the problem of minorities is quite vital and larger than the kind of initiatives taken. This chapter revolves around Muslims as a minority group in India and tries to illustrate the recent problems on the basis of data showing the conditions of Muslims in particular and others in general for the basic reason that other minority groups do not suffer from such marginalization as experienced among Muslims. Surely affirmative action and reservation to slow down and bring back the Muslims from marginalization and backwardness is an important step, but there are other ways too. A few states have given impetus to think upon after implementing the reservation to the backward Muslims from the Muslim as minority. Even in the Ranganath Misra Commission report, it was decided to create 4.5 per cent sub-quota to minorities as per the Section 2(c) of NCM Act, 1992. This was ought to be given within the available 27 per cent reserved for Other Backward Classes (OBCs) and depended upon the list prepared by the states.

Locating Discrimination in Services against Muslim as a Minority

The Mandal Commission helped a small section of Muslims to enter into employment sector but with great difficulty; even the State List of backward classes fails to appreciate the backward classes. This is added with the fact that there are a few suitable candidates available for several government- and private-created employment opportunities. It is relevant to examine certain data to contextualize the concerns of Muslims as discussed in the preceding paragraphs.

Muslims in India were 12.60 per cent in 1991 Census enumeration that slightly increased 0.8 per cent in the nationwide 2001 Census of India of the total population of the country. A country with such a huge population from one community does not find any representation in any sector of employment and political participations. They do not exist in the Parliament of

India, state-level legislatures, central-government services namely administrative, armed, police and even in paramilitary forces. They are far behind in institutions of education either private or public. The most prestigious civil and foreign services find them in much less than a quarter of the Muslims population. It is into the common knowledge of people working on minorities that their share in all kinds of services is minimal and has never improved from a certain level.

All India Milli Council brought up most relevant data before the then prime minister of India, Inder Kumar Gujral, that examined the presence of Muslims in Indian services in the last 50 years. It was found that out of total 3,883 administrative officers, a mere number of 116 were Muslims (2.98%), just 45 (3.14%) among the total of 1,433 were police officers, whereas another small number of 57 (2.64%) out of 2,159 were reported to be foreign-service officers. This figure was much before Sachar Committee (2006) brought out much more stark realities of a Muslim's life in Indian institutions. In cumulative percentage in all the categories, they constituted just 1.6 per cent in Class I officers across the various government organizations, 3.9 per cent are Class II officers and 4.4 per cent are in technical-supervisory jobs.

The Gopal Singh Committee reported a severe disproportion in socio-economic and educational level between Muslims and Hindus. One systematic sample survey in 80 districts at all-India level reflected only 92 students from Muslim community in engineering colleges out of total 2,698 students. Similarly, students (MBBS) in 8 medical colleges across 8 states were just 98 in numbers among 2,895 students. These are a few examples of invisible presence of Muslims in higher education, especially in a profession that could uplift this community at a larger level.

Therefore, the demography of Indian Muslim is necessary to examine in the backdrop of Sachar Committee report due to its implicit and embedded significance while generalizing the socio-economic and demographic aspects of the community. Muslims speak of only one group of minorities listed in the centrally notified minority groups. But the seriousness of educational, employment, health and lack of infrastructural problems appear to be much higher among Muslims than other minority groups.

Sachar Committee report (2006) elaborates the similar pathetic manifestations of inherent problems in the lives of Muslims in India; may be the initiatives taken for all minorities pretend to be only for Muslims, but the veracity is the same. The priority of the state to spend on educational infrastructure and towards better enrollment that ought to be given to Muslims in India gets lost in the name of pseudo-demographic trends and propaganda politics of high fertility among. However, the fact stands clear that the fertility of all religious groups is decreasing including Indian Muslims. The census figure of 2001 remains valuable in 2011 enumeration as well. Muslim community shows most favourable child sex ratio, that is, 986 females for every 1,000 males compared to lesser number (927) for all socio-religious group of people in general for India.

All the demographic trends show a helping nature towards nation's policy of population control where Muslims should get better share in educational fields and increase the attainment. They have low rate of infant mortality in comparison to the entire population. Oddly enough, they have a higher incidence of child under-nourishment cases. The younger-age profile is high among Muslims than the rest of the population in Indian.

One contrast reality is the urban presence of Muslim population which is, perhaps, for historical raison d'être. For the last few centuries, the Muslims have remained more urban than other Indian communities. According to the data of 2001 Census of India, 35.7 per cent were urban compared to 27.8 per cent of their total population. The urban presence of Muslim has also not helped to connect with the formal schooling and increased level of participation in higher education. It is a paradox that the availability of institutions of higher learning is more in urban areas than rural. Despite this fact, the reality is different. On the basis of this fact and the fieldwork done in several cities in India (such as Hyderabad, Delhi, Patna, Lucknow and Ranchi), one finds that availability of educational institutions is not an indicator of higher participation, rather access to those centres of learning is more significant. The Muslims are one such hugely urban-populated group that has not been able to find space in higher education system. The participation and educational status of Muslim women is a more serious challenge. The politics of gender not only operates in one religious group, but this surpasses the religious boundary of one community to another, so it is true for the Muslim women in India (Ziyauddin, 2015).

Do Social Inclusion Perspectives Help Muslims?

'Social inclusion' has increasingly become most dominant concept to help the policy implementation to get the most desired outcome for people with certain disabilities, marginalization and unseen discrimination. The disability is referred to socio-economic and political inabilities of the people unable to find appropriate space in the spheres of public domain. The perspectives of social inclusion have not been properly used to create benchmark success and monitor the effectiveness in view of the outcome required (Gidley and Hampson, 2021). The reference to social exclusion and later, social inclusion emerged in France in the 1970s, (the term was first used by Rene Lenior) predominantly with reference to economic self-sufficiency and work participation (Levitas, 1996), and gradually used in Indian policies and schemes to locate the excluded groups such as the Muslims and Dalits in order to create inclusive space for them (Ziyauddin and Kasi, 2009). Indian context is varied and complex in nature.

There are five most popular social inclusionary forms relevant to contextualize social inclusion and the Muslims: '(a) Economic participation, (b) Health and access to services, (c) Personal independence and self-determination, (d) Education and (e) Interacting with society and fulfilling social roles' (Constantinescu-Sharpe et al., 2015).

The location of the people has minimal role to play in their enrolment to higher education as discussed earlier in this chapter. Major theorists of social exclusion have stressed upon the multidimensional temperament of the concept and application. The widely discussed social exclusion has explicitly brought a paradigm shift in understanding marginalization and inequality, not simply by lacking in material resources but also in inadequate social participation, cultural–educational capital and lagging behind in access to services and power, particularly in social exclusion endeavours to capture the complexities of powerlessness than merely centring its outcomes. The educational attainment of the Muslim community not only depends upon one factor; rather, many other reasons too are responsible (Matin et al., 2013). There is a need to examine the concept of social exclusion while addressing the huge number of people getting marginalized; essentially this demands deeper introspection to the causes and factors responsible for this fate.

The Council of Europe writes, 'Social exclusion is a broader concept than poverty, encompassing not only low material means but the inability to participate effectively in economic, social, political and cultural life and in some characterizations, alienation and distance from mainstream society' (Duffy, 1995).

Manuel Castells, in his analysis on informational capitalism, refers social exclusion associated to the lack of the 'possibility of access to relatively regular paid labour, for at least one member of the household' (Castells, 1998, p. 71). Thinking this assessment to be true, then present-day India has pervasive problems of unemployment and lack of available employment in the market and society.

There is no scope to disbelieve that India is a terra firma (land) of multiplicity or diversity in populations/people, institutions and within societies. Apparently, how do public institutions act in response to and house this vast diversity is a greater challenge to the country. The higher education institutions (HEIs) in India are there to provide 'public purpose'. They shall make available optimum platform to societal diversities and imbibe inclusive ways that act as a symbol to the nation and show the diversities. This was the spirit of the broad discussion held on 'Diversity and Social Inclusion in Higher Education', at the FICCI Higher Education

Summit in 2017 in the national capital of India. The summit debated in sharing the innovative approaches to be brought in the policies, procedures and at implementation levels in order to enable inclusion and strengthen diversities among students, teachers and non-teaching staff. The focus was to have and create environment in institutions 'open to diversity and socially inclusive'.

In 2011, Booth and Ainscow write that prerequisite to inclusion in education involves many steps that included several contents to enable higher inclusion among students while reducing discrimination, barriers and social exclusion (read Booth, & Ainscow, 2011). They further gave several other points to make inclusion part of the action, making society inclusionary.

Impediments in Enrolment: The Dilemma of Indian Higher Education

A country with dynamic policy demands, high-quality education with inclusive vision and implementation are uttermost important. Having the largest youth population of around 600 million, under 25 years of age, of them, 28 per cent are less than 14 years of age. The problem of population explosion is intense in India. The UN projects that the national capital city, Delhi, will emerge as the largest city (37 million) in the world by 2028. India's population policy demands a lot many initiatives namely, improving socio-economic status, increasing the enrollment and attainment in higher education, best inclusionary measures to counter rural and urban poverty, strengthening the existing infrastructures of schools and all publicly funded educational institutions. Therefore, it is not bad to learn how China framed its policy and used their population, modernized their economy, achieved the higher education attainment mark desired globally. This will help India to play a powerful economic role in global politics in the future.

The dearth of data on all Indian Muslims is a challenge to any research on minorities. An all-India survey to study Muslims shows 4.4 per cent students enrolled in higher education (All India Survey on Higher Education, 2014–2015). In spite of almost lagging in the last decade—2010, from 5.2 per cent to 13.8 per cent—Muslim enrolment rate trailed in the national figure at 23.6 per cent, whereas OBCs have 22.1 per cent and Scheduled Castes (SCs) are at 18.5 per cent; Scheduled Tribes (STs) were just 0.5 per cent behind Muslims.

'The rate of enrolment is a measure of the number of enrolment in higher education across the age in a given academic year, compared to the 18 to 23-year old population eligible for higher education in that year.' Muslims fare quite worse in higher education, and that has widened the gap and scale of exclusion between them and other excluded groups. The literacy rate of Muslims is 67.7 per cent, whereby for the females is only 50.03 per cent (Census of India, 2011). The ratio of female education of 50.03 per cent increased from 50.01 in the last 10 years of time. The vital gap between male- and female-educational level is an alarming scene for a democratic and growing economy like India. How can a nation speak of its social development without keeping women in the same coach of the train? The empowerment is nowhere.

The case of higher education is crude. The gross enrolment ratio (GER) of Muslims is 11.3 in the figures of National Sample Survey Office (NSSO) data of 66th round (2009–2010), where Muslims perform lowest among all the minority communities (Sikhs, 23.1 per cent, Christians at 31.3 per cent, Jains at 54.6 per cent and Buddhists at 17.9 per cent).

It would be quite impossible to achieve the given target in GER of the Millennium Development Goals (MDGs) until all socio-religious groups are brought into a common platform including the largest religious minority, the Muslims. Historically, Muslims as a community have been lagging far behind their expectations at educational attainment, employment status, and in reducing poverty level (Sachar Committee Report, 2006). Precisely for all such reasons, the Government of India and several State governments have formed committees and commissions to bring scientific study-based data and suggest the remedial ways.

Poverty has remained another impediment for the minimal visibility of Muslims in higher education. In fact, there is a feeling among a few writings that shows India as an island of prosperity but in a sea of poverty. The cycle of poverty remains one dark reality of Indian society, and it is the home of the second-largest poor population, just next to Nigeria, in the world. The repercussion of being poor demands an immense loss in the form of precious life. The poverty-reasoned illness like tuberculosis kills 435,000 people every year. Another contrasting example is the worst scenario of sanitation which shows 524 million population of Indians who could not use toilet in the year 2017 (World Bank, 2017).

The reason that Muslims remain an excluded group is not alone their 'being Muslim' but also the depressive nature of higher education system in India. Second, the employability of educated youth is also a concern that demands serious introspection. Muslims have survived all forms of poverty due to their self-employability skills in urban informal sector.

Despite successive governments in the past, in the post-independent period, India accomplished in pulling around 133 million people out from the cycle of poverty during 1997–2012 (World Bank, 2017). There has been a contentious position defining the poverty level that brings drastic changes in the figures of people living below or above poverty level in India. Here, in this context, Amartya Sen and Jean Drèze wrote, India is looking 'more and more like islands of California in a sea of sub-Saharan Africa' (Sen and Drèze, 2013). Sen and Dreze argue in their work 'In An Uncertain Glory' that India's major problem lies in not paying attention to the needs of the citizens, especially the poor and large population of women. The failures in creating and fostering participatory growth and not being able to correctly use the public resources by enhanced economic growth to improve the living conditions of the people. The failures to foster participatory growth, and to make good use of the public resources generated by economic growth to enhance people's living conditions (Sen and Dreze, 2013) are responsible for unequal distribution of resources. On one hand, the continual lack of social services in quality schooling and medical health care, safe drinking water, access to electricity, drainage, and sanitation demands serious attention from the state administration. At the same time, apart from this provisioning, Muslims with low socio-economic and educational backwardness need enhanced protection and support by the states and government of India through policy interventions. For such crude reasons, while India still makes efforts to educate and employ the growing population the Muslims remain excluded from educational and employment sectors.

The various forms of exclusionary challenges has not allowed the country to achieve the desirable ratio of GER and somewhere nearer the middle-income economies. India's tertiary gross enrolment rate is mounting fast but remains more than 20 per cent points below China and Brazil.

There is also a need to analyse the employment prospects and educational attainment that remains a neglected subject matter in India. Until enrolment and educational attainment is linked to employability, the relevance of education would remain an unused resource and area in nation-building process. This also brings the kind of quality in education India has carried over the years! One does understand and finds that in 2017, 60 per cent engineering graduates remained unemployed in India. Another study finds that 47 per cent of 60,000 university-graduated students from various disciplines were unemployable in any of the skilled occupation. The most horrifying situation is that overall youth unemployment rate has been lingering above 10 per cent only in the last one decade.

This chapter has already discussed the vast diversity across the country in the context of ethnic, cultural, racial, religious and linguistics that remains a bigger challenge to policy and research. The difference of castes is reflected in the Constitution of India that identifies 1,108 castes and over 700 tribes (SCs and STs), respectively. This degree of diverse and unequal population, speaking entirely different and unique languages, brings complexities to the higher education and how they can be given education. The National Commission for Minority Educational Institutions was set up in the year 2004 and became a statutory body after a bill passed in the Parliament of India on December 4, 2005. This commission protects the rights of minorities enshrined under Article 30 of the constitution of India that states, `all minorities, whether based on religion or language shall have the right to establish and administer educational institutions of their choice.' Therefore, all minorities in India have the right to establish an educational institution and have constitutionally been given the power to administer these. In July 2019, *The Times of India* wrote that there are overall 13,000 educational institutions who have been granted minority status in India. However, these institutions cannot cater to the needs of millions of students who hail from the low socio-economic background—the largest of them from the Muslim community.

The efforts made by the Union of India and all the states have been towards massification of higher education. There are nearly 800 universities, 12,000 stand-alone institutions and 40,000 include all kinds of colleges. These institutions have 40 million enrolled students with over and above 1.5 million faculty members. The pertinent question is despite having huge expansion in higher education, why not the basic purpose is served in the interest of very young and growing population, especially Muslims? How can public institutions uplift and utilize the young Muslim youths by providing apt and skilled education and linking them to employability? How does the policy and system include and have space for the 'last, lost and the least'?

The story is heartbreaking and pitiable. Since 2004, Indian higher education excelled and got widespread expansion; the multiplicities of barriers in higher-education processes have remained the most difficult task and, at times, appear to be left aside. The existing obstruction and exclusionary barriers visibly exist in limited access to the limited number of people. Extending the reservation to Muslims has also been in the political debates after the Sachar Committee data showing backwardness among the large sections and groups of Indian Muslims. But will this single-handedly help to achieve the objective inclusivity in an environment where skyrocketing expenses in higher education is becoming a new trend and new normal? The already segregated and marginalized Muslims (including other excluded groups) cannot bear the burden of higher-education expenses and would remain in the cycle of poverty and less employability. Inclusivity is also seen, if the question is properly addressed, like how far and does scholarship help in increasing the access to HEIs?

The above discussion and framing of questions put the things rightly and suggest to revisit, rethink and rework on the importance and value of 'diversity and inclusion' across higher education and then address those impediments to access higher education among Muslims. Does inclusiveness, and the rich differences and diversity of Indian social structure, allows to leave aside the Muslims or Dalit and Adivasis lagging in educational attainment demands a national discourse. It should be understood that higher education should essentially bring and flourish the diversity through making every step socially inclusive for the basic reason that India still has public education as the best medium and means of higher education. In other words, inclusion or inclusionary efforts in higher education, 'does not only refer to the number of excluded communities, but also exclusion in syllabus, context and pedagogies, and how these can be made more inclusive, given the diversity of our country' (UNESCO Chair in Community Based Research & Social Responsibility in Higher Education, 2018).

All the above discussions also demand to recall the historical challenges in higher education faced just after independence. Independent India had only 17 universities and 636 colleges that taught around 238,000 students in 1947. The leftover problems were different when British created grossly unequal and elitist system of higher education. Higher education in India remained exclusionary in nature and elitist for few decades until very recently. Today, the rapid growth amid rising demand in higher education has not only put pressure on Indian policy makers but also brought a new market for the industrialists and corporate to invest in this sector. The structure and fee on education have further created the divide between poor and rich. In this process, Muslims as the poorest minority group in India lag further in the attainment of higher education unless the state evolves much more inclusionary mechanism and policy interventions.

Rapid Growth amid Surging Demand

The pertinent question remains that several religious groups' population growth rate has gradually been declining over the last decade including Muslims (2001–2011), and this negates all weird excuses given for the failure in attaining better GER. The largest Hindu community in India, their growth rate has slowed down to 16.76 per cent from earlier figure of 19.92 reported during 1991–2001. Similarly, Muslims also managed to show much better population control, and the growth rate went down to 24.60 per cent (2001–2011) from the previous per centage of 29.52 (1991–2001). The significant decrease in the population-growth rate among Muslims is a much greater contribution towards making the nation rise and reduces the population burden on economy, a most rationale contribution by Muslims. This level of decrease has never happened over the last 60 years where Muslims lived more in poverty and illiteracy. The Christians had 15.5 per cent of population growth whereas Sikhs stand with 8.4 per cent of population growth.

Jain community has remained the highly educated and shown least population growth rate at 5.4 per cent during 2001–2011 period. It can be pretended that Hindus, Muslims and Christians would show decreasing trend in their population growth by 2021

Census; however Sikhism, Jainism and Buddhism would remain stable in the next two 20 years because these communities have already slowed down their population growth rate.

Concluding Discussions

Therefore, the chapter negates the idea that inclusive India can develop by excluding the largest group of minorities like Muslims. Any insight and experiences of a developed society suggest that the process of institutionalization by inclusionary measures or of taking social inclusion methods across the university system is of prime significance in policymaking process and also debating the same in higher education, so it is true for Muslims to be given importance as a stakeholder in university structure and not just the receiver.

The process of making higher education curricula inclusive would be only when one transforms the pedagogies of the educational institutions. The literacy rate of minority population, namely Muslims at 59.1 per cent, Christians at 80.3 per cent, Sikhs at 69.4 per cent, Buddhists at 72.7 per cent and Zoroastrians (Parsis) have 97.9 per cent of literacy. Such data shows the real face of impediments in higher education and, consequently, GER that India wants to attain.

The chapter attempted to argue that poverty holds back Muslims from higher education with small difference than northern states; lack of schools also holds an additional factor to hold Muslims from in higher education. The presence of Muslims is shown earlier in the chapter, but it is interesting to see them in the following paragraph quickly. Lastly, it is relevant to conclude by putting the data from 55th round of NSSO (1999–2000) that provides good analysis on the achievement in education among Hindus and Muslims both at India and state level. The participation of Muslims in urban areas was 3.9 per cent and in rural was 0.8 per cent in comparison to Hindus having 11.5 per cent and 1.8 per cent for urban and rural respectively.

Illiteracy rate among urban Muslims was 14 per cent in 1993–1994, which reduced to 11 per cent at the end of the decade. The population of youth below 20 years of age graduated at a very small percentage of 7. There is extraordinary drop out or discontinuation from postgraduate courses or programmes by Muslim graduates. The estimation shows only 1 out of 25 enrolled in undergraduate courses and again 1 student enrolled in a postgraduate course out of 50 students among Indian Muslims. Iqbal (2012), in his elaboration, reflects upon a newer trend where the rate of enrolment of Muslim men for any degree course is lower than women. Another reported data shows that minorities in higher education were merely 4.9 per cent during 2016–2017 (Centre for Educational Research & Training, 2018), and the 90 Muslim-concentrated districts identified in the Sachar Committee report, which were selected with the help of 2001 Census data, still have to travel a long journey if the state gives attention.

There is no doubt that the provisions made in the Indian Constitution in giving rights to all the minority groups shows the commitment and vision of the Constitution makers. They were firm and clear towards making India inclusive so that the multi-religious, multicultural, multilingual and multiracial society of India develops equally and have equity in educational attainment too. The fact that Muslims are a minority group, economically poor, educationally far behind the other religious minorities, their lower presence and participation in higher education is purely an outcome of an exclusionary process that functions in Indian educational setups.

There is a serious need to realize and accelerate the implementation of all forms of inclusionary measures started by successive governments either in States or Centre. Madrasa need not to be the cake of selling political aspirations and dividends, rather the increase in higher percentage of Muslims may gradually make such centres of learning less political than social and religious. The overall development in the states does bring better avenues of higher participation of Muslims than the poorer states, southern states are such examples. The spectacular 'digital divide' between

South and North Indian Muslims (Hasnain, 2009) in the areas of attaining education or having education reflects the political empowerment they would have.

If any measures or interventions of social inclusion have to be working and result oriented, there is a need to frame and evolve long-term policies but not merely a showpiece scheme. It would be benefiting to the nation-building process and also to mark up to the global GER when Muslims are rationally included in any long-term planning in future and/or envisioning the participation of Muslims, who have always remained under-represented in educational structure of the country next after SCs and ST.

References

Booth, T., & Ainscow, M. (2011). *Index for inclusion: Developing learning and participation in schools*. Centre for Studies on Inclusive Education.

Castells, M. (1998). *End of millennium: The information age. Economy, society and culture* (Vol. III). Blackwell.

Constantinescu-Sharpe, G., Phillips, R. L., Davis, A., Dornan, D., & Hogan, A. (2017). Social inclusion for children with hearing loss in listening and spoken Language early intervention: an exploratory study. *BMC Pediatrics*. https://doi.org/10.1186/s12887-017-0823-y

Drèze, J., & Sen, A. (2013). *An uncertain glory: India and its contradictions*. Allen Lane.

Gidley, J., & Hampson, Gary. (2021). Social inclusion: Context, theory and practice. https://www.researchgate.net/publication/265041981_Social_Inclusion_Context_Theory_and_Practice

Hasnain, S. I. (2009). *Muslims in North India: Frozen in the past*. Har Anand Publications.

Iqbal, S. (2012). *Indian Muslims and higher education: A study of select universities in North and South India*. (Unpublished thesis). Jamia Millia Islamia.

Levitas, R. (1996). The concept of social exclusion and the new Durkheimian hegemony. *Critical Social Policy, 161*(46), 5–20.

Matin, A., Siddiqui, F., & Ziyauddin, K. M. (Eds.) (2013). *Muslims of India: Exclusionary processes and inclusionary measures*. Manak Publications.

Rajinder, S. (2006). *Social, economic and educational status of Muslim community of India—A report*. Prime Minister's High-level committee, Cabinet Secretariat, Government of India (pp. 50–51).

Sudheer, G., Bari, M. A., Khan, A. U., & Shaban, A. (2016). *Report of commission of inquiry on socio-economic and educational conditions of Muslims*. Government of Telangana.

UNESCO Chair in Community Based Research & Social Responsibility in Higher Education. (2017). Diversity & social inclusion in higher education: Reflections from FICCI HES 2017. https://unescochair-cbrsr.org/pdf/resource/FICCI%20Doc%20II_Diversity%20%20Social%20Inclusion_4Jan.pdf

Ziyauddin, K. M., & Kasi, E. (Eds). (2009). Dimensions of social exclusion: Ethnographic explorations (Vol. I). Cambridge Scholars Publishing.

Ziyauddin, K. M. (2015). Politics of gender: Issues and challenges on Muslim women in India. In Rekha Pande (Ed.), Gender lens: Women's issues and perspectives. Rawat Publications.

Ziyauddin, K. M. (2017). Manual Scavengers far from dignity and inclusion. In Brahmanandam. T (Ed.), *Dalit issues: caste and class interface*. Rawat Publications.

7

Reaching the Unreachable
Jesuit Worldwide Learning—Higher Education at the Margins

Maxim Dias and Alphonse Pius Fernandes

Globalization offers as many opportunities as challenges, often being opportunities to a lucky few and challenges to many others. There are very few who can turn the challenges into opportunities. Jesuit[1] Worldwide Learning[2] (JWL) plays that role of a midwife in bringing out the best in the last, the least and the lost, by helping individuals to transform challenges into opportunities, and by taking advantage of the global connectedness. Education fosters critical thinking and analytical reasoning. Any investment in education benefits not only the person but also the society, country and the world at large. JWL facilitates that process.

Among the several challenges that the world faces today, there is the challenge of refugees and their education. There had been an increasing number of refugees and internally displaced people reaching up to 79.5 million in 2019 (UNHRC, 2020), the highest since the Second World War. Poverty, political, economic, ethnic and religious conflicts are the major causes of this kind of forcible displacement. The Jesuits have been working with the refugees formally through an international organization called the Jesuit Refugee Service (JRS), which mainly helps forcibly displaced peoples, especially refugees, and asylum seekers around the world. It was founded by Fr Pedro Arrupe[3] in November 1980. At present, it is rendering its service in 51 countries in the area of education and other kinds of dire situations with assistance in healthcare and nutrition, social services and income-generating activities. Having been with the JRS, JWL knows that less than 1 per cent of refugees have access to higher education.

On the contrary, a large number of the refugees are children and those below the age of 18. Therefore, JWL tries to invest its resources, as a top priority, in the education of refugees and especially those living on the margins of society. People living on the margins of the society bear the brunt the most when things go wrong. They often become the targets of conflicts without any fault of theirs (JWL, 2019). Both JWL and JRS remain complementary to each other. On the one hand, if JWL stands for long-term welfare through education and conscientization, JRS, on the other, stands for immediate help. Combined efforts of both these gives great future for the refugees, especially to the youth in imparting higher education.

The charism or the work of the Jesuits embraces a wide variety of services beginning with priestly ministries to all kinds of socially empowering services that are prominent and well-known especially through educational enterprise. Since the inception of the organization, Jesuits were involved in education, especially in higher education. Though the founder of the organization, St Ignatius of Loyola, was initially reluctant, he soon realized the potential that education possesses to impact society at large and gave in to the demands for schools and colleges. He believed in a faith that engages itself in the world, leading to dignity and equality worth of every person. And this was to be achieved by providing education, employment opportunity, medical care, fight against injustice and exploitation, eradicating social evils and improving the social condition of people.

The Constitution of the Jesuits (1548), who also run educational institutions throughout the world having over three million students, in No. 279 # 1 says: 'We must in a special way, help prepare all our students effectively to devote themselves to building a more just world and to understand how to labour with and for others.' Further, in No 289 #5, it says that education should have programmes for spiritual, social and moral formation. A special attention is also required in the area of pastoral care to its students and all the stakeholders who are connected with it.

Pedro Arrupe brings out the main goal of Jesuit education as *creating men and women for others*. Being a person for and with others requires one to take the side of the value system of equality and justice in all aspects for the people who are deprived of it. He intended that Jesuit educational institutions must seek to be the vehicles of transformation in all aspects of society till true social justice for all is realized. Though Jesuit education has a tradition of close to 500 years, it has survived in quality and competence due to its capacity to adapt itself to the changing needs of society. With thousands of Jesuits working in hundreds of institutions, the reach is still too small for the global needs, especially of the last, the least and the lost of the world such as poor, refugees and women. JWL is a giant leap in this direction with its own unique kind of response to the challenges posed by the world. It wants to bring change in the world through education. It wants to make quality education affordable with the best of teachers from the best of institutions across the globe.

The JWL believes that education can foster hope for the hopeless. It, along with higher learning, represents the formation of a global community of learners. It addresses the root causes of social evils such as poverty, despair, conflicts, isolation and displacement. Its aim is to build a more peaceful and humane society. It provides equitable, quality higher education to people and communities at the margins of societies who are deprived of education due to poverty, lack of opportunity, inaccessibility, conflicts or forced displacement. This is undertaken, religiously speaking, 'for the greater glory of God' and existentially to 'create women and men for others.'

JWL venture started with a meeting of the delegates of over 200 Jesuit institutions of higher education from around the world in 2010, where the then head of the Society of Jesus, Fr Adolfo Nicolás, posed the following questions on the nature of Jesuit education in the context of globalization and going beyond the narrow confines of individual institutions. If every single institution, singularly can do so much, how much more can the collaborative venture of all the institutions worldwide, by sharing knowledge, faculty or libraries can do? An agreement was signed at this very conference between Regis University, JC: HEM and JRS to deliver higher education to forcibly displaced persons. JC: HEM, now named as JWL, has its headquarters in Geneva, Switzerland.

The Distinctiveness of JWL

It is true that for a decade or more, there have been several online courses available. However, both in content and delivery, JWL is significantly different and unique. It uses a blended model of online learning which is student centred. It enriches itself on the centuries-long Jesuit tradition of higher education as well as through a blended online and on-site approach. It works by providing university and college professors and facilitators in collaboration with the on-site resources and through worldwide networks of educational institutions. In order to give individual attention and personal care, the student ratio is not more than 15–20 in a class. It admits students of any gender, race, nationality or ethnic origin. However, the focus of the JWL is the unreachable communities or those who are at the margins, such as indigenous people, rural or urban poor, isolated or forcibly displaced people. It forms a multicultural, multi-ethnic and multi-religious global community of learners. It also provides all the rights, privileges, programmes and activities generally provided to students at a formal educational institution.

In the location of learning, which may more often be a refugee camp, the students come together under the leadership of a tutor who facilitates discussion. Each student is given either a tablet or a laptop based on the programme and the need, which they can use to study at home. The whole education and material required by the pupil are given gratuitously.[4] It is funded with a 'cost-sharing model,' in which the onsite partner covers their operating costs and JWL pays the professors[5] and covers the costs of the online programmes (Mackenzie, 2017). However, as it is a service, the professors accept a significantly lower payment for their teaching.

The JWL program covers both credit-bearing courses and professional certificate courses. It also gives importance to lifelong learning as it provides liberal studies which encourages them towards rational, critical and analytical thinking. The programmes of JWL have been planned within the background of Ignatian Pedagogical Paradigm (IPP), which seeks to develop all-round growth of an individual or *cura personalis,* a type of learning structured around the concepts of experience, reflection and action. In addition, the academic contents and subsequent courses are designed with a global perspective in mind. It helps to respond to the global challenges encountered by the societies such as environmental, socio-political, economic issues and others (JWL, 2019).

JWL has trained more than 5,000 students from 25 countries, who are forcibly displaced and marginalized since 2010. More than 50 per cent of the beneficiaries of the programme are women. In the initial stages, the JWL empowered refugees and host community members to study 25 different professional and certificate programmes, which are generally classroom-based courses at all three pilot-study centres located in countries such as Afghanistan, Aleppo, Burundi, Syria, Congo, Thailand, Rwanda, Somalia, Sudan, Uganda, Iraq, Malawi, Myanmar, Sri Lanka, the USA, Chad and Ethiopia (Massey, 2017).

Once the students graduate, some continue their learning by earning scholarships available at different universities around the world. Many continue to remain in the communities either in personal business or providing community service. Most satisfying of all is that quite many of them become agents of change in society by coordinating, collaborating and spearheading the service in their community. Thus, JWL empowers students to become active in their communities (Massey, 2017). The cohort of the students of JWL includes internally displaced people living in refugee camps, other refugees in urban centres and rural villages.

JWL in India

Indian society is highly stratified both economically and socially with small affluent elite having access to quality institutions and millions of poverty-stricken masses having poor quality of education. There is a very large number of institutes of higher education in terms of the absolute numbers, but the proportion of the relevant age group enrolled in higher education is low.

> It is worth noting that while India has the second-largest system of higher education, next only to USA, the total number of students hardly represent six percent of the relevant age group, i.e., 18–23, which is much below the average of developed countries, which is about 47%. (Nigavekar, 2003)

The proportion is even lower in the case of women, Scheduled Castes and Scheduled Tribes. The resource gap for educational needs remains enormous. Most of the educational services in the country are manifestly inadequate and ineffective, especially in rural areas. The educational system in India continues to promote narrow individualism and unhealthy competition. According to Desrochers,

> Education itself is a dialectical process. It leads, on the one hand, to the strengthening and perpetuation of the status quo and on the other, to social change and development. (Desrochers, 1987, pp. 142–176).

Education directly or indirectly promotes liberal structural change. In this context, the single major contribution of the Christian minorities in nation building in India has been education. It has also significantly contributed to the areas of social concern, liberation of the oppressed and in eradicating poverty.

Thus, it has responded to the changing sociopolitical scenario and has made the marginalized groups the primary focus of Christian education through organizing remedial programmes to assist the weak ones and conscientization through social outreach programmes. Still, a large portion of the people on the margins are yet to step into the portals of higher learning. In this direction, JWL has taken some initiatives in giving access to higher learning.

A basic study on the need of education to the marginalized students in India paved a way of opening JWL learning centres in Vettavalam, Tamil Nadu and Sneharam, Anjengo, Kerala. Rural, marginalized students in and around Vettavalam, fisherman community students in Sneharam, Anjengo are given training in Cambridge certified Global English Language (GEL) programme since 2018. Creative writing, peace leader and facilitators' course for teachers are offered at Vettavalam centre, whereas the Anjengo centre in Kerala has applied for BA in sustainable development. Online contents of GEL are offered to these students by JWL and a local facilitator in the centre ensures the success of students in various levels of the assessment conducted by Cambridge certification, administered by JWL. Online courses are offered by JWL at the academic degree level and through professional certificate courses using the Georgetown University learning management system (LMS), Student Information Systems and JWL humanitarian e-learning platform respectively. JWL has its IT team operating from Chennai (since June 2017), with a student record officer (SRO) living in the USA to ensure the availability of these online courses to all of its students across the globe through the respective LMS.

JWL has initiated an academic partnership with St Joseph's College (SJC), Bangalore, St Xavier's College, Kolkata and Xavier University Bhubaneswar (XUB). XUB has already launched a Bachelors programme in arts, specialization in sustainable development (BA-SD) with its first intake from August 2020. BA-SD degree is awarded by XUB and the online courses are developed and produced by JWL-XUB. It is a four-year programme, and the pilot launch has beneficiaries from the marginalized community in Afghanistan and Sri Lanka.

As there is a motive to reach a wide area or network, JWL seeks to explore best educational programmes from experts across various Jesuit organizations. Such an initiative with SJC will pave a way of offering professional certificate courses to JWL students. In collaboration with JWL, SJC is offering creative writing, graphic designing and web designing as one package. The SJC will also be offering e-commerce, accounting and entrepreneurship as a second package under its commerce faculty. All the courses are developed to fulfil the local needs, in a global perspective, and delivered through the global classroom. These course contents not only transform the students in its social, economic status but also lead to a transformation in their community.[6]

Challenges and Limitations

- JWL offers high-quality blended learning educational programmes to those on the margins of society; the major challenge for the students is the local recognition of the degree received from JWL and the awarding institute. Moreover, the credits which the students have earned studying on the academic courses are not easily transferable or accredited by the local universities.
- Some of the JWL centres are located in remote regions which possess the challenge of having easy access to the internet. Due to the remoteness of the locations, the JWL centres are connected using very small aperture terminal connection, which often incurs high running costs. The onsite facilitator for the academic programme has to deal with diverse course contents and that implies finding a highly skilled person to coordinate the academic programmes. Training of these facilitators or the programme coordinators on site is difficult, and there is, sometimes, a big gap between the on-site facilitators and the content creators of courses. Since JWL is an international organization with cross-national programmes, it is indeed a challenge to cater to international students with varied contextual

background and experiences. Moreover, the target group is generally made of refugees and the poor who lack basic facilities. In addition, doing the follow-up of students from across boards and countries is also strenuous.
- JWL programmes being offered by university professors and lecturers increases their workload and also makes monitoring students with timely corrections of the works of the students rather difficult. Finally, as this programme by nature is gratuitous and needs on-site infrastructure and funding, such ventures become a big challenge.

Conclusions

JWL has an outlook that is far-reaching and inclusive. It does not merely aim at taking 'teaching–learning' process beyond the walls of the classrooms but also to open spaces of domination and discrimination (refugees and marginalized), making 'teaching–learning' process viable by backing it up with credits from institutions par excellence, so that the recipients are not only equipped with knowledge but also a valid degree. One can see it as countercultural to the extent that it consciously and systematically aims to blend the structures to the benefits of the marginalized and less privileged. The success stories in Chennai under this project reflects the potential of this programme in making education possible beyond the realms of the classroom without diluting its importance and effect.

The learners have been accorded a degree that is equivalent to a degree of any regular college, thus reducing the gap between the distant learner and the direct learner. This programme makes the best use of the available technology for the service of the less privileged. It seems to assert that any form of discrimination is limited to physical space only, but in the realm of virtual reality one can transcend all these. Therefore, the content that is required for the dissemination of knowledge is converted into an e-format and circulated beyond the boundaries of state and nation. To this extent, the JWL is a revolution in education. It is different from other online learning platforms that do not offer credits and certificates freely. It is different from those institutions that have converted knowledge into a commodity to be sold.

Exploring and navigating the world, a better life is possible only when students have the freedom to wonder, to question, to dream, and without these, learning will never be productive even if one is a storehouse of information (Desrochers, 1987). Any education should be designed to make the students reflective learners. JWL with its clear focus on educating refugees, the poor and marginalized with the best-quality education not only makes the programme a unique one but also a relevant one. It is a step,

> In the pursuit of faith through the promotion of justice, dynamically nurturing cultural and interreligious dialogue and reconciliation. JWL's motto seeks to foster a community of global learners committed to 'Learning Together to Transform the World'. (JWL, 2019)

JWL has a great impact locally and regionally. With its skills of education, critical thinking, it brings transformation in the society through employment opportunities and peace in the communities.

The focus of JWL in India has been a recent one, as it is one of the countries where there is low Human Development Index with a large percentage of persons living on the margins and deprived of higher education. Though the present collaboration is with a few centres of higher learning such as XUB, SJC, Bangalore, St Xavier's College, Kolkata and Loyola College, Chennai, in the post-COVID-19 scenario, efforts are being made to reach out and collaborate with many more institutions so as to have a wider reach and networking towards contextualized content.

Notes

1. Jesuits, otherwise known as members in the Society of Jesus, is an organization of Catholic clergy worldwide founded by St Ignatius of Loyola.
   Jesuit education is characterized by the development of human qualities and openness for critical thinking that are essential for the development

of the whole person. This includes the head and heart, intellect and feelings. It aims at the intellectual, moral, emotional, social and religious formation of a person. The learners are also directed towards community service. The translation of Jesuit educational characteristics is seen in IPP. This invites the active participation of teachers and students. It gives five principles—context, experience, reflection, action and evaluation.
2. Formerly known as Jesuit Commons: Higher Education at the Margins (JC: HEM).
3. One of the former superior generals/heads of the Society of Jesus.
4. JWL fundraises to help meet the initiative's needs and the needs of the students, who typically do not make monetary contributions. Rather, they are expected to do something for the community in exchange for their education.
5. As JWL is a collaborative venture, the teachers are drawn from institutions of higher learning from around the world. Most of the faculty volunteer for free service.
6. Maxim Dias, Unstructured interviews with S. Janaki, J. Chandan, and M. Rodrigues (collaborators of JWL-India), 17 December 2018.

References

Desrochers, J. (1987). *Education for social change*. Centre for Social Action.
Jesuit Worldwide Learning. (2019). *Jesuit worldwide learning*. https://www.jwl.org/en/what-we-do/how-we-do-it/global-thinking?nocache=1494089087
Mackenzie, C. (2017, 20 June). *Jesuit program goes to 'the margins' to bring education to refugees*. CatholicPhily.com. http://catholicphily.com/2017/06/news/national-news/jesuit-program-goes-to-the-margins-to-bring-education-to-refugees/
Massey, W. (2017, 13 January). Learning on the margins. *The Jesuit Review*. https://www.americamagazine.org/faith/2017/01/13/new-jesuit-program-bringing-education-some-worlds-refugees
Nigavekar, A. (2003). *Higher education in India: Issues, concerns and new directions*. University Grants Commission.
UNHRC. (2020, 18 June). *Figures at a glance* https://www.unhcr.org/figures-at-a-glance.html

PART IV

Persons with Disabilities and Higher Education

Chapter 8
Indian Higher Education and PwD: Issue of Access and Opportunities
S. Y. Surendra Kumar

Chapter 9
Right to Higher Education of PwD: Critical Reflections
Sanjay Jain

Chapter 10
Assistive Technology in Higher Education
Udaya Kiran K. T.

8

Indian Higher Education and PwD
*Issue of Access and Opportunities**

S. Y. Surendra Kumar

Over the decades, the primary goal of the international community has been to make education more inclusive, that is, including the marginalized groups and also persons with disabilities (PwD). As a result, PwD's access to higher education has gained the necessary attention globally through various international conventions, resolutions as well as the United Nations (UN) Millennium Development Goals (2000) and Sustainable Development Goals (SDGs) in 2015. Moreover, the UN Decade of Disabled Persons (1983–1992) emphasized the importance of education for empowering PwD. The United Nations Educational, Scientific and Cultural Organization's (UNESCO) World Declaration on Education for All (1990) in Article III argued for special attention towards the learning needs of PwD and also suggested the necessary measures for ensuring equal education for all categories of PwD (UNESCO, 1990). At the regional level in 2000, most of the

---

*This is a revised and an updated version of the article—Kumar, S. Y. S. (2018).

countries from Asia Pacific region also accepted the 'Declaration on the full participation and equality of people with disabilities'.

The landmark convention was the UN Convention on the Rights of PwD (2008) that placed legal obligations on the State to protect and promote the rights of PwD, which emerged as both a development and human-rights instrument. Article 24 of the convention dealt exclusively with education, stressing on the effective participation of PwD in a free society, development of personality, talent and creativity and so on (UN, 2008). Similarly, the resolution of the United Nations Economic and Social Commission for Asia and the Pacific's 58th session, popularly known as Biwako Millennium Framework (2002), agreed for action towards making education inclusive for PwD. The Biwako Plus Five (September 2007) went one step further and directed the member countries to ensure a barrier-free and rights-based society for PwD in the region.

The World Education Forum (May 2015), sponsored by UNESCO and held at Incheon, Republic of Korea, came up with the declaration 'Education 2030: Towards Inclusive and Equitable Quality Education and Lifelong Learning for All'. The declaration argued that 'no education target should be considered met unless met by all [including PwD].' (UNESCO, 1990) The PwD's access to education got a big boost when it became part of the SDG, particularly goals—4, 8, 10, 11 and 17. Goal 4 focused on education and laid major emphasis on (a) ensuring inclusive and equitable quality education and promoting lifelong learning opportunity for all; (b) 'leave no one behind' and pitched for elimination of gender disparities by 2030 in education, and ensure equal access to all levels of education; (c) it emphasized for vocational training for all marginalized communities, and (d) build and upgrade educational facilities for the disabled, with 'gender sensitization and providing safe, non-violent, inclusive and effective learning environments for all' (Deb, 2017; Social Statistical Division, 2016). Hence, the major initiatives at the international level also compelled developing countries like India to frame educational policies and programmes for PwD.

India's commitment to ensure access to education to PwD is well reflected by being a signatory and ratifying most international conventions and endorsing related declarations and resolutions. From time to time, India has initiated policies to make the education system inclusive for PwD. Having realized that the most effective vehicle of social and economic empowerment is education and that India's growth is connected with the education system, India's constitutional provisions, particularly Article 21 A, guarantees education as a fundamental right. In 1974, a centrally sponsored scheme of Integrated Education for Disabled Children (IEDC) was initiated by the Department of Social Welfare, primarily targeting school education providing several facilities, including financial assistance.

In 1986, the National Educational Policy recommended the goal of integrating the handicapped with the general community at all levels as equal partners, laying out provisions for alternative learning material, training of teachers and administrators, accessibility, transportation, vocational training and so on (MHRD, 1986). The Rehabilitation Council of India Act (1992) emphasized the need for training programmes. The main task of the Council was threefold—to regulate and monitor the services provided to PwD, 'standardise syllabus and maintain a Central Rehabilitation Register of all personnel working in the field of Rehabilitation and Special Education.' The National Policy for PwD (February 2006) by the Ministry for Social Justice and Empowerment was a historic framework not just for the state but also for the civil society and private sector to ensure a dignified life for PwD (Ministry of Social Justice and Empowerment, 2006). Moreover, for the first time, the policy recognized PwD as 'a valuable human resource' for the country and aimed to provide them with an equal opportunity in all spheres of life (Social Statistical Division, 2016, p. 7).

Section 26 of the PwD Act, 1995, emphasized on free and compulsory education up to the minimum age of 18 years. By ratifying the UN Convention on the Rights of PwD in 2007 and its Optional Protocol in December 2006, India accepted the obligation to implement the convention as a human-rights instrument with an explicit social development dimension. India adopted a broad categorization of PwD and reaffirmed that all persons with all types of disabilities must enjoy all human rights and fundamental freedoms (Social Statistical Division, 2016, p. 11). Under its flagship policy Sarva Shiksha Abhiyan, launched in 2009, the key goal was to ensure eight years of elementary schooling for age group of 6–14, including the PwD. In 2010, it reformed the IEDC scheme, providing for free education of PwD in the age group of 15–18 years (Social Statistical Division, 2016, p. 49). In April 2016, under its New Education Policy (NEP), the Ministry of Human Resources Development (MHRD) provided for making education accessible to PwD (Verughese, 2017).

The most significant Act related to PwD has been the Rights of Persons with Disabilities (RPwD 2016), which raised the types of disabilities from 7 to 21 and provided for 5 per cent reservation in education and 4 per cent in employment. In April 2017, NITI Aayog also came up with a three-year action agenda to make education inclusive for PwD (NCPEDP, 2017). However, the historic Supreme Court judgement in December 2017, which focused on three critical issues—implementation of reservation, accessibility and pedagogy—provided a big boost to the accessibility of educational and employment opportunities to PwD. The Supreme Court went one step ahead and stated: 'PwD have the right to education and not making adequate provision to facilitate their proper education would amount to discrimination' (Supreme Court of India, 2017). The judgement provided that all government institutions receiving government funds should implement the RPwD Act 2016 in toto. All these initiatives have provided the much-needed space for PwD to access higher education.

Another landmark judgement by the Supreme Court came in July 2020, as it upheld that PwD are entitled to the same benefits and relaxation (age and marks for admission and jobs) as candidates belonging to the Scheduled Castes/Scheduled Tribes (SCs/STs) in accessing education and employment, regardless of their social status (*Hindu*, 2020, p. 8). If this Supreme Court order is effectively implemented, then this will go a long way in making higher education truly inclusive in nature.

Issues and Concerns

Despite all the efforts by the government, there are many challenges confronting PwD in higher education. Some of them are as follows.

1. Challenges in Higher Education

The Indian higher education system is said to be the world's second largest, preceded by the United States of America. However, it is confronted with many contradictions. First, though the gross enrolment ratio (GER) in higher education is witnessing a marginal increase, that is, 24.5 per cent (2015–2016), 25.2 per cent (2016–2017) and 26.3 per cent (2018–2019), it continues to be below the global average of 27 per cent (Chopra, 2018). Apparently, the other BRICS nations like China (48 per cent) and Brazil (36 per cent) have higher GER compared to India. As a result, apart from government initiatives, the University Grants Commission (UGC) in August 2019, pitched for a target of 30 per cent GER by 2020 (Press Trust of India, 2019, also see ANI, 2019). To achieve this objective, it is estimated that India needs around 40 million university students, an increase of 14 million in six years (British Council, 2014).

Second, as per the All India Survey on Higher Education 2019 (AISHE), there are around 993 universities (central, state, deemed and private) and more than 39,931 colleges. There are 16 universities exclusively for women and Bengaluru heads with 880 colleges, followed by Jaipur with 566 colleges (MHRD, 2019). Although there has been an increase in the number of universities and colleges, the quality in many of these institutions remains a concern, as there is an acute shortage of faculty members, lack of quality teaching, outdated and rigid curricula and pedagogy, lack of accountability and quality assurance, separation of research and teaching and so on.

Third, India has a low level of PhD enrolment (0.5 per cent), resulting in not having enough high-quality researchers, very few opportunities for interdisciplinary and multidisciplinary work and lack of early-stage research experience, a weak ecosystem for innovation and low levels of industry engagement. Thus, these aspects hinder the growth of higher education.

Fourth, given that India continues to remain highly divided on socio-economic and religious categories, access to higher education among these communities is uneven, with multidimensional inequalities in enrolment across population groups and geographies. These problems are part of the higher education system, but PwD, being a stakeholder, also have to face these hurdles.

2. PwD in Higher Education: Marginal Improvement

As per Census 2011, there were around 26,810,557 PwD, and the number has increased by 22.4 per cent in comparison with the 2001 Census. Among these, males are 14,986,202 and females are 11,824,355. The majority of PwD reside in rural areas (69 per cent), an increase of 13.7 per cent. The corresponding percentage in urban areas is 31 per cent, having dramatically increased by 48.2 per cent. Uttar Pradesh has the highest number of PwD (16 per cent of the total PwD in the country), followed by Maharashtra (11 per cent) (Social Statistical Division, 2016, p. 39). Although the claims of Census 2011 are different from NSS data (2002), stating that PwD constitute 1.8 per cent of the population, some rights-based organizations claim the numbers to be more than 5 per cent (*Economic & Political Weekly*, 2016). The UNICEF report (2000), *Status of Disability in India*, estimated that there were more than 30 million PwD in India (Singh, (2016). It can clearly be seen that the data on PwD population continues to be widely contested and hinders successful implementation of policies and programmes for the stakeholders.

Apparently, of the total disabled population, nearly 55 per cent (1.46 crore) are literate, males constituting 62 per cent and females only 45 per cent, which is well below the national average (Social Statistical Division, (2016), p. 28). Subsequently, just 13 per cent PwD have had matric/secondary education and only 59 per cent have completed 10th standard. And all India's average is 67 per cent. Nevertheless, Kerala and Goa have the highest literacy rate among PwD (70 per cent) and the lowest literacy rate among PwD is reported from Arunachal Pradesh (38.75 per cent), followed by Rajasthan (40.16 per cent). Due to the low-education levels among PwD, in general, around 63.7 per cent of the PwD are unemployed; however, the employment rate of both rural and urban areas of India is 60.21 per cent (Agarwal, 2019).

The number of PwD students in higher education (graduates and above) is 5 per cent (Salve, 2017). However, the presence of PwD in higher education is increasing. According to AISHE 2019, there are approximately 85.477 (2018–2019) PwD, of which 48,212 and 37,665 are males and females, respectively (MHRD, 2019). Interestingly, majority of them are studying in Uttar Pradesh (14,791), Tamil Nadu (10,199), Delhi (8,346), Maharashtra (7,935) and so on (MHRD, 2019, p. T–15). At the same time, in order to increase the PwD's access to higher education, both Central and State governments have, from time to time, provided national- and state-level scholarships; reimbursed all the expenditure to PwD towards books, fees, uniform, transport, reservation, scholarship; and extended the benefits given to SC/ST and OBC to PwD. Despite these efforts, higher education remains inaccessible for many PwD.

3. Accessibility

Generally, the primary goal of any government would be to ensure inclusive and accessible education for all; however, accessibility continues to be distant dream for PwD in many of the colleges and universities in India. Apparently, legislation and policies focusing on augmenting education and its accessibility for PwD, such as the 1995 PwD Act and the RPwD Act 2016, emphasized on two years of deadline for ensuring a barrier-free access in infrastructure and transport systems for the PwD, still remain to be implemented (Gazette of India, 2016). Even the National Building Code of India 2016 argued that all the new schools and colleges' plan should ensure for 100 per cent accessibility for PwD and elderly persons.

However, accessibility continues to be a major hurdle for PwD in pursuing higher education. According to a forum for disabled students, as of 2017, only 1 per cent of India's 789 universities, 37,204 colleges and 11,443 educational institutions are disabled friendly (HT Correspondent, 2017). A survey conducted by Samarthyam in 2016 in 500 schools in 16 states found that facilities like disabled-friendly toilets and hand railings for visually disabled students did not exist. The survey also found that Tamil Nadu and Odisha did better, and Jharkhand and Chhattisgarh fared the worst. Many of the leading educational institutions still lack adequate ramps, wheelchairs, railings and accessible washrooms. According to AISHE 2019, there are fewer toilets for female PwD; in fact, such toilets were found only in 63 universities, 49 colleges and 48 institutions (MHRD, 2019, p. 25). Even in the university campus—canteens, common rooms, library—toilets and laboratories remain inaccessible to the PwD. Although many institutions and colleges get the infrastructural audit, they fail to get the access audit, which remains unpopular among educational institutions. Unfortunately, the administrators are not aware of these requirements; as a result, accessibility for PwD continues to be a challenge.

However, recently, there are campaigns like #YahanSeWhanTak and #GharSeCollegeTak. Such initiatives are becoming popular in some of the universities and colleges. At the same time, some universities and institutions conduct access audit; unfortunately, the results are not implemented because of financial constraints and the will to act. Due to reduced mobility, instances of dropouts or not making to higher education are more than the admission rate.

4. Implementation of Reservation

PwD Act 1995 stipulated 3 per cent reservation in education. In a significant step, RPwD Act 2016 increased it to 5 per cent. Nevertheless, poor implementation has denied PwD access to education. For instance, according to a survey by the National Centre for Promoting of Employment of Disabled People (NCPEDP), only about 0.56 per cent seats in higher education go to disabled candidates, of which more than 75 per cent go to male candidates. The survey also found that except Jawaharlal Nehru University (JNU), Indian Institute of Management (IIM) and Indian Institute of Technology (IIT), the rest of the institutions offer less than 1 per cent (*Times of India*, 2015). This dismal scenario was acknowledged by the Union Ministry of Social Justice and Empowerment in Parliament and the ministry's statement (2016) said that the employment of PwD is less than the specified 3 per cent reservation in all categories of government jobs. Even the Supreme Court ruling of 2017 stated that there was hardly any representation of PwD in the higher posts, even though certain posts have been identified as suitable for them (Supreme Court of India, 2017). There is hardly any recruitment of PwD even in low-income grades. Moreover, presently, only 9 per cent of the present faculty members in IIT belong to SC, ST and OBC; thus, one can imagine the status of PwD in IIT and other premier institutions (Sharma, 2019). As a result, the number of female faculty (PwD) is just 37 females per 100 male instructors, which is lower than the national average of 73 females per 100 male teachers (MHRD, 2019, p. 20).

Lack of implementation of reservation in higher education and skill-oriented education contributes to low-employment opportunities for PwD. According to NCPEDP, the average employment rate of PwD is just 0.28 per cent in the private sector and 0.54 per cent in the public sector. A World Health Organization report showed that 87 per cent of PwD in India worked in the informal sector. The World Bank report (2007), *People with Disabilities in India: From Commitments to Outcomes*, suggests that the employment rate of PwD was drastically declining; like in 1991, it was 42.7 per cent and it was down to 37.6 per cent in 2002 (NCPEDP, n.d.). The report of the International Labour Organization, *Persons with Disability and the India Labour Market: Challenges and Opportunities*', released in 2011, states that 73.6 per cent of PwD in India are still outside the labour force (NCPEDP, n.d.). Of these, those with mental disability, disabled women and the ones in rural areas are the worst neglected. All these data show that higher education in India is not catering for the skills necessary to ensure job opportunities for PwD. Also, lack of identification of suitable posts for PwD contributes to the sorry plight of PwD in higher education. However, in the recent times, many vacancies for PwD are notified in different premier institutions like IIT, IIM and central universities, also with the allocation of different categories, but it depends on the total number of vacancies, which are shrinking.

5. UGC Initiatives

From time to time, the UGC, catering to higher education, has recommended the establishment of an Equal Opportunity Cell (EOC), an empowerment cell for differently abled (ECDA) and, more recently, the setting up of Higher Education for Persons with Special Needs (HEPSN). HEPSN supports the setting up of disability units in universities and colleges. This policy, however, is yet to become popular, and there are not many takers for it. The funds under this scheme remain unutilized and the possible reasons for this are lack of enthusiasm, fewer numbers of students with documented disabilities, and it is alleged that the scheme was never publicized enough for institutions to apply (Never-the-Less, 2011). In the recent time, the EOC is established in many government and private universities/colleges, by focusing on providing opportunities to SC/ST, OBC, minorities, women and PwD. However, given that PwD are one of the components, not much attention is given to issues concerning PwD under the EOC.

Moreover, in many universities/colleges, the EOC functions as training centres and not beyond that. Interestingly, many universities' websites have a page on EOC with advisory members and co-ordinator, but its activities and initiatives with regard to PwD are missing. In Karnataka, Bangalore University and Karnatak University have functioning EOC. Some universities have ECDA, primarily focusing on addressing PwD problems and also empowering them as in JNU, Bangalore University, Delhi University, University of Hyderabad, Tata Institute of Social Sciences (TISS),

University of Kota and so on also have an EOC. Overall, all the three initiatives—EOC, ECDA and HEPSN—exist in different forms and are performing various functions.

Given that these initiatives are yet to become successful, in 2016, UGC recommended to all universities to establish a Department of Disability Studies. Very few of them, such as Indira Gandhi National Open University, JNU, Ambedkar University, Delhi University, Panjab University, Guwahati University, Central University of Haryana, Dravidian University, National Academy of Legal Studies and Research, Mahatma Gandhi University, TISS, National Rehabilitation University, Lucknow, and National Institute in Andhra Pradesh have established this department/centres (Never-the-Less, 2011). In many states, this department does not exist, such as in Karnataka, Telangana, Odisha and so on. Nevertheless, disability studies is slowly gaining popularity with the increasing enrolment of students—19 students for PhD, 19 for MPhil courses and around 253 for postgraduation. However, the number of pass out is less like 2 (PhD) and 112 (PG) and nil for MPhil (MHRD, 2019, p. T–35, T–13).

In November 2018, the Visvesvaraya Technological University (VTU), Belgaum, directed all the colleges under its control to strictly establish EOC and also to constitute an internal committee to build disabled-friendly campus to promote the education of the PwD. In a similar move, the All India Council for Technical Education has also passed similar instruction to colleges that in all the classrooms, at least 2–5 per cent of seats should be made accessible for PwD, particularly those students using wheelchair. Even the doors, tables and chairs should be adjusted/made suitable for PwD students (Kebbehundi, 2019). Thus, the need of the hour is to strengthen the existing mechanisms in the colleges and universities, before implementing new measures.

6. National Education Policy (NEP), 2020

The Committee for the Draft NEP was constituted in 2017 and was headed by Dr K. Kasturirangan, an eminent scientist. The committee submitted the *Draft National Education Policy 2019* report in May 2019 and was made public in June 2019. However, NEP 2020 was finally approved by the Union Cabinet on 29 July 2020. The policy is a significant step in taking education to a global level and also aims at ensuring universal access to school education at all levels. It emphasizes that it is founded on the principle of access, equity, quality, affordability and accountability, which is very much the need of the hour. The policy proposes drastic reforms in higher education, such as holistic curricula and pedagogy, multidisciplinary education, multilingualism, recruitment of quality teachers and training for them, new parameters for accreditation, setting up of Higher Education Commission of India, promoting/popularizing open and distance learning, use of technology to enhance learning, professional and adult education and so on.

Overall, the policy attempts to make education inclusive, which will have a positive impact on PwD's access to education. However, it fails to address the need/requirements of PwD on a larger scale, for example, it emphasizes on access, but it does not move beyond ramps and handrails for the PwDs. Moreover, many critiques argue that still the policy lacks inclusiveness in terms of access, teaching methodologies and funding for higher studies. At the same time, the requirements of the visually challenged, hearing impaired or wheelchair bound are not addressed adequately.

Although the policy pitches for privatization and commercialization to enhance education, most of the disabled who come from economically poor background are left out. The policy gives an impression that it did not focus on PwD and higher education, and to certain extent, the committee members have not consulted the PwD activists before drafting the policy. Moreover, the draft was neither accessible in Braille nor auto files were available, hence no feedback from the differently abled was accessed. Overall, it is rightly argued that the policy does not convey the notions of *sabka saath*, *sabka vikas* and *sabka vishwas*, at least the point of view of PwD. However, only hope that the grievances of the PwD are taken care by the government, before it is implemented in all states.

The Way Forward

Generally, university/college education is regarded as a vital tool for PwD students to reinvent themselves and revalidate an identity that may have impaired their education. They can not only obtain higher education but can achieve an independent life. To realize this, some of the following measures are necessary.

- There is a need for the Union and State governments to move beyond *divyang* and work towards the actual empowerment of PwD through policies and programmes that encourage them to pursue higher education.
- Anti-discrimination forums at colleges/universities should not only address caste/gender-based discrimination but also the discrimination against PwD, so that prevalent cultural prejudices against PwD in higher education are reduced.
- All the universities and colleges, including private ones, should be made fully accessible with no physical barriers of any type, and the design should be based on universal principles.
- The majority of the teachers in India are not sensitive and adequately equipped to teach PwD. Similar is the case with the non-teaching staff. Hence, training of teachers and non-teaching staff is necessary to boost the confidence level of PwD in higher education (Parasuram, 2006).
- Successive governments have expressed their desire to establish a separate university for the disabled. But the very idea goes against the concept of inclusive education as highlighted in international conventions and also the RPwD Act 2016, which states inclusive education 'as a system of education wherein students with and without disability learn together and the system of teaching and learning is suitably adopted to meet the learning needs of different types of students with disabilities' (The Gazette of India, 2016).
- There is also an urgent need for the teaching and learning methodology, tools, pedagogy, curriculum and evolution mechanisms of students to be adapted to suit PwD.

- Earlier, aid and appliances (software and hardware) for PwD were exempted from taxes, but now all these are under the ambit of goods and services tax (GST) with a slab of 12 per cent, 18 per cent and 28 per cent. This results in making aid and appliances for PwD unaffordable for many of the universities, which are facing a resource crunch. Thus, the union government should exempt the necessary aid and appliances from GST to ensure that the PwD or universities can afford the aid and appliances.
- Although in recent years there has been a great emphasis on higher education with a skill development component, this should also cater for the requirements of PwD.
- For successful implementation of the legislation, policies and programmes, it is important that it should be backed up by adequate resources.
- Finally, suitable placements of PwD in the campus recruitment should be made mandatory.

In a nutshell, developments at the international and national levels related to the empowerment of PwD through education are gaining momentum. But if the issues are not addressed adequately, empowering PwD will remain a distant dream.

References

Agarwal, P. (2019, 21 November). Why we need a new approach towards education of differently abled in new India. *India Today*. https://www.indiatoday.in/education-today/featurephilia/story/need-of-new-approach-towards-education-of-differently-abled-in-new-india-1621248-2019-11-21

ANI. (2019, 22 September). Gross Enrolment Ratio in higher education increases. https://www.aninews.in/news/national/general-news/gross-enrolment-ratio-in-higher-education-increases20190922001402/

British Council. (2014). *Understanding India: The future of higher education and opportunities for international cooperation* (pp. 15–16).

Chopra, R. (2018, 5 January). India's GRE in Higher Education up by 0.7%. *The New Indian Express*. https://indianexpress.com/article/education/indias-gross-enrolment-ratio-in-higher-education-up-by-0-7-5012579/

Deb, S. (2017). SDG's indicators framework and disability in India. *Indian Journal of Human Development, 11*(2), 242.

Economic & Political Weekly. (2016, 9 July). Divine bodied disabled. *Economic & Political Weekly, 51*(28).
Editorial. (2016). Divine bodied disabled. *Economic & Political Weekly, 1.1*(28).
HT Correspondent. (2017, 16 November). With not even one percent being disabled friendly, colleges are difficult to access for many. *The Hindustan Times*. https://www.hindustantimes.com/editorials/with-not-even-one-per-cent-being-disabled-friendly-colleges-are-difficult-to-access-for-many/story-zfemcOhIWQhxiAVT1YNwWK.html
Kebbehundi, R. (2019, 11 September). VTU directs colleges to build disabled friendly campus. *Deccan Chronicle*. http://deccanchronicle.com/nation/current-affairs/110919/vtu-directs-colleges-to-build-disabled-friendly-campus.html
Kumar, S. Y. S. (2018). PwD and higher education in India: The challenges. *Asian Journal of Development Matters, 12*(1), 27-45.
MHRD. (1986). *National policy of education* (pp. 114–120). Ministry of Human Resource and Development, Government of India. http://mhrd.gov.in/sites/upload_files/mhrd/files/upload_document/npe.pdf
MHRD. (2019). *All India survey on higher education 2018–2019* (p. 14).
Ministry of Social Justice and Empowerment. (2006). *National policy for persons with disabilities*. Ministry of Social Justice and Empowerment, Government of India. http://www.usicd.org/doc/IND93612.pdf
National Centre for Promotion of Employment for Disabled People (NCPEDP). (2017). *100 plus points on NITI Aayog's three year action agenda to make an inclusive for PwD*. http://www.ncpedp.org/NITI Aayog
National Centre for Promotion of Employment for Disabled People (NCPEDP). Employment. http://www.ncpedp.org/Employment
Never-the-Less. (2011). *Enabling access for persons with disabilities in higher education and work place* (p. 6). www.g3ict.org/downnload/p/fileld_883/productid_198.
Parasuram, K. (2006). Variables that affect teachers attitudes towards disability and inclusive education in Mumbai, India. *Disability and Society, 21*(3), 231.
Press Trust of India. (2019, 21 August). UGC targets 30% enrolment in higher education by 2020. *India Today*. https://www.indiatoday.in/education-today/news/story/ugc-targets-30-enrolment-in-higher-education-by-2020-1590035-2019-08-21
Salve, P. (2017, 8 April). Why nearly half of India's disabled population is illiterate. https://scroll.in/article/833784/
Sharma, K. (2019, 13 February). Diversity deficit in IIMs and IITs—just 23 ST, 157 SC, in 9604 faculty posts. https://theprint.in/india/education/diversity-deficit-in-iims-iits-just-23-sts-and-157-scs-in-9640-faculty-posts/191246/

Singh, J. D. (2016). Inclusive education in India: Concept, need and challenges. www. researchgate.net/publication/301675529

Social Statistical Division. (2016). *Disabled persons in India: A statistical profile* (p. 66). Ministry of Statistics and Programme Implementation, Government of India.

Supreme Court of India. (2017, 22 December). *Writ Petition (c) No. 292 of 2006, Disabled rights Groups and ANR Versus Union of India and ORS.*

Supreme Court of India. (2017, 22 December). *Writ Petition (c) No. 292 of 2006, Disabled rights Groups and ANR Versus Union of India and ORS.*

The Gazette of India. (2016). *The Rights of Persons with Disabilities Act, 2016.* Ministry of Law and Justice. http://www.disabilityaffairs.gov.in/upload/uploadfiles/files/RPWD%20ACT%202016.pdf

The Hindu. (2020, 17 July). For equal treatment (p. 8).

The Times of India. (2015, 5 April). Disabled get only 0.56% of seats in Higher Education. https://timesofindia.indiatimes.com/home/education/news/Disabled-get-only-0-56-of-seats-in-higher-education/articleshow/46810639.cms

UN. (2008). *UN Convention on right of the PwD.* https://www.un.org/development/desa/disabilities/convention-on-the-rights-of-persons-with-disabilities/article-24-education.html

UNESCO. (1990). *UNESCO World Declaration on Education for All (1990).* UNESCO. http://ncpcr.gov.in/showfile.php?lid=124

Verughese, R. (2017). National policy on education and higher education. *Higher Education for the Future,* 4(2), 158–165.

9

Right to Higher Education of PwD
*Critical Reflections**

Sanjay Jain

In this chapter, an attempt is made to examine role of higher education as an enabler in the lives of persons with disabilities (PwD). Author argues that although there are a lot of articles and books emphasizing and highlighting the role of accessibility in the higher education, very few studies have been undertaken to address the fundamental question, what difference higher education can make in the lives of PwD. To put other way round, whether higher education is a value addition in the quality of lives of PwD. Author demonstrates that higher education, apart from empowering the PwD, is also an enabler in opening numerous vistas of career for them.

It is important to bear in mind that inclusive higher education is a way out to dissolve stereotypes around the overall life pattern of PwD. It is often believed that PwD being weak and vulnerable are unable to contribute productively in the overall growth of society. Political processes undermine them by doubting their

---

* Earlier version of this chapter has been presented at National Conference, Bangalore University. See Jain (2018).

legal capacity and ability to participate in the governance of the country. Economic processes often confine the employability of the PwD to certain very rudimentary sectors of employment. It is often assumed that, because of their disability, PwD lack the ability to hold high positions in both public and private sectors of employment. Till the date, public confidence is very low on the ability of PwD to engage in gainful and monetary employment. Social processes often reduce physical and mental disabilities to inability and depersonalization and locate it in the body of an individual rather than in barriers and hurdles created by the ableist environment (Campbell, 2009).

In this chapter, author seriously challenges and questions the negative and unproductive imagery of PwD, by focusing attention on the role of higher education as an enabler and game changer in their lives. It is also necessary to clarify that United Nations Convention on the Rights of Persons with Disabilities (UNCRPD) does not make any explicit reference to higher education; rather the same is enmeshed in the conception 'tertiary education'. The need of the hour is to contest the same and emphasize on a central role of the right to higher education vis-à-vis PwD perceptibly by grounding it in a next-gen right,[1] like right to personality.

For a systematic discussion, the chapter is divided into five sections. The first section deals with the situational analysis of PwD with reference to relevant data in the sphere of higher education in India. The second section engages with the importance of higher education for every individual including PwD. Third and fourth sections briefly examine the international and national legal frameworks regulating Right to Education with special focus on higher education of PwD. The fifth and final section is a road map sketching an *alternate paradigm* on right to higher education of PwD in the light of republicanism and the capabilities approach.

Situational Analysis

To facilitate discussion and analysis, it is imperative to map the status of PwD vis-à-vis higher education by shedding some light on situational settings in which people with disability prosecute higher education. Equally, it is vital to go for a disability-specific analysis of situational location of PwD in higher education. However, in this chapter, the author does not intend to adopt a disability-specific perspective because of time, knowledge and space constraint. The analysis is mostly influenced by the situation of people with visual impairment in the higher education. Being visually challenged and as a part of the higher education system, author finds it plausible to collate his lived experiences in understanding and analysing the extent of inclusiveness of higher education system qua PwD. The above methodology may be questioned as being sweepingly general to be applicable across all disabilities (to be specific, 21 disabilities enlisted in the Rights of Persons with Disabilities [RPwD] Act, 2016). Though the lived experiences of visually impaired persons are under-represented vis-à-vis other disabilities, for macro analysis and the assessment of non-discrimination or addressing overall exclusion of PwD, in the gamut of higher education, it is not an earnest obstacle. Inductively, it is not difficult to comprehend how higher education system pathologizes the PwD from mainstream by stereotyping their image as incompetent and less eligible.

A leading disability-rights activist Meenu Bhambhani cites a very interesting report about overall educational level of PwD. The figures for 2001 census are very telling to gauge the reach of PwD into the sphere of higher education. Out of total literate people with disabilities, only 6.6 per cent, men and 4.6 per cent women had a degree. Even in 2011 census, the figures did not show notable improvement. Of the 2.68 crore disabled population, 1.46 crore (54.5%) were literates while 1.22 crore were illiterates. In case of disabled women, the rate of illiteracy was much higher at 55.4 per cent compared to 37.6 per cent of men. Only 8.5 per cent among the literate disabled managed to get a degree (Bhambhani, 2016). While 9 per cent (839,702) of the literate disabled men got degrees or above, the figure for women was 7.7 per cent (407,155) (Government of India (GOI), 2016). In terms of numbers, out of the 2.68 crore disabled, only 12.46 lakh had completed degree or qualifications beyond that. The figures of both the census were self-explanatory and directed urgent attention to accelerate participation of more disabled people both quantitatively and qualitatively in the field of higher education.

In this connection, the author would also like to invite attention to an action plan proposed by the government in 2005, which was a welcome reaction to a study conducted by the National Centre for Promotion of Employment for Disabled People (NCPEDP), demonstrating that only 0.51 per cent disabled students were in mainstream-educational institutions at the school level.

While laying the plan on the floor of Rajya Sabha on 21 March 2005, the then minister of human resources, Mr Arjun Singh, had promised to make higher education 'available, accessible, affordable and appropriate' to students with disabilities.[2] All these objectives were to be supposedly accomplished by the year 2020.[3]

Inter alia, the minister highlighted the following objectives under the plan:

- 'All universities will have a disability coordinator to act as a 'one-stop shop' to assist disabled students in their needs;
- All universities will be assisted by UGC in setting up a separate Department of Disability Studies including modules of inclusion;
- A chair of disability studies will be set up in central universities;
- Universities will be encouraged to introduce special shuttle services for disabled students.'

But hardly any significant progress was made to make this plan successful, which is evident from the above figures quoted by Ms Meenu Bhambhani in her article. In fact, a number of non-governmental organizations like National Association for the Blind, Sambhavna, etc., are continuously striving to persuade the government to create rights enabling conditions for pursuing higher education by PwD.

The reference must also be made to the important decision of India of signing and ratifying UNCRPD Disabled World.

(2014). As a State party to this convention, India is under obligation to submit a report to the CRPD committee, detailing the steps it has taken to make Indian legal order including the sphere of higher education compatible with UNCRPD.[4] Author would discuss the relevant provisions of UNCRPD a little later. However, suffice it to state here that India has not much to cheer about the inclusion of PwD in the sphere of higher education, post the ratification of CRPD. While answering a question on the floor of Lok Sabha, the then Minister of Human Resource Development Smt. Smriti Irani had observed that there is an increase in the enrolment of PwD students in higher education, on the strength of the All India Survey on Higher Education (AISHE), MHRD, in the year 2015. Interestingly, in its third national survey on the status of disability in higher education conducted by NCPEDP in 2015, the aforementioned claim of the minister was refuted. The survey reported that about 0.56 per cent seats in higher education went (74% male and 22% female) to disabled candidates; this figure was way below the 3 per cent reservation as per the PwD Act, 1995.

The survey also demonstrated variance across disabilities in respect of pursuing higher education with, out of the total number of disabled candidates, 46.67 per cent being orthopedically disabled, 32.13 per cent being visually impaired, 5.16 per cent being speech/hearing impaired and 16.05 per cent being of other types. Variance in representation of students with disabilities was also visible stream wide with Indian Institute of Management (IIM) coming closest to the 3-per cent quota with 2.49 per cent disabled students out of total enrolled students. Percentage of disabled students in social work colleges and Indian Institute of Technology (IIT) was 1.75 per cent and 1.47 per cent, respectively. However, surprisingly, the general universities stood at the lowest with enrolment of only 0.31 per cent.[5]

The findings of this survey are indeed puzzling and clearly show the indifferent and numb approach of the universities towards inclusion of students with disabilities. It has to be emphasized that rather than IITs or IIMs, where only the most intelligent

Table 9.1 *No. of Scholarship Provided to PwD (Caste Wise)*

Category	Beneficiary	Amount (₹)
GEN	1	42,300
SC	0	0
ST	0	0
OBC	1	44,000
Total	2	86,300

students would get in, the prime responsibility is that of general universities across India to cater higher education to the PwD.

The perusal of Chapter 15 of *Annual Report* of MHRD 2016–2017 demonstrates no change in the indifferent attitude of state towards inclusion of PwD in higher education. Only two disabled students were provided scholarships by the MHRD to pursue higher education as shown in Table 9.1 (MHRD, 2016–2017, p. 341).

A close look on data provided by AISHE 2010–2011 to 2017–2018 in respect of representation of PwD in colleges and universities across India further unfolds the script of the continuous failure of the State. As per the figures in 2015–2016, the highest number of students with disability enrolled, that is, 74,435 (39,718 males and 34,717 females), whereas the lowest number of representation of students with disabilities was in the year 2013–2014, that is 51,954 (31,374 males and 20,580 females). Interestingly, in the year 2017–2018, turn out of the disabled students was lesser than the year 2015–2016, that is, 74,317 (42,630 males and 31,687 females). The data also shows that between the years 2010–2011 to 2017–2018, there is a fair amount of inconsistency in respect to the total of disabled students as well as the percentage of males and females.[6]

It is noteworthy that the method of data collection with regard to disabled students is outmoded and contrary to the mandate of Article 31 of UNCRPD.[7] No attempt has been made even in the year 2017–2018 (post enactment of RPwD Act, 2016) to disaggregate the data disability wise. Figures are also not available about the representation of PwD belonging to variety of disabilities, programme wide and education-level wide.

In fact, the cavalier approach of the authorities is glaring, with AISHE report of 2017–2018 citing the provisions of PwD Act, 1995, repelled in 2016 by the Parliament by enacting rights of PwD Act, 2016 (AISHE report, 2017–2018, pp. A–10).

Table 9.1 and data furnished by AISHE reports, very vividly, show the degree of alienation, apathy and exclusion of PwD from the sphere of higher education. The author wonders, why only two disabled students availed scholarships provided by central government in the year 2016–2017 when the total number of disabled students in the colleges and universities across the country, as per AISHE report of that year, was 70,967 (40,894 males and 30,073 females). It is also to be noted that the 2016 Act has expanded its scope by including 14 more disabilities. Presently, in India, 21 disabilities are covered under the RPwD Act, 2016. In such a scenario, in the absence of disability-disaggregated data, it is impossible for the State to make effective and meaningful interventions.

A close look on the data also shows that there is hardly any attention paid to encourage PwD to join the profession of teaching in colleges and universities. As per the annual report of MHRD 2013–2014, there are only 266 visually challenged teachers in senior colleges across India. Figures are not available in respect of teachers belonging to other disabilities. However, there is no specific scheme barring National Fellowship for PwD, for pursuing MPhil and PhD and post-matric scholarship for pursuing post-matric education till PG (postgraduation). Needless to mention that with the inclusion of 14 more disabilities under the RPwD Act, 2016, responsibility of the State has increased extraordinarily, but it has not been translated into any serious action on the ground.

Right to Higher Education: An Enabler and Game Changer

Sandra Fredman has very aptly amplified the significance of Right to Education, both as a distinct human right and as an enabler for effective realization of other human rights.

> Education is both a human right in itself and an indispensable means of realizing other human rights. As an empowerment right, education is the primary vehicle by which economically and socially marginalized adults and children can lift themselves out of poverty and obtain the means to participate fully in their communities. (Fredman, 2018, p. 356)

While articulating the intrinsic worth of Right to Education, the UN committee on socio-economic and cultural rights has observed,

> Increasingly, education is recognized as one of the best financial investments States can make. But the importance of education is not just practical: a well-educated, enlightened and active mind, able to wander freely and widely, is one of the joys and rewards of human existence.[8]

Rights such as freedom of speech and expression, freedom to carry on profession and right to employment are strengthened by Right to Education.

Sandra Fredman also brings forth the accelerating dimension of Right to Education by observing, 'Education is also an accelerator right: it equips people to enter the labor force, to participate in public life, and to be productive members of society.' Similarly, pivotal role of Right to Education in the alleviation of poverty and various social disadvantages cannot be under emphasized. In fact, one of the commitments underlying sustainable goals of development as endorsed by the world community in 2015 is to ensure 'inclusive and equitable quality education and to promote lifelong learning opportunities for all by 2030' (UN General Assembly, 2015).

Right to Education is a multidimensional right and is a catalyst in closing the gap between socio-economic and civil–political rights. In other words, it synthesizes these two generations of rights into a common whole.

Sandra Fredman identifies the three vital facets of this right as social right, freedom right and equality right. Right to education as a social right calls for conferment of right to free and compulsory primary education to individuals on part of the State.[9] Obligation on the State for the realization of this right is immediate. However, this aspect of the right has received less attention in the sphere of international human rights standards. International courts and tribunals have often downsized its importance by highlighting negative formulation of Right to Education, rather than obliging the States to provide free or subsidized primary education.[10]

As a logical corollary, Right to Education, in its social dimension, continues to remain subject to progressive realization, be it European Social Charter (ESC),[11] International Covenant on Economic, Social and Cultural Rights (ICESCR)[12] or Convention on the Rights of the Child (CRC).[13] However, with changing times, the formulation of right is gradually shifting from negative to positive obligation. Its confined scope to primary education is the obvious limitation of this dimension of Right to Education, and even the obligation to provide free and compulsory primary education to the children of the State parties in all human rights conventions be subject to: (a) progressive realization and (b) the economic capacity and development of the States. Because of Ableist scaffolding around Right to Education and low priority given to right to receive free education of children, policymakers are bound to remain myopic to give primacy to the interests of the PwD in terms of apportionment of resources to create barrier-free and accessible educational architecture and reasonable accommodation. Of course, it goes without saying that obligation to provide higher education, leave alone the accessible and barrier-free higher education, to the PwD is not even in the picture frame of the contemporary international human rights law standards. It is, therefore, interesting to examine whether UNCRPD has made any headway in this matter.

As a freedom right, Right to Education is a guarantee against the State compulsion to use education to further its propaganda or to thrust on citizens and individuals dominant culture, language or religion.[14] This dimension encompasses vital issues such as parental choice of schooling for their children and, particularly, rights of the parents to educate their children in line with their faith.[15] However, this limited focus would mean less attention or almost no attention on other aspects of freedom; for example, freedom of PwD to choose amongst different spheres of education a particular field of their choice. It is worthwhile to examine how UNCRPD addresses this matter.

Right to Education also has an equality right facet. The shrivels and the interstices resulting from weaknesses in its social dimension have been ironed out through its equality dimension in the sphere of international human rights standards. The principle of non-discrimination runs like a thread through all major human rights conventions emphasizing on enjoyment of all rights including Right to Education without discrimination. The overarching compass of this principle influences alike both civil and political and socio-economic rights enshrined in variety of international instruments.[16] It is of particular interest to examine how UNCRPD expands this dimension of this right further.

On the strength of the capabilities rights theory evolved by Sen and Nussbaum, Sandra Fredman guards against viewing aforementioned dimensions of Right to Education in isolation of one another or hermetically sealed and advocates for their convergence by observing, 'education aims to expand positive freedoms for individuals to be and do as they would like to be and do' (Fredman, 2018, p. 357; Nussbaum, 2011). However, she is not unmindful of the inner conflicts between these three prongs, that is, potential conflict of the right to equal education with the right to choose education, for example, minority schools excluding non-minority learners; conflict between its social and freedom dimensions pertaining to distribution of resources (Fredman, 2018, p. 357). Author submits that this inner conflict is very evidently articulated in the framework of Right to Education in UNCRPD.

The author guards against undue focus on Right to Education as an instrumental right, in terms of development of human capital or as an investment in human resources for promotion of economic prosperity. This approach has the danger of exclusion of those individuals and social groups lacking the potential to achieve the aforementioned ends from enjoyment of this right, for example, people with mental disabilities. In fact, over stretching of instrumental dimension of Right to Education may yield undesirable and unethical consequences like formulation of regimented educational policies, thereby keeping the community stagnant or overlooking importance of subjects like arts and humanities, whose mapping in terms of economic productivity is far from easy.

Author, therefore, endorses the enlightening views of Sandra Fredman and John Rawls advocating Right to Education as intrinsic in character and valuable in its own terms.

> The value of education should not be assessed solely in terms of economic efficiency and social welfare. Equally if not more important is the role of education in enabling a person to enjoy the culture of his [or her] society and to take part in its affairs, and in this way to provide for each individual a secure sense of his [or her] own worth. (Rawls, 1999, p. 87)

Professor Amita Dhanda pithily sharpens the intrinsic dimension of Right to Education in the lives of PwD.

> Even as educationists are aware that one size does not fit all, most of education aims to fit individuals into pre-conceived molds. This freezing of liquid personas into rigid shapes is termed standardization. The non-standard, be it in mind, or body, imagination or expression, is not acknowledged or accepted but abandoned. (Dhanda, 2016)

In this connection, the view of eminent psychologist Howard Gardner is also worth noting. He seriously contested the idea that intelligence is something which can be measured and defined in terms of IQ. He evolved the theory of multiple intelligences and observed that in order to capture the full range of abilities and talents that people possess, we have to look beyond intellectual capacities and pay attention to other dimensions of intelligence of the people, such as musical, interpersonal, spatial–visual and linguistic intelligences. This multidimensional view of intelligence is critical because not only it challenges the populist notion of 'scholarship/intelligence' but it also plays a central role in problematizing the 'ableist' conception of education by questioning its focus on core disciplines like science and math (Gardner, 1983).

Right to Higher Education and UNCRPD

To what extent principles underlying UNCRPD in general and Article 24 in particular problematizes the ableist and the exclusionary character of Right to Education is the subject matter of this and subsequent section.

Article 24 of UNCRPD and Higher Education

Commentators have accurately summed up the inhibiting tone of Article 24 by observing 'despite its categorization as in economic, social and cultural right, Article 24 appears to operate in practice primarily as an antidiscrimination measure which inhibits its potential for securing socio-economic justice for all PwDs' (Anastasiou et al., 2018, p. 658). Its formulation is in line with the tradition of international human rights law standards prioritizing negative obligation; whereas to have any meaningful impact on the lives of PwD, focus should have been on imposition of positive obligations on the State Parties such as creation of barrier-free and accessible environment, elimination of inequalities, exclusionary policies and educational stereotypes. This right does not merely entail formal structure of equality of opportunities but obligates institutionalization of substantive equality mechanisms like adherence to principle of equality of result and reasonable accommodation. The commentators advocate 'external criteria for measuring the functional social and economic accomplishments of PwD' (Anastasiou et al., 2018, p. 659).

Article 24 falls short of this vision, unlike Articles 23(2) and 23(3) of CRC, which recognize both economic facet of Right to Education and the necessity for appropriate care to facilitate access to meaningful educational opportunities by the children. With its focus on anti-discrimination paradigm, the article has overlooked the needs-based approach to Right to Education; Professor Bagenstos has very aptly exposed the limitation and lack of effectiveness of anti-discrimination paradigm in respect of PwD. He observes,

> Antidiscrimination law—even when the notion of reasonable accommodation is tacked onto it—is simply too narrow a tool to get at the deep-rooted structural barriers that keep too many people with disabilities from participating fully in the community. To attack those barriers requires something more .... (Bagenstos, 2009, p. 148–150)

This does not mean that Article 24 is completely oblivious to economic justice or need-based dimension of Right to Education. However, the anti-discrimination impulse has unfortunately blunted the economic justice dimension in the tone of Article 24. While advocating the economic-justice and special-needs dimension of Right to Education, the author is not unmindful of its follies and trade-offs. Under this approach, some student would be improperly excluded from the mainstream and forced into classes, unreceptive and insensitive to their social needs. It would amount to deprivation of their right to socialize in school activities and perpetuation of disability-based stereotypes.

On the other hand, being irresponsive to case-sensitive approach to appropriate educational needs and with incommensurate adherence to equality as sameness, anti-discrimination paradigm has the danger to degenerate as a mechanical institution, thereby alienating the number of students from the so-called mainstream. With its undue focus on notions of availability and accessibility, Article 24 of UNCRPD has reduced the anti-discrimination paradigm to espousing inclusive education as the exclusive instrument for the attainment of Right to Education for PwD. By elevating Right to Education of PwD in mainstream educational environments as a solitary and substantive standard rather than a vehicle of quality instruction in an appropriate setting including an individually tailored specialized setting, Article 24 purports to adopt a perfunctory perspective.

Author opines that both anti-discrimination and special-needs approaches to the Right to Education have promise and potential to bring change in the lives of PwD if the same are synergized by striking equilibrium of inclusion, equality and full participation. With the amelioration of mainstream settings, attitudinal deficit and negative stereotypes towards PwD can be effectively redressed and remedied. In other words, equal weight must be attached to the values of inclusive education and addressing the special needs of PwD in appropriate cases.

Thus, having critically analysed the values and principles underlying Article 24 and advocated a synthesis of anti-discrimination-cum-special-needs approach to the Right to Education of the PwD, it is desirable to examine its mandate vis-à-vis higher education.

A close look on language of Article 24 demonstrates that there is explicit absence of the term 'higher education' in its text. However, there is a conspicuous reference to the term 'tertiary education' in Paragraph 5 of Article 24. It reads,

> States Parties shall ensure that persons with disabilities are able to access general tertiary education, vocational training, adult education and lifelong learning without discrimination and on an equal basis with others. To this end, States Parties shall ensure that reasonable accommodation is provided to persons with disabilities.

Paragraph 2(b) deals with primary and secondary education, whereas Paragraph 5 expands the same by covering tertiary education. According to commentators,

> The main function of paragraph 5 is to operationalize the concept of 'lifelong learning' included in paragraph 1. Specifically, it

ensures that the right to education includes the third and higher level of education. This is not unprecedented, as domestic laws in several countries (e.g. the USA, UK, Canada, and Israel) include such provisions. (Anastasiou et al., 2018, p. 703)

With adoption of a broad conception of tertiary education inclusive of non-traditional educational settings like vocational training, adult education and lifelong learning, paragraph 5 enhances the legal rationale for increasing employment opportunities particularly for people with physical and sensory disabilities.

UNCRPD breaks with earlier international conventions in recognizing the notion of lifelong learning. It envisages formal, non-formal and informal learning (Fina et al., 2017, p. 439–470). It is a European policy initiative evolved through Memorandum on Lifelong Learning, 2000.[17] However, in their major empirical study, Gravani and Zarifis have questioned the degree of its efficacy as originally conceived by European Commission (Gravani & Zarifis, 2014, p. 1). Nevertheless, UNESCO continues to emphasize its significance.[18] The relevance of lifelong learning for adults with disabilities is also justified because bulk of the dropouts are from the basic education,[19] and initiatives like second-chance schools may be good intervention points to restart the education of PwD.

In a country like India, an average age for commencing the primary education is comparatively higher than able-bodied children and many times the PwD would reach the age of 20–25 to complete secondary education. In such a scenario, lifelong learning would facilitate late entry of the students in higher education. At any rate, the definition of child as per international standards to be 18 years requires extension in respect of certain physical and mental disabilities as the development of physique and mind is slowed down owing to certain disorders.[20] Factors like lack of availability of and accessibility to educational institutions and extreme financial hardships affect the pursuit of PwD residing in rural areas for higher education.

Even if reservation of seats in public universities and colleges is one of the initiatives for inclusion of PwD, it is very much under-implemented and extremely under-inclusive covering very few disabilities.[21] For example, people with speech impairment or hearing disability have been denied exposure to education of languages; even they find it difficult to pursue college education because of the absence of sign language interpreters in colleges and universities in India. People with visual impairment in the domain of science and mathematics face the same problem as the State has shown very little interest to create accessible higher-education architecture in this area. For example, it is extremely uncommon in India to hear about a visually impaired, speech-impaired or hearing-impaired person pursuing BSc or MSc in science or math, MBBS or MD or other allied courses in the medical science field.

It has been observed that there is restricted access or almost complete denial from pursuing certain professional degrees, and the committee has rightly urged the State Parties 'to introduce legislation regulations on the access of students with disabilities to higher education and vocational training ... while providing reasonable accommodation and the required support services'.[22] The committee has issued General Comment 4 for concretization of ends and goals underlying Article 24. However, its approach on higher education is predictable in line with the earlier international human rights instruments, that is, to emphasize on social dimension of Right to Education and mostly to view the Right to Education from the perspective of anti-discrimination impulse. The committee observes,

> Accessibility requires that education at all levels be affordable for students with disabilities. Reasonable accommodation should not entail additional costs for learners with disabilities. Compulsory, quality, free and accessible primary education is an immediate obligation.
>
> In line with the 2030 Agenda for Sustainable Development, States parties must progressively adopt measures to ensure that all children, including children with disabilities, complete free, equitable and quality secondary education, and to ensure equal access for all women and men with disabilities to affordable and quality technical, vocational and tertiary education, including university,

and life-long learning. States parties must ensure that persons with disabilities are able to access education in both public and private academic institutions on an equal basis with others.[23]

The above discussion shows that Article 24 goes only as far as emphasizing on provision for free and compulsory primary education to the children with disabilities as a progressive obligation and has very little to offer in terms of policy initiatives, schemes or programmes to encourage and enhance inclusion of PwD in higher education and measures to prevent dropouts during primary or secondary education. Although there is focus on tertiary education, it is mainly aimed at providing some kind of vocational or skilled education to the adults with disabilities who have been either denied access to basic education or discontinued the same due to issues of non-availability and non-accessibility. But what about addressing the issues like continuous and uninterrupted education from primary to PG for PwD; contesting barriers and blockages to the entry points of numerous professional programmes and degree courses; ableist curriculum perpetuating the non-productive and burdensome image of PwD? It seems that in terms of priorities, world community has founded it to be appropriate to defer deliberations on these issues at least for the time being.

Normatively, therefore, it has to be observed that international Constitution on the rights of the disabled has not been able to exert any significant influence on community of nations compelling them to eliminate barriers in the domain of higher education and to create enabling environment for PwD to freely pursue the goal of uninterrupted higher education by opting the avocations and the professional programmes and degree courses of their choice. Instead of a twin track, that is, blend of anti-discrimination-cum-special interventions, the focus for the time being appears to be on affording equal opportunities to the PwD to pursue education at equal basis with others. However, what is missing is the pursuit of the goal of equality of result. On this background, the author would now examine position in India vis-à-vis higher education of PwD.

Pursuit of Higher Education by PwD in India: A Legal Perspective

In this section, author would demonstrate how India replicates the half-hearted policy on higher education echoed in UNCRPD. The Constitution of India, apart from guarantying fundamental right to free and compulsory primary education to children in the age group of 6–14 years under Article 21(A), casts a duty on the State to secure Right to Education of disabled as one of the backward classes and to protect them against 'social injustice and all forms of exploitation' under Articles 41 and 46 with a rider of economic capacity and development of State.

However, normatively, obligation on the State to provide free and compulsory primary education including upper-age relaxation is confined to the category of persons with benchmark disabilities under RPwD Act; it is a regressive turn to the conceptualization of Reasonable Accommodation (RA).[24] In the opinion of author, there is no rationale to exclude children with non-benchmark disability from the zone of this right and the upper-age relaxation accommodation. Obligation on the State to provide free and compulsory education to the children being constitutional in nature has to be tailored to the special needs of children with disabilities, and upper-age relaxation is one of the important elements of tailoring. There is no indication of policy initiatives or programmes and schemes to be pursued for encouraging the PwD in pursuit of higher education in RPwD Act, 2016. To establish this claim, the author would examine below the relevant sections of the aforementioned law.

Right to Education under RPwD Act, 2016

The author has already highlighted the regressive turn to Right to Education vis-à-vis PwD by demonstrating how even in the teeth of categorical axiom of Article 21(A) of Indian Constitution and Article 4 Paragraph 4 of UNCRPD, right to receive free and compulsory primary education in the age group of 6–18 is confined only to the children with benchmark disabilities. The direct fall out of this decision is to exclude people with non-benchmark disabilities in the age group of 14–18 from receiving free and compulsory primary education. What is more, the RPwD Act does not even mandate creation of enabling environment to pursue education by children with non-benchmark disabilities. In the guise of obligation, Section 16 whispers in a feeble tone, 'The appropriate Government and the local authorities shall endeavor that all educational institutions funded or recognized by them provide inclusive education ....'

This language nearly imposes 'an endeavour duty' and lacks any policy direction. It is a lacklustre approach and also has a spillover effect on the domain of higher education as Section 32 jumps the gun by providing for reservation in seats in government-recognized educational institutions. It reads,

> (1) All Government institutions of higher education and other higher education institutions receiving aid from the Government shall reserve not less than five percent seats for persons with benchmark disabilities; (2) The persons with benchmark disabilities shall be given an upper age relaxation of five years for admission in institutions of higher education. (RPwD Act, 2016)

This provision sounds like a dole and is also vacuous in absence of obligation to create enabling environment for pursuit of higher education by PwD.

Regressive Turn to Right to Education

The regressive[25] turn by the Parliament on this issue is very glaringly exposed if the said provision is compared with relevant provisions in the final draft bill submitted by the expert committee to the ministry of social justice and empowerment. The provisions repay study and are reproduced below verbatim. Section 47 of the draft bill laid down that:

> There shall be established an Education Reform Commission for such period of time, not less than three years, as the central government may by notification provide.

(1) The Commission shall, to the maximum extent possible, involve an effective participation of all stakeholders in the process of formulation, implementation and monitoring of the curriculum and related Programmes and policies, including disabled and non-disabled children, teachers and parents;
(2) The terms of reference of the Education Reform Commission shall be:
a) To review the existing curriculum being adopted in schools from the standpoint of persons with disabilities and their lived experiences;
b) To develop an inclusive curriculum based on the principles of non-discrimination and appreciation of diversity and tolerance;
c) To make recommendations on the pedagogical methodology to be adopted for the teaching to and learning by persons with disabilities in the creation of such inclusive curriculum;
d) To suggest measures for the adoption and integration of the inclusive curriculum in mainstream education and to monitor its progress;
e) Make such other recommendations, as the Commission may consider necessary.
(3) The Commission may initiate studies and analysis or take any other measures that may be necessary for performing any function in relation to its terms of reference.

Section 49 of the draft bill was a blend of the elements of lifelong learning and reasonable accommodation and had added positive content to the disability rights jurisprudence by vesting right to receive higher education in PwD in contrast with some of the most progressive jurisdictions around the world construing the same very narrowly. It read,

1) No person with disability, particularly women with disabilities, shall be denied admission in a higher-education institution on the grounds of his or her disability, provided that if a person with disability is unable to seek admission to a higher-educational institution at or before the age prescribed for such admission, then he or she shall be given admission in such an institution if he or she fulfils all other eligibility requirements.

'All appropriate governments and educational authorities may if they deem fit to promote equality of opportunity relax according to prescribed procedure the minimum qualification criteria required to be obtained by persons with disabilities who seek admission to a higher education institution.'

Even in respect of provision of reservations, the draft bill was progressive in two respects. First, the percentage of reservation was 6 instead of just 5 per cent at present. The reduction in the percentage would be perceived even more denting if we take into account and compare it to 2011; the present legislation recognizes 14 more disabilities. Second, the provision to Section 50 did not make the inclusion of PwD totally dependent on reservations. It individualized the potential of PwD by providing, 'persons with disabilities shall not be prevented from competing for seats which are not reserved for them.'

The chapter on higher education in the draft bill did not stop here; Section 51 emphasized the creation of support system to make the pursuit of higher education the reality for PwD. It read,

'(1) Every person with disability appearing for an entrance examination for any higher educational institution has a right to adequate, necessary and appropriate support for the purposes of such examination;
(2) Every person with disability has the right to receive necessary, adequate and gender sensitive support for the completion of higher education and for any other extra-curricular and co-curricular activities;
(3) All universities and other institutions of higher learning shall establish equal opportunity offices to ensure the dedicated provision of such support.

The bill had also amplified the necessity of creation of a pool of sensitized and trained pedagogists for PwD. It read inter alia, 'Every school and higher-educational institution shall have a staff of educators who have the requisite qualifications and training to cater to the needs of students with disabilities.'

Section 53 of the draft bill had yet another safeguard by enjoining the educational institutions from charging capitation fees to the PwD. It read, 'No institution of higher education shall charge or collect any capitation fee whilst admitting a person with disability.'

Taking cognizance of the principle that education does not merely mean opening up colleges, Section 54 inter alia laid down, 'All higher-educational institution shall ensure that persons with disabilities have the right to participate in sporting, recreational and leisure activities on an equal basis with others'.

Section 55 then went on to reemphasize the value of lifelong learning echoed in Article 24 of UNCRPD by highlighting the right of disabled adults to pursue higher education. It read, 'All appropriate governments and establishments shall ensure participation of persons with disabilities in adult education and continuing education Programmes on an equal basis with others'.

A careful look on the above provisions in the draft bill amply demonstrates the confluence of normative institutional and personal aspects in the regime on higher education. It is difficult to comprehend, how did the Parliament overlook this important aspect while giving the final shape to the legislation? It is also possible to argue that the expert committee while drafting the bill took a comprehensive account of legal and social mischiefs and suggested a considerably effective redressal mechanism. The draft of the expert committee was expected to positively influence the attitude of the Parliamentarians, particularly because of their relatively low awareness about the issue, but the bureaucrats in the Ministry of Law and Justice in the guise of scrutiny of this draft watered it down completely. On the insistence of some MPs, the bill was referred to a standing committee. But alas, the standing committee also proved below par and nearly brought the dismay with hardly any considerable improvements in the legislation in its report,[26] and to add insult to the injury, the bill was ratified into law by the Parliament with hardly any earnest deliberation. It is submitted that the present regime on Right to Education under RPwD Act is a half-baked idea, and particularly in respect of higher education, it has very little to offer.

Thus, in absence of any normative bite, policies and incentives, the higher-education sphere in India is simply littered with some petty paternalistic and regressive schemes/doles. To substantiate this claim, provided in here is Table 9.2 describing the various scholarships and fellowships.

A close look on above scholarships shows that GOI has imposed some of the most onerous conditions[27] like, discontinuation of scholarship if student with disability is found to be involved in strikes or protests or change of course in between; there is no incentive for creativity and the rules regulating these scholarships are extremely rigid. In the light of addition of new categories of disabilities in RPwD Act, 2016 and growing awareness about learning disabilities, it is imperative on part of the government to evolve an effective scheme for educational empowerment of people with mental, learning, hearing and speech disabilities. The allocation of number of slots per state also has to considerably go up, and complete revamp of the scheme dealing with overseas scholarships is in order. Despite the clear mandate of UNCRPD, there appears to be hardly any progress even post the enactment of RPwD Act to make appropriate disability-specific modifications in curriculum and to strengthen implementation of the principles of accessibility and reasonable accommodation. Of course, amidst this complete negativity reflected in overall policy of the government including its annual budgets and paternalistic glorification of disabled as *divyang*, its initiative to prepare a sign-language dictionary for the speech and hearing impaired deserves appreciation.

Similarly, the scheme evolved by GOI, Department of Empowerment of PwD (DEPwD) for providing free coaching for students with disabilities looks quite good on paper.[28] Idea to involve central and state universities and top-coaching centres in the private sector to prepare and train students with disabilities (SWDs) to pursue competitive exams is commendable. However, empirical research is required to find out the degree of success of this scheme. Author is not aware of any data about the

Table 9.2 Governmental Schemes and Programmes in Higher Education

Name of the Scholarship	Conditions of Eligibility	No. of Slots in 2018–2019	Quantum of Financial Assistance	Author's Observations
Post-matriculation scholarship	• Students with disabilities pursuing class 11th to PG. • Threshold of disability. • Annual family income from all sources—2.5 lakh or less.	17,000	• Depending upon the course, maintenance allowance for day scholars and hostellers is ₹750 and 1,600 per month, respectively. • Non-refundable tuition fees ₹1.5 lakh per annum. • Disability allowance of up to ₹4,000, subject to nature of disability. • Book allowance ₹1,500 per annum.	• Income limit is unrealistic. • This scholarship is not properly publicized. • Disability disaggregated allocation of its scholarship is not done; colleges and universities are not properly sensitized to provide assistance to the PWDs to avail this scholarship. • Allocation of slots to the various states/Union Territories based on the percentage of disabled population therein is irrational; it should be linked with the percentage of no. of PwD pursuing post-matriculation education. At any rate, the number of scholarship is inadequate in the light of the percentage of disabled students in different states. For example, in UP, for population of 4,157,514 only 2,636 slots are available. • Gender disaggregated data is also not provided.

Top class education (for graduate degree/PG degree/diploma in the notified institutes by the Department of Empowerment of Persons with Disabilities	• Students pursuing PG degree/diploma courses in notified institutes of excellence in education till 2017–2018. • Inclusion of graduation level courses in 240 notified institutes from 2018–2019.	150 for boys and 150 for girls

- Tuition fees and non-refundable amount ₹2 lakh per annum.
- Depending upon the course, maintenance allowance for day scholars and hostellers is ₹1,500 and 3,000 per month, respectively.
- Special allowance related to disabilities like reader disability—₹2,000 per month.
- Book and stationery—₹5,000 per annum.
- Expense for purchase of computer with accessories once ₹30,000.

- Only 300 slots for entire country for the PWDs to pursue higher education in top institutes of India very vividly demonstrates the tokenism of Government of India. For example, for disabled population of 2,963,392, only 31 slots (50% for boys and 50% for girls) are available.
- If one goes by the increased number of disabilities covered by the RPwD Act, 2016, then the allocation of this scholarship is just 1.47, that is, less than two persons from each category of disability.
- Interestingly, out of 240 notified institutions, majority represents engineering, medical and management. Although law schools are notified, only two traditional law colleges are mentioned; major government law colleges are left out without any explanation. Faculties of commerce and arts are also completely excluded, establishing the author's criticism of regimented education.

(Table 9.2 Continued)

(Table 9.2 Continued)

Name of the Scholarship	Conditions of Eligibility	No. of Slots in 2018–2019	Quantum of Financial Assistance	Author's Observations
			• Expense for purchase of aids and assistive devices ₹30,000.	• The number of slots in Post-matriculation scholarship (PMS) being already very few, it is necessary to increase the slots in this scholarship. • The rest of the comments in respect of PMS are ipso facto applicable to this scholarship as well.
National fellowship for PWDs (for MPhil/PhD in Indian universities)	• Students pursuing MPhil/PhD from any recognized Indian university/research centre. • Only full-time MPhil and PhD scholars; employees of universities and colleges even on study leave are ineligible. • Two years as JR fellow and subject to satisfactory report, additional three years extension as SR fellow.	200 across universities and colleges recognized by UGC in India.	• Junior research (JR) fellowship—₹25,000 per month, senior research (SR) fellowship—₹28,000 per month. • Contingency allowance for arts and humanities; science and engineering ₹10,000 and 12,000 per annum, (pa) respectively, for	• Only 200 slots throughout India for pursuing MPhil and PhD across 21 disabilities is completely unacceptable. • Absence of an expert in the field of disability from research evaluation committee may prove extremely counterproductive in protecting and safeguarding the interests of students with disabilities.

	• Maximum duration—five years. • Research valuation to be done by three members' committee consisting of supervisor, head of the department and one outside expert in the subject. • Ineligible for other similar scholarships and schemes during the continuation of this fellowship.	first two years and ₹20,500 and 25,000 PA respectively for remaining tenure of three years. • Assistance to the host institutions for all subjects—₹3,000 pa for providing infrastructure. • Escort/reader allowance of ₹2,000 per month for visually impaired and handicapped.	
National overseas scholarship (Master's degree and PhD in foreign universities)	• For pursuing PhD from any university from abroad, preference to be given to experienced candidates, especially to those who are on lien with their existing post and employer.	20 scholarships pa. • For studying in the USA and other countries excluding the UK, annual maintenance allowance is US $15,400 (probably p.a.)	• Age limit of 35 and income limit of 6 lakhs is completely irrational and hints hardly any rationale. • Only 20 scholarships per year across 21 disabilities is too minimal. • The rest of the comments in respect of PMS are ipso facto applicable to all the other scholarships and are not, therefore, repetitive.

(Table 9.2 Continued)

(Table 9.2 Continued)

Name of the Scholarship	Conditions of Eligibility	No. of Slots in 2018–2019	Quantum of Financial Assistance	Author's Observations
	• For pursuing Master's degree from any university from abroad, preference to be given to experienced candidates, especially to those who are on lien with their existing post and employer. • Age limit is 35. • Income limit from all sources should not exceed ₹600,000. • One-time award • Duration for fellowship for pursuing PhD is up to four years or actual, whichever is less; for PG up to three years or whichever is less.		• For studying in the UK, annual maintenance allowance Great Britain Pound Sterling (GBP) 9,900 (probably p.a.) • Incidental journey allowance is $20 (p.m.). • Equipment allowance is ₹1,500 (p.m.) • Reimbursement of poll tax, wherever applicable. • Actual visa fees. • Tuition fees as per actuals. • Medical insurance premium as actual.	

- Extension of duration in absolutely essential cases for facilitation of completion of course subject to recommendation by the host university and Indian mission abroad without any further financial assistance.
- To and fro economy-class air fare through shortest route in Indian national carrier.
- Second-class train fare or ordinary bus fare from the port of disembarkation to the place of study and back and for attending interview for availing this scholarship.
- By way of research/teaching assistantship amount up to US $2,400 and GBP 1,560 p.a. obtained by the awardees is permissible as supplementary grants.

participation of the coaching institutes, nor he is appraised about existence of any such institution in the state of Maharashtra where he is stationed. Recently, this scheme has been given an extremely regressive turn by GOI DEPwD with the introduction of revised guidelines in respect of scribes to be availed by visually impaired students while writing their papers both in examinations while pursuing any degree or diploma course or any competitive examination.

Critical Analysis of Scribe Guidelines

In February 2013, DEPwD had issued a set of guidelines for conducting written exams by PwD in accordance with the erstwhile PwD Act of 1995.[29] A committee was setup by DEPwD under the chairmanship of its secretary in March 2015 'to review the said guidelines based on the issues raised by Union Public Service Commission and others'.[30]

On the suggestions of this committee, adopting the principles of full inclusion and reasonable accommodation, following revisions have been made in these guidelines.

> There should be a uniform and comprehensive policy across the country for persons with benchmark disabilities for written examination taking into account improvement in technology and new avenues opened to the persons with benchmark disabilities providing a level playing field. Policy should also have flexibility to accommodate the specific needs on case-to-case basis.[31]

- As per the guidelines, same criteria have to be evolved to conduct written examinations, both regular and competitive.
- The facility of scribe/reader/lab assistant should be allowed to any person with benchmark disability as defined under Section 2(r) of the RPwD Act, 2016[32] as well as to those with the limitation in writing including speed, on their request.[33]
- In the case of persons with benchmark disabilities in the category of blindness, locomotor disability (both arm affected-BA) and cerebral palsy, the facility of scribe/reader/ lab assistant shall be given, if so desired by the person.

- In case of other category of persons with benchmark disabilities, the provision of scribe/reader/lab assistant can be allowed on production of a certificate from the chief medical officer/civil surgeon/medical superintendent of a government-healthcare institution to the effect that the person concerned has physical limitation to write and scribe is essential to write examination on his/her behalf.[34]
- The candidate can choose his/her own scribe/reader/lab assistant or request the examination body for the same. The examination bodies may also identify the panels of writers at the district/division/state level as per the requirements of the examination. In such cases, the candidates must be allowed to meet the scribe, etc., two days before the examination, so as to enable him/her to verify whether the scribe is suitable or not.[35]

To deal with expediencies, the scribes, etc., may be changed, and it is also permissible to have more than one scribe 'for writing different papers especially for languages. However, there can be only one scribe per subject'.

There is also a provision to allow the candidates to choose the means, that is, audio recording, computer typing or Braille, to write the answers. Besides this,

1. 'Alternative. objective questions in lieu of descriptive questions should be provided for Hearing-Impaired persons, in addition to the existing policy of giving alternative questions in lieu of questions requiring visual inputs, for persons with Visual Impairment'.[36]
2. 'As far as possible, the examining body should also provide reading material in Braille or E-Text or on computers having suitable screen reading software for open book examination. Similarly, online examination should be in accessible format i.e. websites, question papers and all other study material should be accessible as per the international standards laid down in this regard.'[37]

3. 'The candidates should be allowed to use assistive devices like talking calculator (in cases where calculators are allowed for giving exams), tailor frame, braille slate, abacus, geometry kit, Braille measuring tape and augmentative communication devices like communication chart and electronic devices.'[38]
4. 'Proper seating arrangement (preferably on the ground floor) should be made prior to the commencement of examination to avoid confusion or distraction during the day of the exam, The time of giving the question papers should be marked accurately and timely supply of supplementary papers should be ensured.'[39]
5. 'The procedure of availing the facility of scribe should be simplified and the necessary details should be recorded at the time of filling up of the forms. Thereafter the examining body should ensure availability of question papers in the format opted by the candidate as well as suitable seating arrangement for giving examination.'[40]
6. 'The disability certificate issued by the competent medical authority at any place should be accepted across the country.'[41]
7. 'The word 'extra time or additional time' that is being currently used should be changed to 'compensatory time' and the same should not be less than 20 minutes per hour of examination for persons who take assistance of scribe/reader/lab assistant. All the candidates with benchmark disability not availing the facility of scribe may be allowed additional time of minimum of one hour for examination of 3 hours duration. In case the duration of the examination being less than an hour, then the duration of additional time should be allowed on pro-rata basis. Additional time should not be less than 5 minutes and should be in the multiple of 5.'[42]

Revising the earlier guidelines, now the following two regressive changes have been made.

1. 'In case the examining body provides the scribe/reader/ lab assistant, it shall be ensured that qualification of the scribe should not be more than the minimum qualification criteria of the examination. However, the qualification of the scribe/reader should always be matriculate or above.'[43]
2. 'In case the candidate is allowed to bring his own scribe, the qualification of the scribe should be one step below the qualification of the candidate taking examination. The persons with benchmark disabilities opting for own scribe/ reader should submit his/her details.'[44]

As per earlier guidelines,

> Criteria like educational qualification, marks scored, age or other such restrictions for the scribe/reader/lab assistant were not fixed. Instead, the emphasis was on strengthening the invigilation system, so that the candidates using scribe/reader/lab assistant do not indulge in mal-practices like copying and cheating during the examination.[45]

It is submitted that although the revised guidelines replicate old guidelines in all other respects barring the two regressive changes mentioned above, overall, the guidelines have few other lacunas as well. For example, the people with speech and hearing disabilities as well as learning disabilities have been completely excluded from these guidelines. There is also no justification to confine the scope of these guidelines to only people with benchmark disabilities. Third, DEPwD has not made any serious effort to give publicity to these guidelines, through print and electronic media, nor there is any indication that it has tried to coordinate with universities all over India for the implementation of guidelines. For example, Savitribai Phule University Pune, which is ranked amongst top universities of India, has miserably failed to take cognizance of these guidelines by insisting on lower qualification of the scribe. The guidelines issued by it are awfully under inclusive and paternalistic[46]; it has confined the scope of the guidelines to 'blind or disabled' and merely to the provision of writers without any reference to RPwD Act.

It is necessary to briefly analyse the two aforementioned regressions in the revised guidelines. These regressions have been made by the department without conducting any public hearings and consultations with students with disability. Union Public Service Commission (UPSC) cannot unilaterally dictate the terms of policies pertaining to SWDs.

At any rate, UPSC suggestions having been shrouded in secrecy and do not provide any indication about the necessity to make changes. Moreover, it is not correct to ipso facto apply such changes to non-competitive exams. By making such changes, DEPwD[47] has very seriously damaged the credibility of PwD, as it is being speculated in the education sector that the recent revision is in response to malpractices committed by blind students. In the author's opinion, just because of some bad apples, a knee-jerk reaction on part of the department is disproportionate and even unwarranted. However, since these changes have, for the time being, been stayed by the Delhi High Court[48] until the appropriate government creates the pool of writers, the controversy appears to have died down. Whether universities outside Delhi would accept the decision of Delhi High Court is a moot question.

Engagement of the State of Maharashtra with Higher Education for PwD: Mix Bag of Regression and Progression

Author would like to invite the attention towards a recent government regulation issued by the state of Maharashtra aggravating the regression in the educational policy pertaining to PwD. Some of its key features are highlighted below.[49]

1. Provision for additional grace marks of 3 per cent over and above the general grace marking. According to this rule, PwD falling in all categories are now entitled to get additional 3 per cent grace marks of total marks during the examination of a semester; such marks may be either availed by the student in one subject or more depending upon his/her

performance. Thus, in a 1,000 marks exam, the students can avail 30 additional grace marks which he/she can avail in one or more subjects. In the opinion of the author, this kind of gracing is both indiscriminate and irrational. Being a teacher himself, he asks to himself, are we trying to reduce and degenerate the evaluation/examination to a degree-gathering event. A better approach would have been to address the special needs of the SWDs and make them efficient and intelligent to write the exams rather than throwing mercy on them with the dole of 30 grace marks. Principle of inherent dignity is the first causality in this system.

2. Disaggregation of answer books of SWDs with stamp of disability. It is an extremely disparaging instruction, striking at the root of the values of inclusion and mainstreaming. It is also a violation of the right to privacy, as the stamping requirement is not subject to consent of the concerned SWD. In the opinion of author, there are other dignified ways to communicate the examiners about the special needs of the SWDs, for example, the chief examination officer/principal of the concerned college may provide the information about the special needs and disability-related issues of concerned students in a sealed envelope to the university and same may be communicated to the concerned examiner by maintaining both the values of privacy and confidentiality. Of course, the said communication about disability-related issues or special needs must be subject to the written consent of the concerned SWD or his/her parents, depending upon the facts and circumstances.

3. Liberal evaluation ignoring grammar, spelling and description.

The said regulations also provide that 'while assigning the marks, points and understanding of the key concept be given more importance than the length of description.'[50] '... The errors of spellings, grammar, completeness of sentences or minor number or symbol errors committed while answering the questions should be ignored during evaluation.' This instruction to examiners is not merely based on questionable assumptions but also stereotypes the overall image of PwD, as if all PwD lack the capacity to describe or to provide a detailed description of answer, with correct grammar and spelling. In the opinion of author, such an attribution of inabilities lacks empirical basis. Even if it is assumed for the sake of argument that people with speech and hearing impairment, intellectual disability, mental disability, specific disability, specific learning disability, etc., lack effective description ability, the blame has to be squarely and completely placed on the curriculum of universities and boards. Instead of devising tools to create enabling environment to assist SWDs to pursue education with dignity, shortcuts are resorted rather insensitively and ignominiously. For example, instead of training the hearing and speech disabled in different languages, the inclination is to give them wholesale exemptions or to discourage blind students from pursuing math and science. The author laments on this kind of attitude on the part of state universities and governments.

The mandate of UNCRPD is to enable pedagogy by resorting to principles of accessibility, universal design and reasonable accommodation. Irrational exemptions based on unscientific, unverifiable assumptions and stereotypes about the potential and intelligence of SWDs apart from making them lazy and less ambitious would prove to be damaging distortions of their disabilities in the long term. Reasonable accommodation or accessibility should not be confused with simplistic and illogical interventions. Recently unfolded national education policy of GOI is conspicuous for its stoic silence on such and other allied issues.[51] However, the policy has some good points as well; it specifically focuses on the leprosy cured students and those with multiple sclerosis, blood disorders, multiple disabilities, mental disabilities, intellectual disabilities and specific learning disabilities by directing the attention of the colleges towards their special needs and special circumstances. For example, there are clear instructions to provide appropriate furniture and stationery tailored to the needs of such students. There is also the provision for allowing the students with blood disorders to write the papers from their homes. In cases of illness or stress during the examination, the provision is made for retest. Intervention is also conceived by way of provision for writers or promoters in case the students with hearing and speech disability, specific learning disability, mental and intellectual disability find it difficult to complete a particular examination paper by their own, owing to physical exertion.

Despite such seemingly salutary provisions, when looked at from a rights-based perspective, the regulations of the Government of Maharashtra fall flat on the touchstone of the values of dignity, equanimity, accessibility and sensitivity. The regulations appear to have completely lost sight of social model of disability with almost exclusive focus on the medical disorders and bodily conditions of the students. The perfunctory mess of the regulations is further exposed from the myopic aim, that is, somehow pushing the SWDs to pass the exams. There is hardly any indication about transformation in the overall pedagogy and creation of rights enabling accessible and barrier-free environment and nurturance of inclusive higher education.

Last but not least, in terms of sensitizing the institutions, the focus is merely on involving principals and examination-related staff of the college. No attempt is made to explore the possibilities of initiatives like sensitization programmes for students and teachers for raising awareness about the potential of SWDs. Space constraint prevents the author from stretching the discussion any further.

A Road Map for Enabling Andragogy for Higher Education of PwD

In this next section, having briefly critiqued the classical notion of right to higher education as a negative right, author would explore its positive dimension in the light of 'republican liberty' and 'capabilities approach'. This backdrop will be used to reconfigure relationship of Parts III and IV and to ground right to higher education of PwD in Article 46 read with Articles 14, 19 and 21 of the Indian Constitution. The section is concluded with some constructive commendations and suggestions for evolution of effective policy to constitutionalize this right.

Right to Higher Education for PwD vis-à-vis Republican Liberty

Author prefers republican liberty over non-interventionist and contractarian models of liberty, the focus of the latter being on individualism overlooking structural inequalities and biases. For remedying and redressing structural inequalities and biases, interventions are quintessential. Views of noted contemporary republicans like Pettit are worth cognizance as an alternative paradigm, transcending liberty beyond individualism. Pettit opines, 'Freedom as non-domination is defined by reference to how far and how well the bearer is protected against arbitrary interference' (Pettit, 1997). To unpack this idea, every interference on part of the State does not necessarily entail reduction of person's freedom; in fact, at times, interventions prove to be emancipatory. What is objected to in this perspective is both actual arbitrary interference and capacity to arbitrarily interfere as the same contracts person's freedom. To understand this proposition metaphorically, a slave with a benevolent master is more unfree than an impoverished, but free man (Pettit, 1997, p. 65).

The author advocates evolution of the notion of non-domination by critiquing it through the lens of ableism, that is, how societies are predominantly conceived and designed by the able bodied for the able bodied and how PwD are unabashedly excluded from the process of the formation of societies on the ground of their diverse medical conditions. The same is demonstrable at macro level in the domain of higher education as well. The educational sphere, in general, is driven by a regimented and ableist notion of intelligence, debunking and decrying any deflections or deviations, howsoever creative or innovative. In other words, pursuit of higher education by PwD in completely non-congenial and exclusively ableist conditions is merely a subterfuge of the promotion of 'the Right to Education for all'. In reality, the andragogy being entirely tilted in favour of able bodied is nothing but arbitrary hurdle in the lives of PwD and in their quest for exercise of liberty of education.

Thus, the standpoint of non-domination transformed in terms of disability equality would direct attention on the academic ableism and call for freeing the PwD from dependence reinforced and perpetuated through the inaccessible and disabling environment. The best course of action for doing away with dependency in the sphere of education is to make education inclusive and emancipatory. At any rate, for attainment of right of self-determination and to become self-reliant, there cannot be better instrument than right to higher education. Understood this way, PwD have to be endowed with Right to Education as evolving members of public rather than as representatives of a vulnerable group requiring a particular pattern of education. In other words, education has to be synthesized with civic and republican liberty as a foundational value underlying a democratic legal order.

The republicanized conception of education generates public justification for disability-sensitive interventions undercutting the 'narrow Lockean rubric of parental authority, hoisted by proponents of the model of negative liberty (liberty as non-interference)' (Gutmann, 1999). This transformed and broadened conception of education that it cannot be captured by the notion of Right to Education situated by the Indian Supreme Court in right to run a business under Article 19(1) (g), confining it merely to the delivery of a 'service' (Seetharaman & Mukherjee, n.d.). According to the author, the cases like *TMA Pai foundation v. State of Karnataka (2002) 8 SCALE 1: AIR(2003) SC355* were the missed opportunity on the part of the Supreme Court to have captured this vital point, but to be fair to the court, this perspective did not even form a part of the argumentation, and the aspiration of PwD to enjoy impediment-free Right to Education went begging.

Reinforcing the point, it is plausible to argue that Right to Education, synthesized in civic and republican liberty as a foundational value underlying our Constitution, is beyond the conflict of rights issue. Contrary to characterization of right to higher education as an entitlement, calling for non-intervention on part of State, in the judgments of cases such as *Pai foundation,* the *Society for Unaided Private Schools of Rajasthan v. Union of India* AIR 2012 SC 3445, *Pramati Educational and Cultural Trust v. Union of India*, this right as enmeshed in civic and republican liberty posits itself as a positive right and does not object to interventions generated by disability equality sensitive public justifications. It has to be perceived as a recipe to protect the PwD against non-domination by way of academic ableism and handicapping environment. Understood this way, the question of balancing this right with the rights of able-bodied members of the society does not arise, as there is no conflict as such. Able bodied and PwD are entitled equally to exercise and enjoy Right to Education in a non-dominating, inclusive and enabling environment.

From non-domination perspective, even retro-investment to transform ableist higher-educational institutions into inclusive and diversity-enabling platforms is a justified intervention based on public justification of enhancing self-reliance, non-dependence and dignity of PwD.[52] It is erroneous to view the retro action or reasonable accommodations strategy as the markers of conflict between disabled and private rights of the able bodied. There is no question of private rights of abled bodied yielding to the public right to reasonable accommodation of PwD, rather, the latter is a strategy to retroactively ensure right to non-domination in the sphere of education equally to both disabled and able bodied.

Same point can also be captured from the perspective of capabilities approach, which makes the conferment of rights contingent on certain threshold (Riddle, 2017). It is constituted of certain capabilities without the embodiment of which, right conferral appears merely to be an empty formality. The Right to Education of PwD is contingent on attainment of capabilities like accessibility, barrier-free environment, reasonable accommodation, inherent dignity and respect for diversity. Retro action for attainment of these capabilities cannot be perceived as either disproportionate or unduly burdensome in terms of financial resources, in the context of the totally 'indifferent and privileged' default, oblivious to the rights and identity of PwD (Pease, 2010).

Reconfiguring the Relationship between Fundamental Rights and Directive Principles of State Policy (DPSP)

In the light of above-mentioned philosophical blueprint, the author would suggest the reconfiguration of Article 46 of Constitution of India securing Right to Education for weaker sections of society by perceiving PwD as one of the inherent constituents worthy of cognizance. The need of the hour is to abandon the dichotomous relationship between fundamental rights and DPSP as either mutually exclusive[53] or as harmonious.[54] In the opinion of the author, the relationship is a continuum, if we synthesize both these parts by invoking foundational values in the preamble of the Constitution.[55] Equally, we have to appreciate that Article 37 makes all DPSPs cognizable by the government as fundamental principles in the governance and imposes a duty to make laws in the light of these principles. The same in its earnestness amounts to treating conception of directives as unenforceable yet cognizable rules. The point is very well captured in the words of Professor GoodHart and brought home by the Supreme Court of India, 'if a principle is recognized as binding on the legislature, then it can be correctly described as a legal rule even if there is no court that can enforce it.'[56]

To translate the above discussion in the realm of education, the duty to promote right to higher education of PwD when read conjointly through Articles 14, 15(2), 19, 21, 37 and 46 alongside the principles of equality of opportunity and status, liberty and social justice in Preamble and against the backdrop of categorical ratification of UNCRPD by India, then the same is certainly more than 'cognizable' in nature though sceptics may still not view it as 'enforceable'. If categorical ratification of a treaty is seen to be analogous to enactment of new legislation or modifying the existing law, then it is plausible to argue for the case of crystallization of obligation to promote higher education of PwD enshrined in Article 46 as an enforceable duty.

Right to higher education for PwD also has a horizontal dimension, if the word 'shop' deployed in Article 15(2) is interpreted broadly in the context of free market. Article 15(2) read in relevant part:

> No citizen shall, on grounds only of religion, race, caste, sex, place of birth or any of them, be subject to any disability, liability, restriction or condition with regard to... access to shops, public restaurants, hotels and places of public entertainment ....

In *Indian Medical Association v. Union of India*,[57] the question before the Supreme Court was whether a private, non-minority higher-educational institution that admitted students only on the basis of their scores in an entrance test violated Article 15(2). This question was based on the American theory of disparate impact of test-based admissions programmes upon educationally underprivileged castes. However, before dealing with the said question, the Supreme Court was required to answer another striking question that whether the terminology of 'shops, public restaurants, hotels and places of public entertainment', as part of Article 15(2) would include the impugned educational institution, thereby falling within its injunctive sweep. The Court held that Article 15(2) was indeed applicable because educational institutions were covered by the term 'shops'. It quoted—and endorsed—Dr Ambedkar's speech in the Constituent Assembly Debates, where he had observed:

> To define the word 'shop' in the most generic term one can think of is to state that 'shop' is a place where the owner is prepared to offer his service to anybody who is prepared to go there seeking his service ... I should like to point out therefore that the word 'shop' used here is not used in the limited sense of permitting entry. It is used in the larger sense of requiring the services if the terms of service are agreed to.

Thus, the Court abandoned the central meaning of the word 'shop'—that is, a store, 'a building or room where goods are stored', 'a building stocked with merchandise for sale', 'a small retail establishment or a department in a large one offering a specified line of goods or services'—in favour of an extremely abstract, reified, 'generic' meaning, to expand its scaffolding to embrace within it educational institutions.

To borrow the words of young scholar Gautam Bhatia, a 'shop' is merely the concrete expression of the idea of the impersonal, abstract market of the modern liberal–capitalist economy. This is the only way that the court succeeds in bringing educational institutions within the ambit of 15(2) (Bhatia, G).

By invoking the constitutional value of fraternity, it is plausible to argue that even private (public being covered by its vertical dimensions), non-aided higher-educational institutions are obligated to foster enabling environment and open their doors to PwD. Per force, interpretation of Article 15(2) as manifestation of republican liberty in the sphere of education would tantamount to conferment of a positive right on PwD to pursue higher education in the colleges and universities of their choice. The non-performance of this duty would attract the injunctive sweep of Article 15(2). Article 15(5) guaranteeing reservations in favour of socially and educationally backward classes, SCs and STs in higher education, would include by default PwD in the light of categorical ratification of UNCRPD by India and denial of appropriate and accessible environment would amount, to borrow the words of Professor Amartya Sen, 'erection of unfreedom' (Sen, 1999).

Under Article 41, Right to Education being tailored to economic capacity and development of the State provides room for application of the doctrine of margin of appreciation during the allocation of limited resources. But while doing so, State cannot overlook the hitherto continuous marginalization and alienation of PwD from the domain of higher education, and the same has to play a pivotal role during the determination of priorities.

Moreover, since the default being totally oblivious to the special needs of PwD, any retrofitting investment and reasonable accommodation strategies must be regarded as compensatory justice remedies rather than burdens. The aforementioned principle of republican liberty also justifies positive State intervention as long as the enjoyment of this right by all citizens is not free from domination.

In fact, the conception of legal right, be it propounded by Dworkin or Alexy, or, for that matter, by most of the contemporary philosophers, does not account for the disability experiences (Alexy, 1985; Joseph, 1986). Just to give an example, Ronald Dworkin, a very strong proponent of the Right, characterizing the same as Trump's, subordinates the existence of PwD as 'agents born owing to misfortune or bad luck' and by way of compassionate gesture calls for conferment on these agents affirmative action.[58] In the opinion of author, the account of disability provided by Dworkin, apart from being empirically flawed, paints victim-oriented and vulnerable picture of PwD and completely plays down the positive potential in them. At any rate, affirmative action is not a substitute for enjoyment of equal rights by PwD at equal basis with others. It is always viewed as a temporary measure, and UNCRPD, through Article 5 along with the other overarching principles, laid down in Article 3 guards against its adoption by the State Parties as an empowerment strategy. Since the status of the disabled is not going to be assimilated into the able bodied, the conception of the right cannot overlook the fundamental differences between the two. However, the differences must not be the cause for discrimination, rather be the cause of celebration as they are the markers of diversity.[59] Affirmative action perpetuates and reinforces hierarchy between the so-called donors (able bodied) and donees (PwD), whereas UNCRPD calls for elimination of the same and advocates for nurturance of values of diversity and respect for difference.

Viewed against this backdrop, providing doles or few scholarships is not equivalent to recognition of right to higher education of PwD. The need of the hour is the evolution of a comprehensive policy covering all aspects of education. Of course, evolution of such policy is not possible without involvement of the PwD themselves. In other words, right to higher education of PwD being a positive right, its effective enjoyment is squarely dependent on a cohesive non-domination policy.

Policy Inputs

Following may be some of the inputs forming the policy.

1. 'Ensuring active, effective and inclusive engagement of students with disabilities with the overall college environment.' The many ways in which students with disabilities could be engaged include academic programmes, intramural athletics, social entities such as clubs and student organizations, academic courses, programmes events and physical space on a campus. There is a great need for intentional and proactive design for the attainment of the same with focus on accessibility (Kimball et al., 2017).
2. Formation of academic programmes and allocation of resources must be influenced by the special needs of students with severe disabilities, and all educational institutions must scrupulously avoid indifference and neutrality in respect of the disabled students in general and severely disabled in particular. Specially, the tendency to give preference to less severely disabled must be abandoned forthwith.
3. Educational institutions must attach due significance to disability access as a part of institutional engagement and should also incorporate it in their diversity-planning initiatives. In the Indian context, author guards educational institutions against disproportionate showcasing of ramps and wheelchairs, accessible toilets as hallmarks of accessibility. Accessibility programmes would not serve any purpose without the involvement of actual beneficiaries. The repeated emphasis must be on how the accessibility measures are not exclusively for disabled, that is, inclusive and diversity-enhancing utility of such measures must be highlighted.
4. Empirical studies must be conducted periodically to gauze the level of engagement between disabled and non-disabled students and amongst the students with different disability. It means that engagement must be horizontal and vertical. Horizontal engagement involves a cross disability, whereas

vertical engagement promotes inclusion of disabled students into the mainstream.
5. For nurturance of disability identity and to remove stigma attached to it within the educational environment, social barriers preventing access to the PwD must be highlighted, and medical model of disability locating disability in the physical body must be banished from the curriculum.
6. In order to dispense with the ableist conception of intelligence, the notion of multiple intelligence (author has already alluded to) must be endorsed and embraced.
7. Disability studies scholars emphasize on collaboration rather than division between disability studies and disability services. The separation between the two is ahistorical, creating a false dichotomy in the educational campuses (Oslund, 2015).
8. To capture the disadvantageous and vulnerable status of PwD, its intersection with the markers of other disadvantages like caste, sex, economic background, etc., must be carefully studied.
9. Periodical survey must be carried out to examine the implementation of various policy, schemes, programmes and laws in place for PwD.

Time and space constrain prevent the author from going any further in the matter. However, suffice it to say that the list of the inputs is both general and illustrative requiring scientific refinement.

Conclusion

In this chapter, author has argued that right to higher education for PwD is an enabler. It is a multiplier right and enjoyment of all other rights depends on how well people with disability can pursue their higher education. Inclusion of PwD in higher education is also an indicator of degree of respect for diversity and difference in a given society. The author has demonstrated that at normative level, the tentacles of right to higher education of PwD are not spread out because of its confined conception both in the international law as well as at domestic level, and this claim is established by analysing the relevant provisions of UNCRPD, Constitution of India and RPwD Act, 2016. Taking a clue from transformative constitutionalism, author has tried to go beyond the surface of the Constitution and to interpret it in the light of republican tradition of scholarship by emphasizing on the value of non-domination. The reference has also been made to the capabilities approach and ableism to seriously challenge the present unidirectional intelligence model and to question the dole-oriented and perfunctory lip service to the higher-education ambitions of PwD on part of the State and private sector.

By resorting to structural exegesis of the Constitution in the light of republican liberty and categorical ratification of UNCRPD, the author has interpreted Article 46 of Constitution of India as a transformed rule, more than cognizable in degree. Author has located the site of right to higher education of PwD in Article 46, read with Articles 37, 14, 15(2), 19, and 21 alongside values of equality of opportunities, social justice and liberty in the Preamble by characterizing them as one of the backward classes. Author has argued that as a part of republican liberty, right to higher education being one of the defaults and every member of civilized society is equally entitled to exercise it, and the same being anterior to other rights, there is no question of any 'rights conflict'. Emphasizing on the positive nature of right to higher education, author has also ventured to randomly identify some inputs for an effective educational policy on which this right is grounded.

Notes

1. Z. Kramer (2019) observes,

    Modern discrimination is the product of a complex web of cultural norms, stereotypes, and unconscious biases. Together, these forces make discrimination messier and more individualized than ever before. Accordingly, the work of civil rights needs to be about the universal experience of being different. We need a right to personality. Imagine a civil rights regime that seeks to carve out space for people to be themselves fully, a regime that values expressions of individuality as central to the human experience. Imagine that the law recognizes a right to shave your head; a right to be fat; a right to be open about your same-sex partner; a right to wear your hair in braids; a right to transition from one sex to another; a right to have tattoos; a right to speak a language other than English.

Space and time constrain prevent the author from articulating this idea in detail in this chapter.
2. To make this plan more participative and to consult with all the stakeholders, NCPEDP had conducted a number of consultations based on which government had also made certain revisions in the plan. See, DNIS (2005).
3. Action Plan for Inclusive Education of Children and Youth with Disabilities, (2005). www.unicef.in/PressReleases/288/Government-of-India-announces-plan-to-make-education-disabledfriendly-by-2020
4. Article 35–36 of UNCRPD 2006.
5. The sample for the survey was very large with responses from more than 150 institutions throughout India covering 1,521,438. Disabled get only 0.56 per cent of seats in higher education; refer TNN (2015).
6. See the reports of AISHE from 2010–2011 to 2017–2018.
7. Article 31, UNCRPD.
   1. States Parties undertake to collect appropriate information, including statistical and research data, to enable them to formulate and implement policies to give effect to the present Convention. The process of collecting and maintaining this information shall:
      a) Comply with legally established safeguards, including legislation on data protection, to ensure confidentiality and respect for the privacy of persons with disabilities;
      b) Comply with internationally accepted norms to protect human rights and fundamental freedoms and ethical principles in the collection and use of statistics.
   2. The information collected in accordance with this article shall be disaggregated, as appropriate, and used to help assess the implementation of States Parties' obligations under the present Convention and to identify and address the barriers faced by persons with disabilities in exercising their rights.
8. Office of the High Commissioner for Human Rights. (1999).
9. In India, it manifests in Article 21A of Constitution of India. See also, Article 13, ICESCR, 1966.
10. See generally, *Belgian Linguistic Case (No 2)* (1979–80) 1 EHRR 252 (European Court of Human Rights)

Right to Higher Education of PwD / 203

11. See Article 17(2) of revised ESC, 1966.
12. See Article 13, ICESCR, 1966; obligation to provide free and compulsory education to the children, on the state parties, is subject to progressive realization and economic capacity and development of the State Parties, Article 2, ICESCR, 1966.
13. See Article 28(1) (a) of CRC, 1989.
14. It manifests in Article 29 of Constitution of India.
15. See Article 18(4) of ICCPR, 1966; the crux of Right to Education recognized in Protocol 1, Article 2 of ECHR, 1950, does also echo the same idea.
16. See Article 10 of CEDAW, 1979; Article 28, CRC, 1989; Article 3 of ICESCR, 1966; Article 14, ECHR, 1953.
17. See generally, Yang et al. (2015).
18. See Hamburg Declaration (1997). Cape Town Statement on Characteristic Elements of a Lifelong Learning Higher Education Institution. (2001); UNESCO World Conference on Higher Education (2009); Report of the Special Rapporteur on the right to education devoted to technical and vocational education and training from a right to education perspective (2014).
19. See Domna Michail and Dimitris Anastasiou. (2010).
20. Supreme Court gave regressive turn to the notion of mental age in the context of Protection of Children from Sexual Offences Act, 2012 in *Ms Eera v. State of NCT Delhi 2017 SCC On Line SC 787*.
21. See generally, CRPD Committee (2017).
22. See generally, CRPD Committee (2017)..
23. See General Comment 4 Para 23; adopted by UNCRPD committee on September 2016.
24. See Section 31, read with Section 2(r). Ironically, when obligation to provide free and compulsory primary education was crystalized in Article 21(a) of the Constitution of India as a fundamental right, the right was conferred on every child falling within the age group of 6–14. In the light of the same, the Parliamentary attempt of levelling down the structure of this right in Section 31 of RPwD Act is questionable. In the teeth of Article 4 Paragraph 4, guarding against regressive steps on part of State Parties post UNCRPD, is Section 31 incompatible with UNCRPD?
25. Section 4(4) of UNCRPD: Nothing in the present Convention shall affect any provisions which are more conducive to the realization of the rights of persons with disabilities and which may be contained in the law of a State Party or international law in force for that state. There shall be no restriction upon or derogation from any of the human rights and fundamental freedoms recognized or existing in any State Party to the present Convention pursuant to law, conventions, regulation or

custom on the pretext that the present Convention does not recognize such rights or freedoms, or that it recognizes them to a lesser extent.
26. Standing Committee on Social Justice and Empowerment. (2014–2015).
27. See detailed guidelines on central sector scheme of scholarships for students with disabilities at www.https://www.vidhyaa.in/public/uploads/images/scholarship/5b72b5d67ea7e3939.pdf
28. The stipend of ₹2,500 for local students and ₹5,000 for outstation students along with special allowance of ₹2,000 appears to be very meagre. For detailed guidelines of this scheme, see central sector scheme of scholarships for students with disabilities at www.https://www.vidhyaa.in/public/uploads/images/scholarship/5b72b5d67ea7e3939.pdf
29. See OM No. I 6- I I 0/2003-DD. TH 26 February 2013 at www.http://disabilityaffairs.gov.in/upload/uploadfiles/files/Guidelines-29_08_2018%20(1).pdf
30. See revised guidelines for conducting written examination for persons with benchmark disabilities, F. No. 34-02/2015-DO-HI (p. 1) at www. http://disabilityaffairs.gov.in/upload/uploadfiles/files/Guidelines-29_08_2018%20(1).pdf
31. Ibid.
32. (r) 'Person with benchmark disability' means a person with not less than 40 per cent of a specified disability where specified disability has not been defined in measurable terms and includes a person with disability where specified disability has been defined in measurable terms, as certified by the certifying authority.
33. RPwD Act Section 2(r).
34. Ibid., p. 2.
35. Ibid.
36. F. No. 34-02/2015-DO-HI, id at pp 04.
37. Ibid, p. 3.
38. Ibid.
39. Ibid.
40. Ibid.
41. Ibid.
42. Ibid.
43. Ibid, p. 2.
44. Ibid.
45. See OM No. I 6- I I 0/2003-DD. TH dated 26 February 2013, p. 2.
46. University has decided to reimburse ₹150 per paper till graduation and ₹175 till PG for writers. It is fantastic to conceive that somebody would spend his/her four hours to write a paper for blind person with aforementioned ridiculous amount; see letter reference number 163 examination coordination available at www.unipune.ac.in dated 24 January 2019. University has not even taken cognizance of the recent judgement of Delhi High Court staying the aforementioned regressive

changes in the revised guidelines; see *Aditya Narayan Tiwari & ANR v. Union of India & ANR W.P.(C) 12222/2018* dated 4 December 2018.
47. Recently, Supreme Court of India has expressed its disquiet about the policy disconnect between UPSC and DEPwD on the issue of Scribe. See Vikash Kumar vs UPSC [MANU/SC/0067/2021]. Pre-published version of this chapter has been cited by D. Y. Chandrachud, J. in Para 65 and 71.
48. See *Aditya Narayan Tiwari & ANR vs. Union of India & ANR W.P.(C) 12222/2018* dated 4 December 2018.
49. See government regulation 302 dated 4 March 2017.
50. See *Individuals with Disability/Special Needs in Higher Education: Guidelines of Mumbai University* dated 11 May 2017 at https:// www.google.com/url?sa=t&rct=j&q=&esrc=s&source=web&cd =1&ved=2ahUKEwiY9OPPrbDgAhVMWisKHSc4CWkQFjAAe gQICRAC&url=http%3A%2F%2Fmu.ac.in%2Fportal%2Fwp-content%2Fuploads%2F2016%2F06%2F4.29-Disability-Guidelines. pdf&usg=AOvVaw1DVr_JegmFo--y4No37B4N
51. See, for critical analysis, Muralidharan (2019); Ali (n.d.); Roy (2019). The draft policy is available at http://www.iiitu.ac.in/documents/NEP-2019.pdf
52. See overarching principles enshrined in Article 3 of UNCRPD, 2006.
53. *The State of Madras v. Srimathi Champakam Dorairajan 1951 AIR 226*
54. *Minerva Mills v. Union of India AIR 1980 SC 1789*
55. *M Nagraj v. Union of India AIR 2007 SC 71.*
56. Cited by Mathew J. in *Kesavananda Bharati v. State of Kerala, (1973) 4 SCC 225 Para 1701.*
57. *Indian Medical Association v. Union of India, (2011) 7 SCC 179.*
58. See generally, Dworkin (1977). For critique of his position from disability rights perspective, see, Mark (2006).
59. See generally, Kramer (2012).

References

Alexy, R. (1985). *A theory of constitutional rights*. Oxford University Press.
Ali, A. (n.d.). Draft New Education Policy ignores persons with disabilities yet again: Are special children not supposed to go to school? *India Today*. https://www.indiatoday.in/education-today/featurephilia/story/draft-new-education-policy-ignores-persons-with-disabilities-yet-again-are-special-children-not-supposed-to-go-to-school-1597687-2019-09-10
Anastasiou, D., Gregory, M., & Kauffman, J. M. (Eds.). (2018). Article 24: Education. In I. Bantekas, M. A. Stein & D. Anastasiou (Eds.), *The UN Convention on the rights of persons with disabilities: A commentary* (p. 658). OUP.

Bagenstos, S. R. (2009). *Law and the contradictions of the disability rights movement* (pp. 148–150). Yale University Press.

Bhambhani, M. (2016, 16 July). Role of higher education in building stable careers for persons with disabilities. *Deccan Herald.*

Bhatia, G. (n.d.). *Transformative constitutionalism* (Unpublished manuscript). Cambridge University Press.

Campbell, F. K. (2009). *Contours of ableism: The production of disability and abledness.* Palgrave Macmillan.

Cape Town Statement on Characteristic Elements of a Lifelong Learning Higher Education Institution. (2001). UNESCO. https://unesdoc.unesco.org/ark:/48223/pf0000199256

Comprehensive Action Plan for Inclusive Education. (2005). http://ap-iedss.blogspot.com/2014/01/comprehensive-action-plan-for-inclusive.html

CRPD Committee. (2017). *Concluding observations on the initial report of Bosnia and Herzegovina* (para. 49).

Dhanda, A. (August 2016). Reasonable accommodation for all. *Café Dissensus.* www.https://cafedissensus.com/2016/08/14/reasonable-accommodation-for-all/

Disabled World. (2014). Signed on 30-03-2007 and ratified on 01-10-2007 'India had not signed or ratified the optional protocol to this convention'. www.disabled-world.com/disability/discrimination/crpd-milestone.php

Dworkin, R. (1977). *Taking rights seriously.* Harvard University Press.

Fina, Valentina Della. (2017). The right to inclusive education according to Article 24. In V. D. Fina, R. Cera & G. Palmisano (Eds.), *The United Nations Convention on the Rights of Persons with Disabilities* (pp. 439–470. Springer.

Fredman, S. (2018). *Comparative human rights law* (p. 356). OUP.

Gardener, H. (1983). *Frames of mind: The theory of multiple intelligences.* Basic Books.

Government of India. (2016). Disabled persons in India, a statistical profile 2016. www.mospi.nic.in/sites/default/files/publication_reports/Disabled_persons_in_India_2016.pdf

Gravani, M. N., & Zarifis, G. K. (2014). Introduction. In M. N. Gravani & G. K. Zarifis (Eds.), *Challenging the European area of lifelong learning* (p. 1). Springer.

Gutmann, A. (1999). *Democratic education.* Princeton University Press.

Hamburg Declaration. (1997). www.http://unesdoc.unesco.org/images/0011/001161/116114eo.pdf

Jain, S. (2018, 11–12 December). *Right to higher education of PwD: Critical reflections,* paper presented at National Conference on higher education in India With special reference to Dalits, minorities, women and persons with disabilities, Bangalore University.

Jain, S. (2021, 20 February). *The supreme court's judgment in vikash kumar: Some reflections.* Available at https://www.barandbench.com/columns/usps-of-the-supreme-courts-judgment-in-vikash-kumar-some-reflections

Joseph, R. (1986). *The morality of freedom.* Clarendon Press.

Kimball, E., Friedensen, R, E., & Silva, E. Engaging disability trajectories of involvement for college students with disabilities. In E. Y. Kim & K. C. Aquino (Eds.), *Disability as diversity in higher education policies and practices to enhance student success* (p. 70). Routledge.

Kramer, Z. (2019). *Outsiders: Why difference is the future of civil rights* (p. 60). Oxford University Press.

Mark S. (2006). *Distributive justice and disability: Utilitarianism against egalitarianism.* Yale University.

MHRD. (2016–2017). *Educational development of persons with disability* (Chapter 15 https://www.education.gov.in/sites/upload_files/mhrd/files/document-reports/HRD%20AR%202016-17%20SE.pdf

Michail, D., & Anastasiou, D. (2010). Gender discrimination and learning as the main reasons of dropping-out from basic education: A retrospective study in the context of second-chance schools. In P. Cunningham & N. Fretwell (Eds.), *Lifelong learning and active citizenship, proceedings of the twelfth conference of the Children's Identity and Citizenship in Europe Academic Network* (CiCe, pp. 435–444).

Muralidharan. (2019, 3 July). New Education Policy 2019 Draft unacceptable: It Perpetuates inequality & discrimination. *Enabled.in.* https://enabled.in/wp/new-education-policy-2019-draft-unacceptable-perpetuates-inequality-discrimination/

Nussbaum, M. (2011). *Creating capabilities.* Harvard University Press, Belknap Press, 2011.

Office of the High Commissioner for Human Rights. (1999). CESCR General Comment No. 13 (para 1). https://www.refworld.org/pdfid/4538838c22.pdf

Oslund, C. M. (2015). *Disability services and disability studies in higher education.* Palgrave Macmillan.

Pease, B. (2010). *Undoing privilege—unearned advantage in a divided world.* Zed Books.

Pettit, P. (1997). *Republicanism: A theory of freedom and government* (p. 109). Oxford University Press.

Rawls, J. (1999). *Theory of justice* (Rev. ed., p. 87). Harvard University Press.

Singh, K. (2014). Report of the special rapporteur on the right to education. https://www.ohchr.org/EN/HRBodies/HRC/RegularSessions/Session26/Documents/A_HRC_26_27_ENG.DOC

Riddle, C. A. (2017). *Human rights, disability, and capabilities.* Palgrave Macmillan.

Roy, K. (2019, June). Examining the Draft National Education Policy, 2019. *EPW (engage)*. https://www.epw.in/engage/article/examining-draft-national-education-policy-2019

Seetharaman, B., & Mukherjee, G. (n.d.). *A republican solution to the conflict of rights dilemma: The case of the Right to Education*. Unpublished paper.

Sen, A. (1999). *Development as freedom*. Oxford University Press.

Solomon, A. (2012). *Far from the tree: Parents, children and the search for identity*. Scribner.

Standing Committee on Social Justice and Empowerment. (2014–2015). (Sixteenth Lok Sabha) The Rights of Persons with Disabilities Bill, 2014: Fifteenth report. Ministry of Social Justice and Empowerment, Lok Sabha Secretariat. https://www.prsindia.org/sites/default/files/bill_files/SC%20report-%20Persons%20disabilities.pdf

TNN. (2015, 5 April). Disabled get only 0.56% of seats in higher education. *The Times of India*. www.timesofindia.indiatimes.com/home/educatiohttps:n/news/Disabled-get-only-0-56-of-seats-in-higher-education/articleshow/46810639.cms

UN General Assembly. (2015, 21 October). *Transforming our world: The 2030 agenda for sustainable development*. www.sustainabledevelopment.un.org/post2015/transformingourworld

UNESCO. (2009). World conference on higher education. The new dynamics of higher education and research for societal change and development. https://unesdoc.unesco.org/ark:/48223/pf0000183277

UNICEF. (n.d.). www.unicef.in/PressReleases/288/Government-of-India-announces-plan-to-make-education-disabledfriendly-by-2020

Yang, J., Schneller, C. & Roche, S. (Eds.) (2015). *The role of higher education in promoting lifelong learning*. UNESCO Institute for Lifelong Learning (UIL).

10

Assistive Technology in Higher Education

Udaya Kiran K. T.

The highest result of education is tolerance.

—*Helen Keller*

Introduction

Education provides opportunity to make most out of perceiver's faculties. Higher education brings people together by breaking barriers. Inclusive education builds an idyllic society where people with special needs can have access to information and contribute their best. The present chapter aims at discussing some of the technological possibilities for the visually impaired, which can make the teaching–learning experience in higher education better. The present chapter does not include technical information related to software or statistical information about various factors pertaining to disabilities.

The terms assistive technology, higher education and differently abled or disabled are defined by the concerned authorities. A few relevant definitions are quoted here. Differently abled students and teachers have special needs which can be fulfilled by providing accessibility, assistive technology and adaptive technology. The Rights of Persons with Disabilities Act, 2016, defines differently abled as—'"Person with disability" means a person with long term physical, mental, intellectual or sensory impairment which, in interaction with barriers, hinders his full and effective participation in society equally with others.'

The Act also defines benchmark disability as

'Person with benchmark disability' means, a person with not less than forty percent of a specified disability where specified disability has not been defined in measurable terms and includes a person with disability where specified disability has been defined in measurable terms, as certified by the certifying authority.[1]

Higher education can be defined as education at a college or university where subjects are studied at an advanced level. The term assistive technology can be understood as any item, piece of equipment or product system, whether acquired commercially off the shelf, modified or customized, that is used to increase, maintain or improve the functional capabilities of persons with disabilities. The above explanation of terminologies makes it clear that higher education for people with special needs, differently abled or disabled requires assistive or adaptive technology to provide equal participation in education and at workplace.

Education taught at college and university level involves advanced teaching methods or pedagogy which in turn necessitates the use of assistive technology for accessing information and also managing daily routine related to teaching, learning and research. Understanding assistive technology as expensive equipment is a common misconception among people with less information about the differently abled. The fact is, making any technology, device, structure or information easily accessible by differently abled can be categorized under this terminology. There are number of assistive technologies in vogue, ranging from locally available resources to high-end gadgets. Starting from initiating persons with disability towards education up to

---

[1] According to Section 2(r) of the Rights of Persons with Disabilities Act, 2016

enabling them to take up research or a profession of their choice, the use of technology depends mainly on its application and given situation rather than its functionalities.

Assistive technology devices can be categorized from users' point of view as the following:

- Based on disability
- Based on use/application
- Based on manufacturer or makers
- Low-technology and high-technology devices

Among these classifications, there can be further sub-classifications based on type, technology, software, hardware and so on. The main purpose of these devices or technology is to provide the differently abled an equal opportunity to have access to resources which are available for able-bodied people. The key focus here would be on people with eyesight impairment. There are software applications ranging from word processors to programming and remotely accessing computer or servers. The technology which is directly related to higher education is, predominantly, taken into consideration. Braille, speech, tactile and other alternative formats, which provide the user access to resources related to higher education ranging from scripts to software programmes, enable equal access to differently abled aspirants to study their choice of subject with less or no barrier.

Technology innovations in campus can open the doors for individuals with disabilities.

Screen Readers

A screen reader is a software programme which provides speech output for actions performed on the computer either by navigating with keyboard or mouse. Screen readers come with many features which are user friendly for the vision impaired or visually challenged such as text editing, screen navigation, menu options, web browsing and so on. Screen reader users can operate computer and perform common tasks using the software specially designed for the purpose. There are various screen readers available in the market based on operating system of the device. Windows PC supports Job Access with Speech (JAWS), Window Eyes, Macintosh computers/Apple supports Voiceover for both computers and mobile devices including tablets.

These screen readers also support some touchscreen tablets and Windows PCs. Main functionality of the screen reader is to provide speech output for all commands performed on the computer or mobile device. These screen readers provide access to vital information, which in turn helps visually challenged users to gain knowledge, teach, carry out research, participate in e-world with full potential. Some screen reader also come with Braille drivers. Braille driver is an additional piece of software integrated into screen readers, which provides Braille output along with text on either visual screen or speech or both. This helps users in reading the information present on screen in Braille simultaneously.

Mobile devices also support screen reader. Some of the major platforms include Android, Windows phone, iPhone Operating System (IOS) devices. Talkback is the major screen reader for Android, Narrator is the screen reader for Windows phone and Voiceover is the screen reader for IOS devices as mentioned above. Similar functionalities with a few device-specific restrictions such as size, upper limit for simultaneously opening multiple windows exist in these screen readers but greatly helps users in having access to essential information which are significant for both day-to-day and specific academic activities. These screen readers also come with Braille support which helps accessing information with Braille output.

Optical Character Recognition

Optical character recognition or OCR solutions are scanning and reading software helpful for visually challenged users to scan, convert data into editable format, process and read. These software range from add-ons to stand-alone applications and specific device designed for the purpose. Some of the major solutions include Freedom Scientific, ABBYY FineReader and so on. These software programmes allow visually challenged and low-vision users to scan and read printed documents. These solutions also make it easy to preserve documents which are not digitized. OCR software provides users with number of options including scanning–reading, editing, OCR correction under processing menu and saving to multiple formats such as Word, PDF, large text, Braille, audio and so on.

Kurzweil is another software well known among screen reader users. KNFB Reader is also an OCR solution which has both portable and stand-alone versions. These developments have provided visually challenged users great opportunity to access information, which is vital for research, teaching–learning and emerging as professionals in various fields. The accuracy of these software is still a challenge as it has not reached the peak. This is not because of the lack of technological advancement but the quality of source document, the software used to capture the image, the technology used, the awareness about the features of the software, the processing engine and the like.

Some of the software have reached considerable perfection in scanning–reading solutions with a few flaws, which is making the users to work around for optimum result. Significant feature in most of the OCR software is compatibility regarding orientation of the document, that is, the software can process the scanned document even if it is placed upside down on a printed page which makes visually challenged users to scan and read independently. Some software's come with orientation guide and other useful features which helps the users place documents in perfect position for better result. In India, there is still scope to develop these technologies for regional language in order to enable users from remote places to encourage towards the use and application of technology for knowledge dissemination.

Braille

Braille is a universal script which is adaptable to any language across the globe with permutation–combination of dots arranged in two rows and three columns making it six dots per cell. A letter or a character is represented by dots ranging from one to six, which is preceded by number sign, letter sign, capital sign and other indicators. Traditionally, Braille is embossed on thick paper with an embosser or Braille printer. Advent of technology has opened up new possibilities in Braille scripts. Presently, users can have Braille documents digitally on a Braille display or note taker which makes it easy to carry. The price of these devices is usually high because of the component used which makes the users to abstain from buying. However, there are number of options in these devices ranging from small display containing 12 cells to large displays with 80 cells in order to cater to the needs of the users.

Developing a low-cost device in Braille display is the need of the hour as it would enable Braille users to read, write and analyse a document without compromising on formatting, spelling and other parameters. It would be ideal to read in Braille for a visually challenged user rather than audio books, as it gives the option to read by character, line, paragraph and page with ease when compared to other alternative formats. Unfortunately, using Braille has not got its due in this technology era. Studies have suggested that Braille reading simulates the visual cortex. Experts opine that Braille users have the chances of being efficient with regard to academics when compared to the users of other alternative formats.

Braille displays or note takers come in different variants. The major manufacturers of Braille displays and note takers are Freedom Scientific, Optelec, PerkinElmer, Seika, Baum, HIMS, Humanware and so on. These devices display Braille characters in both six- and eight-dots mode. These displays are called refreshable because the dots are temporarily raised to communicate the actual character on a computer screen in Braille and refreshed as the text or display progress or the character changes. When a user navigates the document, the display changes accordingly, providing Braille output for the lines presently under focus. These Braille displays are capable of providing Braille output for math, science, computer notation, music notation/score along with the regular text. Many Braille displays come with Braille keyboard which helps in typing Braille on to a note taker or display and later saving either on device, computer and universal serial bus flash drive, depending on the model of the device. Braille displays also contain commands to navigate through character, line, page and so on.

Regional Language and Braille

Internationally, English is the prominent communicative language; hence computer-based applications are designed to suit English language. These developments have posed challenges to those who prefer to access documents in Indian regional languages. Efforts are on to develop full-fledged screen reader in regional languages. From past two decades, many attempts have been made to bring out the synthesizer voice for Indian regional languages. This includes the Indian Institute of Science and other research bodies. Though there is some progress, evident results are yet to come. Of late, a few software developers have ventured providing Braille and speech output in regional languages focusing Indian languages. NVDA, which stands for non-visual desktop access, is a group of volunteers who have come up with a screen reader software which is free. Though the software lacks some features, it provides an option for including Indian language voices. Commercially available JAWS has many features including support for Indian languages, speech and Braille. The software mentioned above is being used across the globe as a major screen reader. JAWS supports Hindi, Kannada and many Indian languages. With this option, users can read and write documents, check mails and perform regular tasks on computers that run Windows.

Braille Support

Presently, efforts are on to provide Braille support for many software. The leading Braille translation software is Duxbury Braille Translation (popularly known as DBT among Braille users), which converts any text to Braille in a given language. This software supports many Indian languages. The unique features of this software include back and forth Braille conversion, save to alternative formats, support for math text, support for music xml files and so on. Apart from DBT, there are a couple of Indian software working towards Braille support. Baraha could be the best example for software supporting English, Indian languages and Braille. Baraha contains commands which convert documents into Braille with a few clicks. This software also supports music notation writing for Indian music. Text can be converted to and from Braille in both ways, that is, from text to Braille and Braille to text including Unicode. This software also supports script convert giving user the choice of reading scripts of other languages in his/her native language. Braille embosser comes with driver software which also supports basic Braille conversion. Mobile phones also support Braille, hence, can be hooked up to Braille displays. Apple devices also come with Braille support built in, which can be enabled using Voiceover screen reader, which is a native software for all the Apple devices.

Web Accessibility

Presently, making most of the information accessible is part of many projects. Efforts in these directions are significant. Making the web page accessible is one more step closer to inclusive atmosphere. There are prescribed guidelines which explain web accessibility. The World Wide Web Consortium or W3C has issued guidelines to be followed while making the web content accessible. There are provisions in law to accommodate web accessibility. Mobile-based web browser accessibility and related guidelines are issued by Web Content Accessibility Guideline (WCAG), which is the authority related to mobile accessibility. With all these developments related to web-based and mobile-based accessibility, accessing data has become much easier and simpler.

Web accessibility includes—making web page easy to navigate with screen reader, providing alternative text for graphics, providing separate link to accessibility features, adapting screen-reader friendly layout design for web pages without compromising look and feel of the website. Mobile accessibility is including all the above features in mobile-based browsing via mobile devices and enabling accessibility mode or providing link which leads to accessible mode of a particular webpage. These developments have provided the differently abled with ample scope to accomplish their professional and academic goals.

Alternative Formats

Alternative formats provide differently abled users access to many mainstream data which is inaccessible otherwise. Alternative formats include large print, Braille, high contrast, audio, daisy and editable PDF which makes differently abled users have access to available resources without barriers. Alternative formats can be both converted and created with minimal technical help depending on the task involved. Creating accessible materials using locally available resources can also be useful in making the society more inclusive and congenial place for people with special needs.

Media and Accessibility

Media today serves information faster than ever before. Stream of media, including social media, web media, print media, audio and video media, acts as a bridge between people and nations. Challenges related to accessibility vary between these sources, situations and technology used. Though television can be called hub of information, accessibility is still inadequate. Some attempts have been made in making television accessible through speech feedback for menu navigation, described movies, accessible set-top box steps travelled and journey ahead is still skimpy. Web accessibility, as discussed above, makes it clear that the progress is significant in this regard. Print media and accessibility is in progress at different levels at various channels and situations. Audio and video media is partially accessible, but efforts are on giving a ray of hope for differently abled users. Availability of contents in alternative formats are still in the preliminary stage in India.

Considering all the above aspects related to accessibility in higher education, India is definitely marching towards becoming an accessible nation in the future. Many projects are aiming at making the public buildings more accessible. Public transport and related domains are gradually adapting accessibility feature. Booking ticket, getting information about arrival and departure of public transport is presently more accessible. Overall pace of making the society inclusive and information accessible is mixed as the effort at various facets of development is taking a different dimension with a different approach.

Academics and Accessibility

Examination system and related information are being made more accessible. Preparing question paper in alternative formats, providing examination-related information on the web in accessible formats, making online application accessible, making financial transaction accessible are in progress and visually challenged users are benefitted by these developments. Writing examination has become more accessible as the Government of India and University Grants Commission have issued order allowing visually challenged candidates to write exams using computer with screen reader. Effective implementation of the use of computers in examinations will make writing for candidates and evaluating for teachers trouble free. Spreading awareness about this can be considered significantly essential as it would solve the problem of getting scribes on time and boost the morale of differently abled.

Providing pace with accessibility feature might be challenging for a few organizations, where technology and trained persons are not in enough numbers. Such organizations can collaborate with centres that have these facilities. Making question paper and syllabus accessible is less complicated due to the availability of software which can convert the text into Braille with less or no information about Braille, that is, sighted users can also perform the task of converting text to alternative formats including Braille. Availability of Braille keyboard and Braille input methods in software have increased the option for Braille users to write in Braille and, later, convert it to text or other editable and viewable formats. This facility can be used to evaluate the answer scripts written by visually challenged candidates.

Accessible software which helps to collaborate remotely has provided an option to conduct examinations remotely. Audio and video calling software have made the job of conducting interviews and discussions easy for those who have difficulties in travelling to different places due to restricted mobility. Online libraries have made accessing information convenient, enabling differently abled to browse text and audio from their location. Indian repositories like Shodhganga and Inflibnet are providing updates about research by giving access to thesis which not only serves as resource but also provides food for thought, inspiring to carry out unique research in the respective fields.

Limitations

Every technology comes with its own advantages, but there are a few limitations which pose challenges to the users. Here are some of the limitations related to various technologies designed for differently abled.

Screen Reader

Screen readers are major source to acquire knowledge for visually challenged. However, these software's are designed in a few languages; hence, this could be a barrier for users of regional languages as the support is limited or constrained. Delay in updating scripts, compatibility-related issues, limitations in accessing some of the on-screen content are some impediments related to screen readers which necessitate sighted help.

OCR

Accessing printed materials for various tasks are part of activity for visually impaired today. Many of the OCR software have still not reached total accuracy in data recognition and processing. This greatly limits the access to available printed material. Handwritten documents are still not accessible. Many of the OCR software are designed in a few languages; thus, number of accessible languages is also limited. Due to high price and inaccuracy in OCR software, the technology is not yet free of challenges.

Braille Format

Braille format can be used both online and offline. Due to nonavailability of reliable software in all the languages, production and use of Braille documents are restricted to very few users. Braille hardwires such as Braille display are high priced and proprietary formats further limits the exchange of data between various platforms. Braille drivers and scripts are designed for specific platform, which is a great limitation in today's cloud computing world in accessing data over the internet. Regional differences in Braille code further makes it complicated in conversing or exchanging data internationally through this medium.

Daily Living

Presently, use of technology is inevitable in day-to-day activities. Identification of currency, colour, temperature, bills are some of the areas in which visually challenged are struggling to obtain the required result in spite of walking an extra mile. Though the advancement in this direction is commendable, it has many challenges which makes the visually challenged, in particular, and differently abled to look for workaround or trouble shooting.

In a nutshell, with all the facilities and advancement in technologies, a visually challenged professional can contribute his/her best to the society. Differently abled students can have access to mainstream resources in various formats. Visually challenged can opt to study subjects which has graphs, charts and equations, which has opened doors to science and mathematics, encouraging research in the field. New job opportunities can be considered as against conventional stereotype jobs which require basic skills. Change in thought process and innovation in technology has made a few skill-based jobs accessible for differently abled. Though the development in technology is not completely free of challenges or accessibility issues, there is definitely a ray of hope that further improvements in the technology and change in the mindset of able-bodied people and differently abled aspirants can work together with mutual cooperation and contribute through their knowledge and skills to the field of higher education and research.

PART V
Women and Higher Education

Chapter 11
Locating Women in India's Higher Education
Vagishwari S. P.

Chapter 12
Addressing Gender Parity in Higher Education:
Challenges and Concerns
Priyanca Mathur and Roshni Sharma

11

Locating Women in India's Higher Education

Vagishwari S. P.

Introduction

A major debate in feminist historiography has been that women are hidden in history or from history. Sheila Rowbotham argues about this issue succinctly, stating that women on the periphery of history is a foundational issue that contests the epistemological identity of the discipline itself. Joan Scott defending feminist historiography against accusations of ideological bias argued as to how traditional historians have established a mastery over history by segregating history as knowledge arising through neutral enquiry and ideology arising through consideration of interest, whereas there is no such thing as objective history. These arguments reflect issues of visibility of women not just in history but in all streams of theoretical frameworks, as well as in structuring of institutions too. The social learning theorists posit that behaviour and observable events override thoughts and feelings while framing opinions. By this rationale, it must be assumed that children, and later as adults, get rewarded for behaviour that is consistent with their gender (Donelson, 1998). Thus, while masculinity decides permissible roles for women in a professional space, socially determined notions of femininity prevents women from reaching out and reaching beyond, specifically in their professional lives. Hence, one of the most pertinent query for scholars and researchers working on marginalization of identities would be why should gender be considered and how does it become an issue in higher-academic spaces too.

Higher education is accepted as a formative space that facilitates crystallization of cultural practices and nuances. It is a space where debates of the communities are widely expressed and heard, resulting in the formation of identities, defining of roles and responsibilities. Very interestingly, all hierarchical power structures, from political to social, too, get firmed up here. It is these possibilities that interests non-state players to heavily be involved in higher-education sector. In addition to all of these, higher education also becomes a contested space because of the dominos effect, wherein gendered beliefs and practices of high school enters into college and university environs too. Thus, from being considered a liberal space, higher education, many a time, becomes a conforming space for marginalization of caste, class and gender.

Contextualizing Women in Higher Education

Higher education, as a domain representing the intellectual capacities of societies, experienced a significant shift in its identity, with liberalization and privatization of economies all over the world. An interesting aspect of it is the fact that there has been an increase in the enrolment of women in higher education between 1999 to 2005. It has been accepted that there are now more women in higher education sector all over the world. This introduces the question, is there a feminization of higher education underway. This is a relevant query because there has been a significant increase in the number of women who are accessing higher education, all over the world, including North America and Europe. However, there are immense dichotomies accompanying this new change. It is stated that despite this increase, women have been marginalized within universities, by being excluded 'not just from the classrooms, offices and meeting places, but also from the discourses, texts and subjects on which university education is based'. (Hills & Rowan, 2002 p. 2)

Thus, a hierarchical organization of university identity has gradually emerged in terms of responsibilities, activities and functions, wherein who has access to what is also, by and large, gendered. Interestingly, research, considered as a knowledge-construction pursuit, has become privileged above teaching and administration. And the entire process of research is social, financial and associated with power. A constant factor that women in higher education have to grapple with is the holding and wielding of power, in a professional set up. Patriarchy determines that all power of decisions is executed by male faculty, or women as heads or deans or directors have to comply with the structural arrangement, outlined by their male authorities. This reflects, in turn, over remuneration, project allotment, financial gains and returns. As Reskin (Reskin, 1988) states, 'basic cause of income gap is not sexual segregation, but by their ability to establish rules to distribute valued resources in their favor'. This privileging of power is seen through the protégé system too, where powerful men within universities and higher education system serve as sponsors for the entry of a novice, as well as for the advancement within the hierarchy.

This protégé system is used to favour the 'boys' or also used as an exploitative tool against women. To quote Linda Lindsey (Lindsey, 1997), professional networking, which is inaccessible to women, due to their multiple social and familial responsibilities, creates old-boy system that operates to keep power in the hands of a few designated men. Women are under-represented and are constantly concentrated at the lower levels of administration, without any access to policymaking strata of the university. They are also more engaged with teaching, documenting and organizing activities outside of the curricula. They have less say in formulation of curricula too, which they, ultimately, have the responsibility of carrying it to class room. While this is true of women in higher education in India, similar situation exists in major areas of Asia, Africa and South America. Women are also globally under-represented in science, both theoretical and application oriented, as well as technology-based disciplines.

Higher Education as a Gendered Space

All of these are not just an act of segregation and denial. The malady goes deeper than that. The issue here is severe gendering of higher education space itself. It is gendering of roles, responsibilities and opportunities. The gendered division of labour (Lynch, 2010) suggested that academia is constructed as a 'carefree zone', which assumes that academics have no commitments other than to their profession. This assumption transforms into an ideal at certain phases to be realized at all costs. This premeditation disqualifies women from academia to a large extent, due to their inherent role of being a caretaker and caregiver that formulates her social identity. It is a 'negative equity' at workplace for women (Guillaume & Pochic, 2009). The entire discourse of women in higher education needs to be rooted within the framework of postcolonialism and modernism.

The essentiality of locating it arises in the context of how modernity placed women within a didactic arrangement of progress and control. As Jürgen Habermas noted, modernity refused to accept tradition unreflectively. Modernity was a process of moving away from tradition and designing of a rational future world. 'It remains my essential point that modernism amounted to a double psychological, liberation for consumers of high culture as much as for its producers' (Gay, 2007). The irony was, in this liberation, women neither figured as consumers nor producers of high culture. Modernity was intended only for the White bourgeois male, with the exclusion of women, workers and non-Whites. Education, which was rooted in this Euro-centric modernist movement, inherited the passive-aggressive policy of ascribing marginal roles to women. Postcolonial feminist thinkers have questioned this marginalization. While debating the issue of non-visibility of women in public spheres such as education, they have progressed beyond just the inclusion of White, middle-class, English-speaking women. Postcolonial and postmodernist feminist thinkers have even questioned as to whom they are representing, when they speak for 'women'.

This self-reflectionis crucial in the context of discussing women in higher education because of the prevalence of widespread imbalance in terms of social, economic and cultural background that they are from. The issue for women is compounded with the additional burden of having to be conformists in the choice of disciplines as well as roles and positions that they aspire to. 'Will an education geared towards femininity weaken the growth of the mind' (Friedan, 2001). This has been the ever-lurking question. This is evident in the area of higher education, where determinants such as gendered space and social roles limit women to a great extent. As Runte and Mills claimed (Runte & Mills, 2004) that women who invariably 'navigate between parental and employee roles, they have to pay the "toll" for crossing the boundary between work and family'. Here, one needs to acknowledge that unmarried, without children or parent women, who are traditionally considered as not being burdened by 'personal/familial responsibilities' are also not the visible faces of higher education. All levels, categories of leadership in higher education, which range from administration to academia, have a common feature of marginalization of women.

Such approaches obviate the possibilities of women functioning in these spheres as contributors or producers of knowledge. By far, higher education envisages women more as consumers of created knowledge. Hence, increasing number of women in higher education does not necessarily translate into formation of a space for a discourse on it. This is primarily due to the process of systemic operations, wherein all systems are inclusive of only contributors. Systems and institutions hold themselves responsible for providing leadership, which will move, sustain and help in overall growth. By an internal systemic default, women are not a part of this clique and are as consumers who have no role to play in any of the decision-making processes. One of the more pointed notes in relation to women and the roles that they are accredited is the gender-stereotyping imagery that revolves around their role and position.

Gender stereotypes are an organized set of beliefs about the personal attributes of women and men (Ashmore & Del Boca, 1979). Thus, the lens through which women as educators are viewed is coloured by their gendered attributes rather than their acquired capacity to perform the role. The media intensifies this stereotyping imagery of women by upholding the traditional construct of thought and culture. In their representation, while men are the norm, women are less visible and confined to the role of being a nurturing and serving agent, which is devoid of any intellectual vibrancy. Hence, such reinforcement of retrograde views frames the responses of the system towards women in the field of education.

Framing and Executing the Content: Issues and Concerns

This in turn also raises another question of what does and should constitute content and pedagogy in higher-education spaces? This search is clearly delineated by Joan Scott, when she traces the evolution of history of gender over decades up to the 1990s. She states that within three decades, from political feminism to women's history to gender, a congruent de-politicization of the academic study of feminine has taken place (Scott, 1991, pp. 42–43). Continuing this, Alan Munslow argues that there are words or concepts that defy signification because they carry culturally contradictory meanings (Munslow, 2000, p. 228). This deconstructionist notion of language affects content too, when it is placed in the context of curricula in higher education. For instance, the idea of women as supplement falls in this category. Here, supplement means both an addition to or a substitute for what pre-exists.

This effectively captures the dilemma of what should constitute content in higher education. Should the content be with women's issues as an added part, or should it reflect a thorough restructuring of epistemology from feminist perspective? The former will appear more as an appendage to traditional constructions of disciplinary boundaries. The latter is more problematic in terms of the foundations of disciplines itself. However, that does not eliminate the need to reconstruct from women's perspective. Because anything otherwise will be contradictory to the principles of democracy and equity.

Pedagogical practices are considered as a way of raising consciousness of the receiver/learner. In relation to content with aspects of gender/women, pedagogical process involves seeking non-traditional or non-established sources of knowledge. One has to move away from accredited texts, due to their inherent imbalances towards gender representation. This then brings to the forefront the practice of looking at lived-in experiences, narratives, autobiographies and oral narratives and histories. These have to be contextualized and analysed as they are powerful empirical sources for constructing new frontiers of knowledge. Such an approach will create new frontiers of exploration of experiences, which will then reflect on the process with which the complexity of issue is understood.

Feminist historiographers have always stated that this is a very required orientation, as the structural context is closely interlinked with societal actions and ideas. Teaching and implementing feminist perspective, by using gender-conscious pedagogy, stimulates students to confront their acceptance of 'false consciousness'. (Cuesta & Witt, 2014). It should always be remembered that the stakeholders/learners are constituents of societal identity and are endowed with civil rights. So, it is imperative to have a shared experience between the teacher and the taught for a greater understanding of the society that they live in as well as for a better interpersonal relationship.

This experiential understanding as part of pedagogy is needed because the context from which such experiences emerge is always analysed as well as problematized. This is constantly upheld by libertarian educationists, who argue that people must feel invested in the thoughts and ideas that are being discussed. It brings in a certain proprietorial feeling, when their lived-in experiences are the focus of study. This is very much required both as content and as pedagogy in higher education spaces, specially while dealing with women and the marginalized. Such an approach is enriching because there is a conviction that content and pedagogy cannot be insulated from the voices of the oppressed. Rather it has to be dialogically constructed. (Freire, 1993, p. 105). This self-reflexivity is apparent in higher-education spaces that are engaged in humanities and social science discourses. Here, it becomes a challenge for facilitators to design pedagogic methods that interrelates experiences with knowledge. This is extremely difficult due to the underpinnings of nuances that exists within each experience.

It is also complicated due to experiences being relative in nature and dominated by considerations of caste, class, gender, religion, ethnicity, political formulations and cultural determinants. These considerations change the trajectory of the discourses as well as the idea of how they can be conceived, taught and understood. These subjective considerations always dominate the thought process of both the teacher and the taught, meaning gender-conscious pedagogy requires a certain effort to move away from subjective positions, in order to create critical thinking so that it can contribute to social justice, inclusiveness and equality.

One of the major issues in relation to learners in higher-education spaces is that many are not familiar with the theoretical framework that binds concepts of equality, justice, egalitarianism and rights. They are aware of these violations in passing but are unable to refute these violations logically. This in turn makes them unaware of the impact that these concepts have on social distinctions. A major factor in gender-conscious pedagogy is to: (a) make students from marginalized sections aware of the inherent 'wrongness' of these violations and (b) sensitize students in general about the unacceptability of these violations, not just as an act but as thought too. The emphasis here has to be that these concepts are independent of social background and are fundamental to human existence.

Ruptured Approach towards Women in Higher Education: India

In India, locating women in education, both at elementary and higher level, is fraught with the difficult task of first retrieving her identity and roles in society. This process is, in itself, complex due to redefinition of women's position in the Indian society by colonial intervention and sensibilities. Colonial restructurings of gender and the curricular institutionalization of literature both worked to undermine the authority in Indian literatures and undercut the societies that gave rise to them (Tharu & Lalita, 1993). The first generation of educated women found a voice; they wrote about their lives and about the conditions of women. The second generation acted. They articulated the needs of women, critiqued their society and developed their own institutions (Forbes, 1998).

Colonized Indiawitnessed tentative steps towards including women within the streams of education, supported by political leadership and sociocultural movements. Post-independence India saw education commissions being set up from the 1950s and five-year plans, all of them struggling to create space for women's education. Even the Kothari Commission of 1964, credited with heralding major changes in education, devoted very less attention towards women in education, both at primary and higher levels. All the committees failed to envisage a link between women's education, their position of equality and national development. Paradoxically, while these committees concentrated on elementary education, women's enrolment in higher education was not as dismal as in primary levels. The impetus to technical education in India after independence saw women being visible here. However, as Karuna Chanana remarks, the national agenda helped women of the upper-middle class and upper castes to enter the portals of higher education (Chanana, 1988). Even with this composition of upper-caste elite women, the dilemma of adopting gender-sensitive pedagogy has been one end of the spectrum. An equally important point is the case of empowering women through information and communication technology (ICT) education in higher-education centres.

ICTs are the driving forces of change in a globalized world and a liberalized world economy. An important area of this process is trade. Trade liberalization and flow of foreign capital has penetrated into various levels from export processing zones to that of agriculture. It has also resulted in an unmitigated expansion of informal sector in rural and urban India. A notable part of this process is women not being defined as workers but only as home producers. They do not appear in labour statistics and are not protected by labour laws and, therefore, are not organized (Mies, 1998). Thus, devoid of a status as organized labour, women also face the herculean task of adapting to the extensive use of ICT in workspace.

ICTs provide access to information and resources that help in transcending social barriers and gain entry to mainstream development. However, their uneven distribution and non-availability in terms of access to it for women in semi-urban and rural India has been a major stumbling block. Women are yet to cross this digital divide to be an integral part of the digital world. Lack of access to ICT, thus, becomes a significant factor in their marginalization from economic, social and political participation (Huyer & Carr, 2002; Mitter, 1999). Access, here, needs to be relooked at, not just from the perspective of availability of technology but also the required training to understand, use and adapt to it. While basic literacy is needed to learn to use and navigate the Internet, advanced learning systems, in relation to research, are essential in higher education.

The ability to manoeuvre through ICT for purposes of research must also be the content part of the curricula. If this is not considered, then women end up choosing the well-travelled path of majoring in humanities and social sciences only. A study shows that 40 per cent of women, who enter college wanting to be scientists, switch to other majors (Masters, 1994). Though the situation has witnessed a vast improvement, two decades down the line, it is still not significant enough to be considered as mainstream development.

Despite these changes, scholars have mapped out distinct, gender-specific patterns at undergraduate, graduate and doctoral-degree levels. 'As would be expected, women are concentrated in nursing, literature, home economics, certain of the social sciences, education and library science, with men dominating areas such as mathematics, the physical sciences and architecture' (Lindsey, 1997, p. 284). There are psychological roadblocks accentuated with competition for grades and grants at universities for projects and funding. Women have to deal with restrictive admission policies too, wherein a certain proportion of seats get reserved on the basis of gender too. It is widely accepted that academic careers, in universities, are based on protégé practices, where talented students are under the supervision of an established faculty. It is here that women students are at a disadvantage. They spend less time with faculty advisors, are susceptible to sexual exploitation and are also burdened by familial responsibilities.

The position of female faculty is no better than this. It has been observed that women operate in adjunct positions, without reaching the most senior organizational positions. It has to be acknowledged that extensive reforms have been initiated in higher education from 1990's that have accommodated women in managerial positions, quality assurance and in HR areas. However, many women find themselves in 'ivory basements' (Eveline, 2004) or the 'velvet ghettos' of communication, finance and human resource management (Guillaume & Pochic, 2009). Ryan and Haslam (2007) theorized the way women are placed very frequently in not-so-desirable and management areas, that is, 'glass cliffs', in which the parameters for selection of men and women are heavily gendered. Selections of employees for rewarding and unrewarding organizational tasks are also based on genders. All these place women at a disadvantageous position.

In some locations, there has been a feminization of penultimate leadership positions. In Australia, for example, women constitute 40 per cent of the pro-vice chancellors but only 18 per cent of the vice chancellors (Bagilhole & White, 2011). Absence of women from senior positions, such as directors, heads of departments, professors is also a major issue. The criteria laid down by their structural prioritization itself is very gendered. For instance, women are denied often because they have fewer publications in lesser-known journals. However, their teaching loads are either not considered as one of the significant qualifiers or, even when done, is marked down. In contrast, research projects and publications are up on the ladder and marked high. This kind of prioritization as well as hierarchically privileging certain categories of academic work disqualifies women.

Higher educationis plagued by discriminations of caste, class and gender. Women are entering into higher education spaces but in lesser numbers, specifically in certain domains. This entry itself should provide a momentum to establish sustainable growth environment that is more inclusive. Transparency, clear demarcation of rules of selection and policy statements of an inclusive culture alone do not provide satisfactory results. There needs to be a paradigm shift in organizational structures and approaches towards being inclusive. While content and pedagogic practices need to be gender sensitive, there must also be a drastic shift in valuing various academic initiatives in higher-education spaces. There is no scientific validation in deciding that mentoring, teaching and documenting are lower-order skills, in comparison to publications, networking and socializing. Academic audits in higher-education spaces need to be redesigned, wherein individual strengths and institutional experiences will emerge as major qualifying determinants. Strict adherence to gender ratio in terms of leadership within an organization will also be a positive step.

References

Ashmore, R. D., & Del Boca, F. K. (1979). Sex stereotypes and implicit personal theory: Toward a cognitive-social psychological conceptualization. *Sex Roles, 5,* 219–248.
Bagilhole, B., & White, K. (Eds.). (2011). *Gender, power and management: A cross-cultural analysis of higher education.* Palgrave Macmillan.
Chanana, K. (Ed.). (1988). *Socialisation, education and women: Explorations in gender identity.* Orient Longman.
Cuesta, M., & Witt, A. K. (2014). How gender conscious pedagogy in higher education can stimulate actions for social justice in society. *Social Inclusion, 2*(1), 12–23.
Donelson, F. E. (1998). *Women's experiences: A psychological perspective* (p. 159). McGraw Hill.
Forbes, G. (1998). *Women in modern India* (p. 61). Cambridge University Press.
Freire, P. (1993). *Pedagogy of the oppressed.* Penguin.
Friedan, B. (2001). *The feminine mystique* (p. 172). W. W. Norton and Company.
Gay, P. (2007). *Modernism—The lure of heresy* (p. 30). William Heinemann.
Guillaume, C., & Pochic, S. (2009). What would you sacrifice? Access to top management and the work–life balance. *Gender, Work & Organization, 16*(1), 14–36.
Hills, E., & Rowan, L. (2002). Feminist academics as nomadic subjects: Reconceptualizing women in universities. Advancing Women in Leadership. www.advancingwomen.com
Huyer, S., & Carr, M. (2002). Information and communication technologies: A priority for women. Gender *Technology and Development, 6*(1), 85–100.
J, Eveline. (2004). *Ivory basement leadership: Power and invisibility in the changing university.* University of Western Australia Press.
Lindsey, L. L. (1997). *Gender roles: A sociological perspective* (p. 258). Prentice Hall.
Lynch, K. (2010). Carelessness: A *hidden doxa* of *higher education.* CHEER/ESRC Seminar series 'Imagining the University of the Future', Seminar 2: What are the Disqualified Discourses in the Knowledge Society? Centre for Higher Education and Equity Research (CHEER), University of Sussex. www.sussex.ac.uk/education/cheer/esrcseminars/seminar2
Masters, B. (1994, April). Staying the science course. *Washington Post Education Review, 3*(8), 10.
Mies, M. (1998). Globalization of the economy and women's work in a sustainable society. *Gender, Technology and Development, 2*(1), 3–37.
Mitter, S. (1999). Globalization, technological changes and the search for a new paradigm for women's work. *Gender, Technology and Development, 3*(1), 1–16.

Munslow, A. (2000). *The Routledge companion to historical studies.* Routledge.

Reskin, B. F. (1988). Bringing the man back in: Sex differentiation and the devaluation of woman's work. *Gender and Society, 2*(1), 58–81.

Runte, M., & Mills, A. J. (2004). Paying the toll: A feminist post-structural critique of the discourse bridging work and family. *Culture and Organization, 10*(3), 237–249.

Ryan, M. K., & Haslam, S. A. (2005). The glass cliff: Evidence that women are over-represented in precarious leadership positions. *British Journal of Management, 16*(2), 81–90.

Scott, J. W. (1991). Women's history. In P. Burke (Ed.), *New perspectives on historical writing* (pp. 42–66). Pennsylvania State University Press.

Tharu, S., & K, Lalita. (Ed.). (1993). *Women writing in India 600 B. C. to the Present, Volume I: 600 B.C. to the Early 20th Century* (p. 10). Oxford University Press.

12

Addressing Gender Parity in Higher Education
Challenges and Concerns

Priyanca Mathur and Roshni Sharma

Introduction

Governments across the globe have been working to balance out the Gender Parity Index especially in the field of higher education, in order to facilitate a more inclusive development. Though at a slow pace, there has been a humongous growth in the numbers of women enrolling for higher education and the global gender parity, which is 68.6 per cent to be precise.[1] However, the status of the same in developing countries is a different picture, as there, the gender parity in the field of education is yet close to 20 per cent of the gaps (Global Gender Gap Report, 2020). Thus, the picture remains gloomy, despite the significant progress been made in the said field to promote equality and social justice.[2] The marginalization of women is even further when it comes to access to higher decision-making levels in higher education. Working women, like all women, face 'double jeopardy'—the reality of confronting discrimination because of their gender and by virtue of being a minority.

Contextualizing the same in the Indian model, last seven years have witnessed a minimal gender gap in higher education. The gross enrolment ratio suggests that there were 85 females as against 100-male enrolments in higher education in 2018–2019.[3] Despite these figures, studies still focus on the embedded inequalities with respect to women being under-represented at the higher positions in higher education. In the *Global Gender Gap Report*, India ranked at 87th position in terms of gender equality. This has been a norm despite the National Policy for Empowerment of Women (2001) focusing on the vital need to condense the gender gap in higher education and the focus of the last Twelfth Five-year Plan (2012–2017) on decreasing the gender imbalances in higher education. Alongside, voices from academia have repeatedly argued the significance of having diverse perspectives on board (see Catalyst, 2013). Interestingly, this feature is not limited geographically. Rather, a similar kind of situation exits in most of the countries of the world. For instance, nations like the UK, USA and Australia also have similar stories.[4]

This chapter seeks to interrogate the reasons behind the low representation of women as leaders, such as VCs and administrators within higher education, despite studies showing a worldwide boom in higher education of women.[5] The question that needs to be asked is—why does this 'gap' exists even after a rise in the enrolment of women in higher education? Despite improved access of women to higher education, there still remain many educational inequities when it comes to women faculty, as most of them remain concentrated at the lower rungs of the academic ladder and not many reach managerial leadership positions.

Theoretical Background—Why Study Women in Higher Education?

There is ample empirical evidence globally that demonstrates the glaring absence of gender in the analysis of higher-education policy. While studies focus on female enrolment into courses, there isn't much data available on the percentage of women as staff or other higher positions in the domain of higher education. Existing studies show that while some women are able to occupy senior-leadership positions, their number still remains dismally low. Two decades ago, Wenniger and Conroy had highlighted that while women students were slowly becoming majorities in college campuses, they still lacked the rights they deserved as, 'the cultural tradition of male dominance still prevails in academic leadership, teaching, curricula, and standards for promotion and tenure' (2000, p. 3). This has been attributed to a variety of complex interplaying factors.[6]

While, until the 1990s, women entered institutions of higher education in countries like India to mainly study arts subjects or general education, today, they study both new and traditionally labelled 'masculine' disciplines like hard sciences and engineering. However, their percentage still remains significantly low. The *Global Gender Gap Report* of the World Economic Forum stated that in the STEM field (i.e., science, technology, engineering and mathematics), women still are under-represented. Such an under-representation has also been the result of the stereotyping image of a scientist as 'a man who wears a white coat and works in lab' (Mead & Metraux, 1957, p. 386). This, in result, has only strengthened in associating the 'masculine' traits with such disciplines.

There has been research to study the gendered impact of changes like these on social change and gender equity and to interconnect the participation and subject choice of women in India's system of higher education (Chanana, 2000, 2006). However, Chanana (2020) recently has dismissed the argument of feminist scholars of the 'double burden' borne by women and the conflict between their professional and personal roles as insufficient in explaining this exclusion of women from senior academic roles. She points out that while attempts to address the gender inequality in the corporate world have been made by pumping up the figure of female employment in senior positions, the higher education institutions (HEIs), however, have not been positively impacted by such a strategy.[7]

The process of 'othering' the women as a group is not a new phenomenon (Brons, 2015). Women across the globe have witnessed tough times to make their voices heard in the decision-making process, regardless of the space that they are in, being excluded, and therefore, the position of women in leadership roles in higher education cannot be treated in isolation from the general status of women in society. Davis and Maldonado (2015) have studied the implications of race and gender for African–American women in academia.[8] Fitzgerald has examined the contribution of women as senior leaders in universities across Australia and New Zealand to reveal the challenges and complexities they face; how, in academia, they 'undertake a great deal of labour and emotional toil and, despite decades of affirmative action strategies and equity legislation, still struggle to claim a leadership space as their own' (2014, p. 2). The field of higher education does not show any different picture. Though there has been improvement with more women taking part in university-leadership roles than before, the percentage is still lower, especially in research institutions (Berg, 2019). Besides, the gender gap increases with the levels of seniority.[9] As a matter of fact, only 6.67 per cent of Indian institutes are headed by women.[10] The scenario is no different in the Western world. According to the American Council on Education's American College President Study, 2017, only 30 per cent of the university president positions were handled by women, which has only been a 4 per cent increase since 2011 (Bartel, 2018).

Policy Questions: Barriers and Enablers

One of the primary reasons for the low percentage of women in this sector is attributed to the traditional patriarchal role that women have been performing as caretakers in the private sphere (Ghaus, 2013). The role of women being associated within the four walls of the household while men's role being associated with productivity (Kameshwara & Shukla, 2018). Unfortunately, this practice continues to exist in the

Indian society, where men take up more challenging roles in decision-making and women's role is assigned for supporting (Khandelwal, 2002). After seven decades of gaining independence, the continuous existence of such prejudices within the Indian society has added significantly to the deepening of gender inequalities in the system.

Deshmane, in her study of women employees at Bangalore University, Karnataka, India, has thrown light on the persisting dominating patriarchal culture which deters and undermines their efforts for academic leadership and progress (2014). Verma (2015) did a similar study in Lucknow University and found that despite visible accomplishments, a persistent gender gap remained at the top administrative–academic positions; female administrators faced subtle barriers in academia, which were not faced by male administrators; expectations from female-university leaders was higher than from their male counterparts, and finally, female-academic leaders received limited support from the top administration at their institutions which, time and again, has discouraged women from seeking leadership roles. Even if women who manage to climb up the ladder and seek promotion and supervision, they become targets of workplace bullying (Hollis, 2016).

Howe-Walsh and Turnbull (2016) have examined perceived barriers by science and technology faculty in assuming leadership roles in universities in the UK. They highlight the existence of male-dominated networks, the effects of organizational influences such as short-term work arrangements and psychological reasons like harassment and intimidation, leading to their own lack of self-confidence.

There is an absence of gender equality in recruitment and selection right at the beginning of the career followed by the absence of accountability and transparency in the institutional processes during the commencement of the career. Besides, in the peer-review-scoring process for publication, gender discrimination has been found and women faculty also find themselves deprived of the social capital of social networks.[11] Women find themselves in an institutional culture, wherein they have few female role models to look up to, and unfortunately, also at times in situations, they are at the receiving end of sexism and harassment at the workplace. Thus, to survive at such work cultures, women need greater self-efficacy beliefs, perseverance and resilience to push away the 'imposter syndrome' that stops them from internalizing their accomplishments and believing in their self-worth. 'Doubting their own ability to gain promotion is a reason in its own right to create a barrier to career advancement' (2016, p. 9).

Another factor that acts as a barrier for lesser number of women in leadership positions in higher education can be attributed to the mindset of viewing women as the 'second class citizens of the university' (Phadke & Roy, 2017). This phenomenon does not just persists in the aforementioned field. A similar situation also exists in the medicine, where women surgeons are 'bullied, harassed and discriminated by their male counterparts'.[12] Such an attitude cushions the male perspective of being able to achieve and perform stronger and challenging roles than women. The general perception of associating traits like competence and authority is attached with people at the higher positions, and because of the stereotypical beliefs, it is assumed that men are more efficient in taking up such roles, constituting a major structural barrier with respect to women's entry into the top positions (Lühe, 2014). All India Survey on Higher Education data for 2016–2017 indicates that as low as 17 per cent of VC, pro-VC and director positions across universities in India are held by women; that's one woman for every five men. And in no state is the share of women professors more than 40 per cent.[13]

As recent as the last year, for the first time, Jamia Milia Islamia got its first woman VC, Dr Najma Akhtar, and recently, a public state university—Ambedkar University, Delhi, appointed its very first woman VC, Professor (Dr) Anu Singh Lather. Adding on to the list, Dr Sonajharia Minz also got appointed in May 2020 as the VC of Sido Kanhu Murmu University, Jharkhand. She is also the second woman tribal VC in the history of India.[14]

Further, this gender disparity aggravates because of the existing intersection of other identities, such as caste, religion, region and tribe, adds on to a much more vulnerable position of women in the field of higher education (Nath, 2014). Referring to the USA model, Armstrong and Jovanovic (2015) argue that such an intersectionality has been playing a crucial role in the under-representation of women associated with different identities, especially in the STEM fields, which are considered to be 'masculine' in nature. Similarly, the supremacy of White men informed by efficiency and dominance continues to serve as the basis for strengthening the gender disparity at leadership roles (Agosto & Roland, 2018). This has led to the further discrimination especially for women of colour, keeping them locked out of opportunity (Smith, 2013). In the USA, Black women face unfair treatment, get bullied and are threatened about losing their jobs, which affect the career of these women (Hollis, 2018).

Balancing childcare and family responsibilities become an additional challenge for women in academia as in all other professions, as here it gets compounded with competitiveness of the additional burdens of acquiring grants and funding for research projects. Often, women choose to take a career break when they plan to start a family, and this plucks them out of networking and tenure which is crucial in their careers. Often, thus, childbirth and marriage are said to be the two biggest barriers for women in academia. It has even been seen that during recruitment women face the invisible barrier that their prospective employers think that she may become a liability if/when she marries or has a child. Thus, they also face differential treatment.

Women in academia often complain of the quantitative lack of women role models at higher positions for them to look up to and learn from. This also ends up perpetuating the cycle of male leadership and an institutional gendered culture. Women often refer to hurdles in approaching the informal networks which are usually governed by men. They need to be heard so that they don't feel that they are outliers, as often they are forced to become assertive so that they are not silenced (Davis, 2012).

Thus, more women at higher levels need to support the entry of women amongst them. Women need to become their own biggest enablers. What is primarily needed is a shift in the mindset of people in the society, men and women alike, to accept and allow women into the 'boys clubs'. Women need stronger professional networks which create pipelines that empower them.

While the few women at the top demonstrate the resilience that they have developed over the years, there are still so many others who are still struggling in their own battles confronting entrenched discrimination and disparity. There is a necessity for universities to conduct an audit of the gender breakdown of brief contracts so that efforts can be made to provide greater job security to women. This can cut the pervasive organizational myths that women are not good enough for these jobs and reiterate, instead, the truth that women actually perform skilfully in negative environments and demonstrate their ability to perform tenaciously and rise above it all. Women know when the playing field is not level, how to sit and remain at the table in order to make their presence known (Davis, 2012, p. 151)

Conclusion

There is a need to make policies more inclusive and diverse with the approach of promoting gender diversity and being more sensitive in mainstreaming the role of women leadership within higher education. A strong stance could be taken in the aspect of developing ambition amongst women in society, so that they are in a better position to take up challenging roles, which otherwise gets sidelined in prioritizing their family responsibility (Sandberg, 2013).

Despite all advancements, studies still show that diverse contexts of gender consideration still influence the choices made for women when it comes to choosing what they can study, that in the family the father still played the prominent role in deciding the subject choice, and so, gender still mediated the entire decision-making process (Gautam, 2015). This surrender of agency goes right up to the top and impacts the entry of women in higher levels of decision-making in higher education. When gender concerns deprive women from their agency of determining their subject choices, the process of deprivation only adds up to the top, as it makes women believe that they do not deserve this.

From childhood, women are reared to believe that the major attributes found in most professional and occupational roles, such as persistence, drive, personal dedication, aggressiveness and emotional detachment are considered to be masculine. So, when a woman exercises her agency and aims for positions at higher levels, her choice 'involves her in conflicts and ambiguities, and given societal and biological demands on women, her choice may require her to adopt a complex life-style to accommodate both home and work responsibilities' (Estler, 1975, p. 378). What stood true and was discovered empirically nearly four decades ago stands true even now.

Notes

1. https://www.weforum.org/reports/gender-gap-2020-report-100-years-pay-equality
2. For instance, the Millennium Development Goals and the Sustainable Development Goals.
3. https://mhrd.gov.in/sites/upload_files/mhrd/files/statistics-new/AISHE%20Final%20Report%202018-19.pdf
4. The gender divide in leadership positions in higher education has been highlighted by Karen Jones et al. (2018), in their study 'Perspectives on Women's Higher Education Leadership Around the World'. On similar lines, Morley (2014) provides numbers of women vice chancellors (VCs) across the globe, and in this list, right at the bottom is Hong Kong with no female as a VC. Next on the ladder are Kuwait (2%), Japan (2.3%), India (3%), Turkey (7%) and the European Union (EU) which has only 13 per cent of VC positions being held by women, while the UK reports 14 per cent. All these countries' numbers are quite dismal.
5. Lower inequality of non-cognitive skills among women than men imply that, for the currently relevant portion of the supply curve,

elasticities of supply to college would be greater for women than men since heterogeneity in total costs of college attendance would be lower for women. Greater average non-cognitive skills of women than men imply that the supply of women to college would be greater than that of men when their total benefits were the same. The gender differences in mean non-cognitive skills implies that as total benefits from college narrowed over time between men and women, the lower average full college cost of women could help explain why women overtook men in their likelihood of graduating from college. (Becker et al., 2010, p. 21)

6. Morley and Crossouard (2015), in their study titled 'Women in Higher Education Leadership in South Asia: Rejection, Refusal, Reluctance, Revisioning', examine various reasons that lead to women being denied senior leadership positions and cite them to be the following—discriminatory recruitment, selection and promotion procedures, gendered-career pathways or exclusionary networks and practices in women-unfriendly institutions.
7. In her work, Chanana (2020) has discussed the nationwide orientation and training programme for women faculty of the University Grants Commission (UGC). It cuts across discipline areas in Indian HEIs, attempts to support gender inclusivity by establishing a broad-based network of women faculty, helping them gain higher visibility, leave the 'sticky' floor and help them claim their rightful place in senior leadership positions.
8. When a phenomenological research method was used to put forth the participants' stories and comprehend their common experiences, the results showed that the women confirmed that race and gender informed their development as leaders in academia.
9. http://www3.weforum.org/docs/WEF_GGGR_2020.pdf
10. https://www.hindustantimes.com/education/only-6-67-indian-institutes-headed-by-women-report/story-YXgkKKg64HlWlED5pop3WP.html
11. This discrimination further aggravates when/if the first-author position is predominated by male authors and women faculties are pressurised to demonstrate their ability to obtain grants and publish research papers in peer-reviewed journals in order to secure their promotions amidst the 'boys clubs'.
12. https://blogs.scientificamerican.com/voices/female-surgeons-are-still-treated-as-second-class-citizens/
13. https://www.newslaundry.com/2018/02/03/women-academia-india-teaching-harassment-ugc-data
14. https://enewsroom.in/jharkhand-tribal-vice-chancellor-university/ accessed on 12 July 2020

References

Agosto, V., & Roland, E. (2018). Intersectionality and educational leadership: A critical review. *Review of Research in Education, 42*(1), 255–285.

Armstrong, M. A., & Jovanovic, J. (2015). Starting at the crossroads: Intersectional approaches to institutional supporting underrepresented minority women stem faculty. *Journal of Women and Minorities in Science and Engineering, 21*(2), 141–157.

Becker, G. S., Hubbard, W. H. J., & Murphy, K. M. (2010, September). *Explaining the worldwide boom in higher education of women* (Working Paper Series No. 2010-09). Milton Friedman Institute for Research in Economics, University of Chicago.

Berg, Gary A. (2019). *The rise of women in higher education: how, why, and what's next*. Rowman & Littlefield.

Brons, L. (2015). Mothering, an analysis. *Transience, 6*(1), 69–90.

Chanana, K. (2020). Women and leadership: Strategies of gender inclusion in institutions of higher education in India. In C. Gail (Ed.), *Strategies for supporting inclusion and diversity in the academy: Higher education, aspiration and inequality*. Springer.

Chanana, K. (2006). Gender and disciplinary choices: Women in higher education in India. In N. Guy (Ed.), *Knowledge power and dissent: Critical perspectives on higher education and research in knowledge society* (p. 256). UNESCO Publishing.

Chanana, K. (2000). Trending the hallowed halls: Women in higher education in India. *Economic & Political Weekly, 35*(12), 1012–1022.

Catalyst. (2013). *Our history*. https://www.catalyst.org/what-we-do/

Davis, D. R. (2012). *A phenomenological study on the leadership development of African American women executives in academia and business* (PhD Thesis). Submitted to University of Nevada.

Davis, D. R., & Maldonado, C. (2015). Shattering the glass ceiling: The leadership development of African American women in higher education. *Advancing Women in Leadership, 35*, 48–64.

Deshmane, S. B. (2014). Discrimination in the university in India: Special reference to Bangalore University women employees in Karnataka. In A. Vongalis-Macro (Ed.), *Career moves: Mentoring for women advancing their career and leadership in academia* (pp. 35–46). Sense Publishers.

Estler, S. E. (1975, Winter). Women as leaders in public education. *Signs, 1*(2), 363–386.

Fitzgerald, T. (2014). *Women leaders in higher education: Shattering the myths*. Research into Higher Education, Routledge.

Gautam, M. (2015). Gender, subject choice and higher education in India: Exploring 'choices' and 'constraints' of women studies. *Contemporary Education Dialogue, 12*(1), 31–58.

Global Gender Gap Report. (2020). World Economic. http://www3.weforum.org/docs/WEF_GGGR_2020.pdf

Hollis, L. P. (2016). Socially dominated: The radicalized and gendered positionality of those precluded from bullying. In L. P. Hollis (Ed.), *The coercive community college: Bullying and its costly impact on the mission to serve underrepresented populations diversity in higher education* (pp. 103–112). Emerald Publishing.

Hollis, L. P. (2018). Bullied out of position: Black women's complex intersectionality, workplace bullying, and resulting career disruption. *Journal of Black Sexuality and Relationships, 4*(3), 73–89.

Howe-Walsh, L., & Turnbull, S. (2016). Barriers to women leaders in academia: Tales from science and technology. *Studies in Higher Education, 41*(3), 415–428.

Jones, K., Ante, A., Longman, L. A., & Remke, R. (Eds.) (2018). *Perspectives on women's higher education leadership from around the world.* MDPI.

Kameshwara, & Shukla. (2018). Towards social justice in institutions of high learning: Addressing gender inequality in science and technology through capability approach. In K. Jones, A. Ante, K. A. Longman, & R. Remke (Eds.), *Perspectives on women's higher education leadership from around the world.* MDPI.

Khandelwal, P. (2002). Gender stereotypes at work: Implications for organisation. *Indian Journal of Training and Development, 32*(2), 72–83.

Lühe, J. (2014). In search of the glass ceiling: What mechanisms and barriers hinder qualified women from progressing in academia? B. Thege, S. Popescu-Willigmann, R. Pioch, & S. Badri-Höher (Eds.), *Paths to career and success for women in science.* Springer.

Mead, M., & Metraux, R. (1957). Image of scientist among high school students. *Science 126,* 384–390.

Morley, L. (2014). Lost leaders: Women in the global academy. *Higher Education Research & Development, 33*(1), 114–128.

Morley, L., & Crossouard, B. (2015). *Women in higher education leadership in South Asia: Rejection, refusal, reluctance, revisioning* (Project Report). British Council, University of Sussex, Centre for Higher Education Equity Research.

Nath, S. (2014). Higher education and women participation in India. *Journal of Business Management & Social Sciences Research, 3*(2), 43–47.

Phadke, S., & Roy, A. (2017). Women walk out: Tired of being harassed and treated as second class citizens, Indian women are taking to the streets. *Index on Censorship, 46*(4), 50–53.

Ghaus, B. (2013). *Amidst the barricades: Pakistani women as managers in higher education* (pp. 27–28). 3rd international conference on Business and Management, (ICOBM), University of Management and Technology (UMT).

Sandberg, S. (2013). *Lean in: Women, work, and the will to lead.* Random House Audio.
Smith, S. (2013). Black feminism and intersectionality. *International Socialist Review,* (91), 6–24. https://isreview.org/issue/91/black-feminism-and-intersectionality
Verma, S. (2015). Gender, power, and knowledge: Deciphering the dialectics of inclusion–exclusion in academia in India. In E. Rodriguez & B. Wejnert (Eds.), *Enabling gender equality: Future generations of the global world.* Research in Political Sociology, Vol. 23, pp. 57–66. Emerald Group Publishing Limited.
Wenniger, M. D., & Conroy, M. H. (2000). *Gender equity or bust: On the road to campus leadership with women in higher education.* Jossey Bas Publishers.
Bartel, S. (2018, 19 December). Leadership barriers for women in higher education. *BizEd.* https://bized.aacsb.edu/articles/2018/12/leadership-barriers-for-women-in-higher-education

PART VI
Prospects of Indian Higher Education

Chapter 13
Marginalized Communities and Higher Education:
The Way forward
D. Jeevan Kumar

13

Marginalized Communities and Higher Education
The Way Forward

D. Jeevan Kumar

> *The right to inclusive education encompasses a transformation in culture, policy and practice in all educational environments to accommodate the differing requirements and identities of individual students, together with a commitment to remove the barriers that impede that possibility.*
>
> —*The United Nations Convention on the Rights of Persons with Disabilities (2008)*

The United Nations (UN) 2030 Agenda for Sustainable Development, with its objective of leaving no one behind, provides humankind with a talisman to build more inclusive societies. Sustainable Development Goal (SDG) 4 emphasizes that inclusive and equitable education must be made available for all by 2030. To ensure this, countries should take a series of steps to prevent and address all forms of exclusion, marginalization, disparity, vulnerability and inequality in educational ecosystems. (UNESCO, 2017)

The Cali commitment to equity and inclusion in education (UNESCO, 2019) reiterates inclusion in education as a critically transformative process that ensures full participation and access to quality learning opportunities for all young people. It implies respecting and valuing diversity and eliminating all forms of discrimination, in and through education. This vision of inclusion emphasizes the concept of intersectionality (i.e., the recognition that a disadvantage is compounded when it intersects with other disadvantages associated with discrimination and marginalization). It simultaneously highlights the magnitude and complexity of the transformations required at the educational, social and cultural levels.

It must also be recognized that this discussion is taking place at a point of time when the world is facing new challenges, manifested, among others, by pandemics, climate change and the Fourth Industrial Revolution. As pointed out by UNESCO, it is vital that education powered by artificial intelligence is accessible to all, irrespective of the individual's environment, nationality, culture, gender, disability status, sexuality or age (UNESCO, 2019). Notwithstanding the enormous potential of new technologies, there is the real possibility that they may accentuate existing structural and related disparities.

How is India doing here? This chapter intends to look at the current education scenario in India from the perspective of the marginalized communities and wonders whether the latest policy initiative in the form of the National Education Policy (NEP) 2020 (Government of India, 2020) has the right prescription to address the ever-elusive goals of access, inclusion and equity. The chapter attempts an analysis of what ails our educational ecosystem and identifies a way forward that can only come from a deeper introspection of the roots of structural inequality and violence that is inherent in our social and cultural ethos.

The Problem

Although it cannot be denied that the higher education ecosystem in India has expanded rapidly since its inception, the reality is that it still remains far behind in addressing issues of inclusion and equity (Tilak, 2013). Although literacy rates and education levels among the marginalized communities have improved greatly, they still fall short of the national average. Despite the existence of reservation and affirmative action, Kumar (2016) highlights that only 13.5 per cent and 4 per cent of the total students in higher education belong to Scheduled Caste (SC) and Scheduled Tribe (ST) categories, respectively. The caste profile of faculty reflects a similar scenario. According to 2011 statistics from the University Grants Commission, only 4.9 per cent of the faculty positions reserved for SCs, STs and Other Backward Class (OBC) were filled in central and state universities (see Pathania & Tierney, 2018). It is very obvious that Indian higher education is found wanting in terms of the virtues of diversity, representation, inclusion and equity.

The 12th Five-year Plan document on higher education (Planning Commission, 2013), quoting data of National Service Scheme 64th round, pointed out that the gross enrolment ratio (GER) in the ST category is one-fourth of the general category students; less than half for the SC; and more than half for the OBC students. The participation of SCs, STs and OBCs in higher education is significantly lower than the national average. The document acknowledged the reality that there is no evidence of a reduction in relative disparities, there is only a marginal change in inter-group inequality and that the low percentage of students from the marginalized communities in the domain of higher education is a persistent problem that refuses to go away. Access to higher education continues to reflect inherited privileged social backgrounds. The presence of multidimensional inequalities compounds matters. It is obvious that all the plans, policies and programmes have cumulatively not quite ensured the goals of access, inclusion and equity in higher education.

Deshpande (2006) states that 'higher education, by its very nature, presupposes access to a minimum level of economic, cultural, and political resources'. He notes that higher education in countries like India usually involves two variations of de facto discrimination, summarized as resource discrimination and merit discrimination. Resource discrimination is when parents are unable to invest monetarily in the higher education of their wards. Merit discrimination happens when members of upper castes do not want the lower castes to receive this entitlement.

As Bhikhu Parekh (1995) puts it,

> Every society includes large sections who are disadvantaged and unable to develop their human potential. Victims of a long history of exploitation, repression, discrimination and marginalization, these groups have, for centuries, been denied adequate opportunities for growth and treated as 'naturally' inferior, almost as if they belonged to a separate species.

According to Anirudh Krishna (2017), the ladders that lead talented people from the marginalized communities upwards are deliberately broken in many places. These breakages are detrimental not just for the affected individuals and their communities; they limit the achievements of an entire society.

In the words of Ajantha Subramanian of Harvard University, 'What is understood as merit in India's educational institutions is only another name for the accumulated cultural capital of India's upper caste elites.'

Miranda Fricker describes the phenomenon as 'hermeneutical injustice', where certain sections of society are overlooked or ignored because of a gap in our collective interpretive tools (Fricker, 2007). In other words, as a society, we may not notice that an injustice is occurring because we lack a way to name, recognize or interpret what is happening. For Fricker, this type of injustice is caused by structural inequalities of power and unnoticed or unacknowledged systemic prejudice. For example, if a subject is marginalized and the forces that produce this marginalization are systemic, then the source of prejudice will likely go undetected.

NEP 2020 and Implications for Marginalized Communities

NEP 2020, in Part II dealing with higher education, has devoted a whole chapter to 'Equity and Inclusion in Higher Education', where it is explicitly stated that *the Policy envisions ensuring equitable access to quality education to all students, with a special emphasis on SEDGs.* This new acronym goes much beyond our traditional understanding of marginalized communities.

Who exactly are these Socio-Economically Disadvantaged Groups (SEDGs)? According to NEP 2020, SEDGs can be broadly categorized based on the following characteristics:

1. *Gender identities* (particularly female and transgender individuals): NEP 2020 notes that women cut across all under-represented groups, making up about half of all SEDGs, and that the exclusion and inequity that SEDGs face is magnified for the *women* in these SEDGs.
2. *Sociocultural identities:* Such as SCs, STs, OBCs and minorities.
3. *Geographical identities:* Such as students from villages, small towns and Aspirational Districts.
4. *Disability-based identities*: Including learning disabilities.
5. *Identities based on socio-economic background:* SEDGs coming under this category include migrant communities, low-income households and the urban poor.

It cannot be denied that NEP 2020 has several innovations intended to bring cheer to the marginalized communities in the country.

1. The policy deserves appreciation because it brings into its fold gender identities, including transgender. It clearly recognizes the fact that women are found in all under-represented groups, making up about half of all SEDGs. It cannot be denied that the exclusion and inequity that SEDGs face is compounded many times, for the women in these SEDGs. This is indeed a very positive development that will be cheered by right-thinking people, in particular, by gender activists.
2. The inclusion of geographical identities—students from villages, small towns and Aspirational Districts—is another innovation that deserves credit. For a variety of reasons, students from these backward and neglected regions of the

country have been suffering from neglect, for no fault of theirs. In their quest for admission to the portals of higher education, they have been falling by the wayside.
3. Persons with disabilities (PwD) also find a place in the NEP, which deserves another cheer. Apart from physical disabilities, which are clearly evident, there is a mention in the policy to learning disabilities, which may be harder to fathom but which deserve to be taken into account too.
4. And finally, what about those who have not found a place in the existing scheme of categorization of marginalized communities? The reference is to the children of migrant communities, low-income households and the urban poor. The NEP takes note of their predicament, too.

While the NEP 2020 has done well in identifying all those who deserve to be brought under the category of marginalized sections of the population, the *methodology* proposed to ensure access, inclusion and equity to them leaves much to be desired. The document makes two sets of recommendations to be implemented, one by the government and the other by higher-educational institutions.

The steps to be initiated by the government include ones like allotment of adequate funds for the education of the SEDGs; ensuring that clear GER targets are established for them; making sure that gender balance is maintained during the admission process itself; setting up top-quality higher education institutions (HEIs) in Aspirational Districts and in special education zones in remote areas where a large number of SEDGs are located; establishment of HEIs that can impart instruction in local languages; monetary assistance and scholarships to SEDGs studying in both government and private educational institutions; arrangement of outreach activities to spread information about the opportunities available in the sphere of higher education; and ensuring that they become proficient in the use of information and communication technology.

The other set of recommendations are for HEIs. These are mostly similar to the ones meant for the government, and largely repetitive, except for the following: Making the curriculum more inclusive; ensuring the employability of the SEDGs; seeing to it that buildings and facilities are wheelchair accessible and disabled friendly; devising bridge courses for weak students; providing psychological support and mentoring for weak students; and offering sensitization programmes for teaching and non-teaching staff, as well as students on matters pertaining to gender, disability, etc. HEIs are also expected to strictly enforce zero-discrimination and zero-harassment rules and regulations.

A perusal of the above set of recommendations, in the important chapter on 'Equity and Inclusion in Higher Education' in NEP 2020, raises several questions pertaining to the comprehension of the terms 'equity' and 'inclusion'. One is reminded of the fact that one of the overarching objectives of both the 11th and 12th Five-year Plans was 'ensuring equity and inclusion in higher education'. Both the above documents also had a long list of policy measures to ensure the incorporation of these elusive values into the ecosystem of higher education in the country.

NEP 2020 is obviously influenced by this methodology and does likewise, without undertaking a serious introspection of the *real* reasons behind the absence of these elusive values, thus far. It is therefore hardly surprising that the recommendations made by NEP 2020 seem too pedestrian and unimaginative to make a meaningful difference to the problem. All of these and much more have already been tried and tested, without much success. One cannot but get the impression that the NEP wishes to address the huge problem of exclusion and marginalization of the SEDGs (who make up 80% of the population, by its own admission) through sheer tokenism.

An even more significant lacuna in the NEP 2020 is the absence of a commitment towards *affirmative action* for the marginalized sections of the population. As has been pointed out by many, there is no reference to reservation anywhere in the entire document, either for students or for teachers. Does NEP 2020 wish to bring down the curtains on the policy of affirmative action? If so, would this be a wise move? It would be useful to recall the words of Marc Galanter (1984) in this context:

> Preferential treatment may be viewed as needed assurance of personal fairness, a guarantee against the persistence of discrimination.... Second, such policies are justified in terms of beneficial results that they will presumably promote: integration, use of neglected talent, more equitable distribution, etc..... With these two—the anti-discrimination theme and the general welfare theme—is entwined a notion of historical restitution or reparation to offset the systematic and cumulative deprivations suffered by lower castes in the past.

The benefits of official policies and programmes of compensatory/protective discrimination (CPD) are well substantiated: These policies ensure equality by erasing the effects of systematic subordination; they compensate for historic and systemic discrimination that unfairly penalize members of the marginalized communities; they redistribute resources and opportunities; they improve the motivation of marginalized communities to rise above their predicament; they ensure greater diversity, which in turn ensures better performance and more productive efficiency; they enable marginalized communities to gain better access to social capital; and they foster a more representative, inclusive and legitimate democratic order. In the long run, such policies diminish the effects of historic injustice and promote greater homogeneity and integration within society.

An unstated premise of NEP 2020 is that the failure of policies of CPD to ensure access, inclusion and equity in higher education warrants a serious rethink on their continuance. This could explain the silence in the NEP 2020 on reservation, its rationale or its efficacy. What is instead warranted is a serious analysis, coupled with introspection, of why and where the CPD policies are not succeeding, and then taking corrective steps.

In Dr B. R. Ambedkar's last speech in the Constituent Assembly of India as the chairman of its drafting committee (Government of Maharashtra, 1994), popularly referred to as 'The Grammar of Anarchy' exposition, he spoke about the importance of not just political democracy but, critically, social democracy, in order to achieve equality and emancipation of the downtrodden. He argued that

> Political democracy cannot last unless there lies at the base of it, social democracy.... What does social democracy mean? It means a way of life which recognizes liberty, equality and fraternity as the principles of life. These principles are not to be treated as separate items in a trinity. They form a union of trinity in the sense that to divorce one from the other is to defeat the very purpose of democracy....

It is this lack of social democracy which allows social stigma and negative stereotypes to flourish in the environment of higher education and makes it traumatic for students from marginalized sections to negotiate.

The Way Forward

The earlier articles in the present volume have attempted to identify the problem from the perspective of specific marginalized communities and have suggested several policy guidelines and initiatives.

Mainstream economic theory indicates that discrimination has multiple consequences. It hampers economic growth, induces income inequality and creates potential for inter-group conflict, by denying equal opportunity to discriminated groups. Therefore, remedies against discrimination—legal, affirmative action or compensatory discrimination—are required both for equity and economic growth.

It is essential to address discrimination in a more effective way that binds institutions with stringent legislation and laws. In most HEIs, orientation of students is rudimentary, without mention of the intricacies of marginalization, diversity and other factors. It is essential to break the conventional structure of teaching, research and orientation in HEIs. The incorporation of pedagogy on democracy, 'difference' and social justice will facilitate in evolving a social culture, free from all prejudices. The deepening divide of caste in HEI spaces has only amplified discrimination and exclusion. It is vital to have effective interventions from policymakers, along with a serious introspection among the privileged communities, to address a variety of hierarchies of which they are torchbearers.

A closer look at the Muslim religious minority reveals that they come next to the SCs and STs in terms of being under-represented in the educational ecosystem of the country. A pioneering 2018 intergenerational mobility study indicated that in the current economic liberalization period, most of the upward mobility gains in India had accrued to other traditionally disadvantaged groups, but for 'Muslims these opportunities have substantially deteriorated' (Asher et al., 2018). Clearly, Muslims are now the most insecure and politically marginalized in India and are among the least prepared to cope with the educational and developmental challenges of contemporary India.

The educational deficit of this significant minority cannot be bridged without Muslim organizations and other civil society organizations chipping in to provide a variety of 'learning-enabling' interventions for them—including policy advocacy, capacity building and community-based initiatives—to complement government policies and programmes. Community-based programmes additionally need to focus on building capacities of different vulnerable Muslim stakeholders.

With specific reference to PwD, several measures may be suggested to bring them into the educational mainstream of the country. Educational institutions must attach due significance to disability as a part of institutional engagement and diversity-planning initiatives. There is a need for the Union and State governments to move beyond tokenism and work towards their actual empowerment, through policies and programmes that encourage them to pursue higher education. Anti-discrimination forums in colleges/universities should not only address caste/gender-based discrimination but also the discrimination against PwD, so that prevalent cultural prejudices are reduced. There is also an urgent need for the teaching and learning methodology, tools, pedagogy, curriculum and mechanisms of students to be *adapted* to suit PwD. Empirical studies must be conducted periodically to gauge the level of engagement between challenged and non-challenged students and amongst the students with different forms of disability. This engagement must be horizontal and vertical. To capture the disadvantageous and vulnerable status of PwD, their intersection with the markers of other disadvantages like caste, gender and economic background must be carefully studied. There should be adequate emphasis on higher education with a skill-development component that caters to the requirements of PwD. Placements for PwD in campus recruitment should be made mandatory.

In order to overcome the gender deficit in higher educational institutions, one suggestion is that there is a need to make policies more inclusive and diverse with the objective of promoting gender diversity and being more sensitive in mainstreaming the role of women leadership within higher education. But we need to go beyond this. There needs to be a paradigm shift in current thinking and methodology. While content and pedagogic practices need to be gender sensitive, there must also be a drastic shift in valuing various academic initiatives in higher-education spaces. There is no scientific validation in deciding that mentoring, teaching and documenting are lower-order skills, in comparison to publications, networking and socializing. Academic audits in higher-education spaces need to be redesigned, wherein individual strengths and institutional experiences will emerge as major qualifying determinants. Strict adherence to gender ratio in terms of leadership within an organization will also be a positive step. A strong stance could be taken with regards to developing ambition among women in society, so that they are in a better position to take up challenging roles, which otherwise gets sidelined in prioritizing their family responsibilities.

Last Word

For government efforts to be qualitatively successful, policies and programmes need to look at the denial of access, inclusion and equity in the realm of higher education for the marginalized communities squarely in the face. This implies calling a spade a spade; in other words, recognizing the casteist, patriarchal and exclusivist nature of HEIs and acknowledging the variety of sociocultural prejudices that lurk and prevail in those hallowed portals. Without understanding and addressing structural barriers (like caste, meritocracy, patriarchy and communalism as structures and their continuing propensity to inflict structural violence), social justice cannot be achieved. What is missing in our systems of education is the methodology to confront and deal with structural barriers that negate and impede the values of community and fraternity. This is because primordial factors are visualized as a part of culture, tradition or *karma* and *not* as a structural shortcoming. It is no surprise, therefore, that the quest for equity and inclusion in the form of social justice for the disadvantaged and marginalized communities continues to remain elusive.

Let us not forget that the most important and urgent reform needed in education is to transform it, to endeavour to relate it to the life, needs and aspirations of all sections of the people, in particular the marginalized, and thereby make it a powerful instrument of social, economic and cultural transformation necessary for the realization of national goals. This is indeed the need of the hour.

References

Asher, S., Novosad, P., & Rifkin, C. (2018, September). Intergenerational mobility in India: Estimates from new methods and administrative data (p. 7). https://www.dartmouth.edu/~novosad/anr-india-mobility.pdf

Deshpande, S. (2006). Exclusive *inequalities*: Merit, *caste* and *discrimination* in Indian *higher education today*. *Economic & Political Weekly*, *41*(24), 2438–2444.

Government of Maharashtra. (1994). Dr. Babasaheb Ambedkar: Writings and *speeches*. Vol. XIII, p. 1216. Department of Education, Government of Maharashtra.

Fricker, M. (2007). Epistemic *injustice*: Power and the *ethics* of *knowing*. Clarendon Press.

Galanter, M. (1984). Competing *equalities*: Law and the *backward classes* in India. Oxford University Press.

Krishna, A. (2017). The *broken ladder*: The *paradox* and the *potential* of India's *one billion*. Chapter 5. Penguin Random House India.

Kumar, V. (2016). Discrimination on campuses of higher learning: A perspective from below. *Economic & Political Weekly, 51*(6), 12–15.

Government of India. (2020). *National Education Policy*. Ministry of Human Resource Development, Government of India.

Parekh, B (1995, October–December). Cultural pluralism and the limits of diversity. *Alternatives: Global, Local, Political, 20*(4), 431–457.

Pathania, G. J., & Tierney, W. G. (2018). An *ethnography* of *caste* and *class* at an Indian University: Creating *capital*. Tertiary Education and Management. https://doi.org/10.1080/13583883.2018.1439998.

Planning Commission, Government of India. (2013). *12th Five Year Plan (2012–2017)*. SAGE Publications.

Tilak, J. B. G. (2013). Higher education in Trishanku: Hanging between state and market. In J. B. G. Tilak (Ed.), *Higher education in India: In search of equality, quality and quantity* (pp. 391–407). Orient BlackSwan.

UNESCO. (2017). *A guide for ensuring inclusion and equity in education*. UNESCO.

UNESCO. (2019). *Cali commitment to equity and inclusion in education*. UNESCO.

ABOUT THE EDITORS AND CONTRIBUTORS

Editors

M. J. Vinod is a Professor in the Department of International Studies, Politics and History, Christ (Deemed to be University), Bengaluru and former Dean (Faculty of Arts) and syndicate member in Bangalore University, India. He received his MA, MPhil and PhD degrees from Bangalore University. He was awarded the Fulbright Fellowship, where he taught as a scholar in residence at Morgan State University, Baltimore, from August 2015 to May 2016. He is recipient of Salzburg Fellowship; Ford Foundation Fellowship at the University of Maryland, College Park; Swiss Foreign Ministry Fellow at the Graduate School of International Studies, Geneva; visiting fellow at the Henry L. Stimson Center, Washington, D. C. He has been a visiting professor at the Department of Geopolitics, Manipal University; Department of International Relations, Jadavpur University, Kolkata, and regularly visits the Jawaharlal Nehru University (JNU), New Delhi. His areas of specialization include higher education, Indian foreign policy and political theory.

Dr S. Y. Surendra Kumar is an Associate Professor, Department of Political Science, Bangalore University, Bengaluru, India. He holds MPhil and PhD degrees in South Asian studies from School of International Studies, JNU, New Delhi. He is a recipient of Mahbub ul Haq Research Award and Short Duration fellowship. His recent book is titled '*Ballots, Bullets and Bhikkhus: The Role of Buddhist Sangha in Sri Lankan Politics and Ethnic Conflict*'. He has contributed more than 20 chapters in various edited books and published more than 30 research articles in leading national and international journals. His areas of interests are public policy studies and South Asian security.

Contributors

T. Brahmanandam is an Associate Professor at Centre for Multi-Disciplinary Development Research, Dharwad, Karnataka. He obtained his MA and MPhil degree from JNU, New Delhi, and PhD from University of Hyderabad. He has several projects and published several research articles and chapters in edited books on the issues concerning marginalized communities. His latest edited books include *Dalits Issues: Caste and Class Interface* (2018) and *Voices Unheard: Methodologically Articulated* (2018).

Krishnaswamy Dara is an Assistant Professor, Department of Political Science, JMI, New Delhi. He obtained his MA, MPhil and PhD degree from Centre for Political Science, JNU, New Delhi. He has written several research articles on the issues concerning Dalits, social and political movements in India and Indian political ideas.

Prakash Desai is an Assistant Professor, Department of Political Science, Goa University, Goa, India. He received his PhD from JNU, New Delhi. His area of research interest is Indian political thought. His recent publications are- 'Quest for Egalitarian Socio-spiritual Order: Lingayats and Their Practices', *Journal of Human Values* (25, no. 2 [2019]: 87–100) and 'Karnataka: BJP's Spectacular Victory over the Congress and JD(S)', in Paul Wallace (ed), *India's 2019 Elections: The Hindutva Wave and Indian Nationalism* (New Delhi: SAGE, 2020).

Maxim Dias, Assistant Professor, Department of Political Science and Peace Studies at St Joseph's College (autonomous), Bengaluru, was formerly the principal of St Joseph's Evening College (autonomous), Bengaluru. He is pursuing his doctoral studies from Bangalore University. His research areas include higher education, religion and religious extremism, secularism and peace studies.

Alphonse Pius Fernandes, Assistant Professor in the Department of Sociology at St Aloysius College (autonomous), Mangalore, is pursuing his doctoral studies from Mangalore University.

His research areas include education, religion, marginalized groups and civil society.

Sanjay Jain is an Associate Professor and Director (PhD Research Centre), ILS Law College, Pune. He specializes in constitutional and administrative law. He has a total teaching experience of more than 19 years. His areas of interest include feminist jurisprudence and gender justice with special reference to India, comparative constitutionalism, sociological jurisprudence, disability rights jurisprudence, human rights of marginalized groups, legal theory and jurisprudence and international economic law. He is the recipient of National Award in 'employee category' on the occasion of World Disabled Day in 2004. He is co-editor of the book *Basic Structure Constitutionalism: Revisiting Kesavananda Bharati*.

Areesh Kumar Karamala is an Assistant Professor at St Joseph's College (Autonomous), Bangalore University, Bengaluru. He obtained his MPhil and PhD from the Centre for Russian and Central Asian Studies, School of International Studies, JNU, New Delhi. He has participated in various workshops, national and international (London, Bhutan, Canada) seminars and presented more than 30 research papers. He has contributed chapters for various journals and edited books. His main areas of interest are international politics, nationalism, political parties and party system, caste and social exclusion.

D. Jeevan Kumar is the Honorary Professor at Karnataka State Rural Development and Panchayat Raj University, Gadag, Karnataka. He has 38 years of teaching experience in political science at Bangalore University, where he served as dean (faculty of arts) and special officer to the vice chancellor. He was visiting professor at the National Law School of India University, Bengaluru. He is a recipient of international fellowships like Schomburg fellow, Fulbright fellow and Salzburg fellow. His areas of interest include development politics, administration and subaltern studies.

About the Editors and Contributors / 271

Vagishwari S. P. is a Professor in the Department of International Studies and History, Christ (Deemed to be University), Bengaluru. Her master's and MPhil degree is in history. Her doctoral dissertation was on *The Architecture of Western Gangas* and her areas of specialization are history and visual aesthetics, historiography, international relations and Karnataka studies.

Roshni Sharma is Assistant Professor in BMS College of Law, Bengaluru and is a doctoral candidate at Jain (Deemed to be University), Bengaluru.

Chetan Singai is an Associate Professor at the School of Social Sciences, Ramaiah University of Applied Sciences, Bengaluru and Deputy Director, Ramaiah Public Policy Center, Bengaluru, India. He obtained his doctoral degree (PhD) from the National Institute of Advanced Studies, Bengaluru. He completed his MPhil in law and governance and MA in political science at the JNU, New Delhi. He received the prestigious Erasmus Mundus Scholarship to pursue Master in Lifelong Learning: Policy and Management, joint degree from University of London (UK), University of Aarhus (Denmark) and University of Deusto (Spain). He was nominated as a Chief Consultant, Technical Secretariat, Committee for Draft National Education Policy 2017–2019, Ministry of Human Resource Development, Government of India, New Delhi, and National Assessment and Accreditation Council, Bengaluru, Karnataka.

Udaya Kiran K. T. is an Associate Professor in the Department of Music and Fine Arts, Central University, Tamil Nadu. He is recipient of several awards such as Karnataka Sangeetha Nritya Academy, Louis Braille award, Swaraalaya Ratna and so on. His areas of interest include Carnatic music and PwD and higher education. He regularly performs at national and international concerts.

Priyanca Mathur is an Associate Professor in Centre for Research in Social Sciences and Education (CERSSE), Jain University, Bengaluru, and also Gender Advisor and International Trainer with the Forum of Federations (FoF) for its work in Myanmar. She gained her master's, MPhil and PhD degrees from JNU, New Delhi and an M.Sc in Forced Migration from the University of Oxford, United Kingdom. She has helped devise modules for FoF on gender and decentralization and conducted workshops, both gender and federalism workshops and 'training of trainers (ToT) workshops on gender', for parliamentarians and civil society actors in Myanmar and Thailand. She teaches politics to undergraduate, MBA, MPhil and PhD students at Jain University and is known for drawing out a gender angle in everything. She has written many opinions and editorial articles in the *Deccan Herald*.

K. M. Ziyauddin is a teaching faculty in the Department of Sociology and is also associated with Al-Beruni Centre for the Study of Social Exclusion and Inclusive Policy, Maulana Azad National Urdu University, Hyderabad. He obtained his master's degree in sociology from Jamia Millia Islamia (JMI), an MPhil in Social Medicine from JNU, and a Ph.D. in sociology from the Delhi School of Economics, University of Delhi. His research mainly involves the sociology of minorities (Muslim), Dalit studies, health and illness, sanitation and gender politics. A few of his book publications include, Muslims of India: Exclusionary Process and Inclusionary Measures, (Ed. 2012); Dimensions of Social Exclusion: Ethnographic Explorations (Ed. 2009) (Cambridge Scholars Publishing); Sociology of Health in a Dalit Community: Axes of Exclusion of Hadis (2021 upcoming by CSP) and Reading Minorities in India: Forms and Perspectives (2021 upcoming by Rawat). He is currently working on three manuscripts: Communalism in India: Socio-Historical and Legal Perspectives (co-authored) and Illness and Health: Sociological Narratives of Dalits. He is an alumnus of the United States Exchange Programme on International Visitors Leadership Programme (IVLP), and the convener of Research Committee on Minority Studies (RC26) of Indian Sociological Society.

INDEX

academics and accessibility, 218
administrative injustice, 62–66
  Supreme Court case, *Dr Subashkashinathmandan v. State of Maharashtra and Others*, 65
  Upendra Baxis view, 63
Agenda for Sustainable Development, 2030, 170
All India Survey on Higher Education (AISHE), 10, 244
alternative formats, 217
American Council on Education (ACE), 242
Article 24 of UNCRPD and higher education
  2030 Agenda for Sustainable Development, 170
  anti-discrimination paradigm, 168
  formulation, 166
  special needs approaches, 168
assistive technology
  academics and accessibility, 218
  alternative formats, 217
  Braille, 214
  Braille format, 220
  day-to-day activities, 220
  devices category, 211
  limitations, 219–221
  media and accessibility, 217
  OCR, 212
  screen reader, 211
  web accessibility, 216

Baraha, 216
Bharat, 30

Biwako Millennium Framework (2002), 140
Braille, 214
  regional language, 215
  support, 216

caste discrimination
  against Dalit students, 92
  Dalit Media Network's point of view, 91
  institutions based, 92
  patterns in higher education, 90–92
Chinese universities, 2
Constitution of the Jesuits (1548), 127

Dalits
  higher education in India, 8–10
  social spaces, 9
Dalit students
  committing suicide in India's higher educational institutions, 93
democratic citizenship, 4
Directive Principles of State Policy (DPSP)
  policy inputs, 199–200
Directive Principles Of State Policy (DPSP)
  fundamental rights, reconfiguring relationship, 195–198
Duxbury Braille Translation, 216

education, 2
educational institutions, 27

empowerment cell for differently
abled (ECDA), 148
Equal Opportunity Cell (EOC),
148

favouritism, 61
fundamental rights
DPSP, 195–198

Gender Parity Index, 239
Goal 4, 140
gross enrolment ratio (GER)
gender equality in higher
education, 240

Hermeneutical injustice, 60
higher education
communal agenda, 29–31
political consensus on
commercialization, 31–34
higher educational institutions
(HEIs)
gross enrolment ratio (GER), 98
social category-wise distribution
of non-teaching staff, 97
Higher Education Commission of
India (HECI), 150
Higher Education for Persons with
Special Needs (HEPSN), 148
higher education in India (HEI),
21, 38, 226
addressing gender parity,
239–246
assistive technology, 209–221
caste-based discrimination, 9
caste discrimination and
exclusion, 92–98
caste discrimination patterns,
90–92
challenges, 1
contextualizing women,
226–228
Dalits, 8–10
definition, 210

evolution and growth, 4–6
governmental schemes and
programmes, 178
Illustration of key policies and
committees, 42
Jawaharlal Nehru University
(JNU), 24
JWL, 130–132
marginalization, 2–4
marginalized, challenges, 6–8
marginalized communities,
258–263
market, 26
merit concept, 89–90
MHRD's report, 96
Muslims, 10–11
persons with disabilities (PwD),
12–13
engagement of state of
Maharashtra, 188–191
republican liberty, 192–194
road map for enabling
andragogy, 191
policy questions, barriers and
enablers, 242–246
private universities and freedom
of social research, 26–28
right of PwD, 155
Section 51 highlights on reality
of PwD, 175
software revolution, 3
structure and contents, 13–17
study women, 240–242
teaching community numbers, 84
transformations, 5

Ignatian Pedagogical Paradigm
(IPP), 129
Indian Council of Historical
Research (ICHR), 29
Indian Council of Social Science
Research (ICSSR), 29
Indian Higher Education (IHE)
PwD, 139–150

information and communications technology (ICT) growth, 2
Integrated Education for Disabled Children (IEDC), 141
International Labour Organization (ILO), 147

Jawaharlal Nehru University, 24
Jesuit Commons
  Higher Education at the Margins (JC HEM), 128
Jesuit Refugee Service (JRS), 126
Jesuit Worldwide Learning (JWL), 15, 125, 133
  academic partnership, 131
  challenges and limitations, 133
  distinctiveness, 128–130
  India, 130–132
  learning centres, 131
  programme, 129
  starting, 127
Job Access with Speech (JAWS), 215

KNFB reader, 213
Kurzweil, 213

marginalization, 2
media and accessibility, 217
merit
  Anoop Kumar's view, 90
  views, 90
Ministry of Human Resource Development (MHRD)
  report on higher education in India, 95
minorities
  discrimination in services against Muslim, 109–112
modernity, 228
Muslim
  higher education, 10–11
  minority discrimination in services, 109–112
  social inclusion perspectives, 112–114

National Democratic Alliance (NDA), 24
National Education Policy (NEP) 2020, 17, 40, 149
  implications for marginalized communities, 258–263
National Policy for Empowerment of Women (2001), 240
New Economic Policy (NEP), 22

optical character recognition (OCR) solutions, 212

persons with disabilities (PwD), 16
  accessibility, 145
  Act, 139
  challenges in higher education, 143
  higher education in India, 12–13
  implementation of reservation, 146
  issues and concerns, 143–150
  marginal improvement, 144
  NEP 2020, 149
  right to higher education, 156
  Section 26, 141
  UGC initiatives, 148
polarization, 3
protégé system, 227

Rehabilitations Council of India Act (1992), 141
Rights of Persons with Disabilities Act, 2016, 12
Rights of Persons with Disabilities (RPwD) Act, 2016, 142, 172, 210
  right to education, 173

right to education, 156
  critical analysis of guidelines, 184–188
  enabler and game changer, 162–166
  legal perspective on pursuit, 172
  objectives, 158
  Sandra Fredman's observation, 162
  scholarship provided, 160
  Section 47, 173
  Section 49, 174
  Section 51 highlights, 175
  Section 53, 175
  Section 55, 176
  situational analysis, 156–161
right to education under RPwD Act 2016, 172
  regressive turn, 173–177, 184
right to higher education and UNCRPD, 166
  Article 24, 166–171

Sachar Committee, 10
Sarva Shiksha Abhiyan (SSA), 142
screen readers, 219
  mobile devices, 212

social inclusion
  helping Muslim, 112–114
  systematic testimonial injustice
    Miranda Frickers view, 62
testimonial injustice, 61

United Nations Convention on the Rights of Persons with Disabilities (UNCRPD), 159
United Nations Development Programme (UNDP), 3
United Progressive Alliance (UPA), 24
University Grants Commission (UGC), 29

Visveswaraya Technological University (VTU), 149

web accessibility, 217
women in higher education, 11–12
  contextualizing in higher education, 226–228
  framing, executing, content, 230–233
World Education Forum, 140